"Chap Clark's classic book [is] highly recom
and educators who write about teenage stress. .. .. .uunuauonai reading
that provides valuable insight into the hurting hearts of young people."

—**Peggy Kendall**, *YouthWorker Journal*

"This book does a great job of framing the issues affecting adolescents. It provided me with some powerful insights. No wonder adolescents identify with the movies I have been making—the characters are on the same journey of trying to find hope and authenticity. This book is a great look inside the adolescent world, the world beneath the one exposed to adults."

—**Ralph Winter**, movie producer, *X-Men Trilogy*, *Fantastic Four*,
Star Trek series, and *Cool It*

"What makes *Hurt* so valuable is that it marries the very best of careful scholarship with a deep compassion for kids. Clark is not just an academic who offers thoughtful ethnographic research. He's a frontline youth worker who still spends time with these students even after all the data has been collected. This important book will be very helpful to youth workers, parents, counselors, and educators alike."

—**Duffy Robbins**, associate professor of youth ministry,
Eastern University

"This book is a must-read for anyone who has any contact with adolescents, for as Clark points out, overriding the negative forces of abandonment means each teen needs multiple positive voices in their world. Written accessibly, this book could be given as a resource to volunteers in a youth group, but the depth of research displayed makes it invaluable in an academic setting as well."

—**Anna E. Aven**, *Journal of Youth Ministry*

"[Clark's] lucid writing style combines warmth and compassion with sociology-textbook straightforwardness, backing his observations with extensive research—his own and others'. . . . *Hurt* is must-reading for every parent, educator, and youth worker in America."

—**Gary Hassig**, *CBA Retailers + Resources*

Youth, Family, and Culture Series

Chap Clark, series editor

The Youth, Family, and Culture series examines the broad categories involved in studying and caring for the needs of the young and is dedicated to the preparation and vocational strengthening of those who are committed to the spiritual development of adolescents.

hurt 2.0

inside the world of today's TEENAGERS

CHAP CLARK

Baker Academic

a division of Baker Publishing Group

Grand Rapids, Michigan

Published by Baker Academic
a division of Baker Publishing Group
P.O. Box 6287, Grand Rapids, MI 49516-6287
www.bakeracademic.com

Hurt 2.0 is a revised edition of *Hurt*.

Printed in the United States of America

Library of Congress Cataloging-in-Publication Data
Clark, Chap, 1954–
    Hurt 2.0 : inside the world of today's teenagers / Chap Clark—[2nd ed.].
        p.   cm. — (Youth, family, and culture)
    Includes bibliographical references (p.   ) and index.
    ISBN 978-0-8010-3941-6 (pbk.)
    1. Teenagers—United States—Social conditions. 2. Teenagers—United States—Attitudes. 3. Adolescent psychology—United States. I. Title.
HQ796.C553 2011
305.2350973—dc22   2011000494

        13   14   15   16   17   7   6   5   4   3

In keeping with biblical principles of creation stewardship, Baker Publishing Group advocates the responsible use of our natural resources. As a member of the Green Press Initiative, our company uses recycled paper when possible. The text paper of this book is composed in part of post-consumer waste.

green press INITIATIVE

contents

Part 3 Where Do We Go from Here?

preface to *hurt 2.0*

t is hard to know when a second edition of a book is needed. On the one hand, the issues and cultural changes detailed in the original *Hurt* led many people to such a new way of thinking about teens and the world we have handed them that the first edition's basic conclusions should have a relatively long shelf life. Yet at the same time, one thing that has become clear to me since I first embarked on the *Hurt Project* (as it is now sometimes called) is that *Hurt* was only the beginning. The world is changing so quickly, and the way our young must adapt to those changes far outpaces adults' assumptions and axioms about who teenagers are, how they feel, and what growing up is like from their perspective. Moreover, there have been sweeping changes in the systems and structures that adults have carefully crafted over the decades to guide our dealings with youth. From education to youth sports to media to parenting, just about every institution has become more complex, more demanding, and more relationally disengaged than when *Hurt* first came out. Adults themselves are scrambling to survive, and whenever a child or adolescent happens to throw a wrench in our plans or agenda, the child becomes the problem, or as therapists put it, the "identified patient."

When *Hurt* was first published, I encountered a fairly significant amount of pushback from just about every side (except from the youth themselves, for in every case where a teenager has heard me speak or read *Hurt* or its more popular cousin, *When Kids Hurt*, they have nearly universally exclaimed, "Finally, somebody gets us! Listen to him!"). The two statements I heard during the first year or two the book was out were, "Not *my/our* kids; you're talking about those kids in LA," and "You're just focusing on the extreme or fringe kids, not the _____ (fill in the blank: smart, stable, gifted, etc.) kids." Today, whenever I speak or interact with those who deal directly with teens on the field, including parents—and I get to speak to thousands every year on this topic around the world—the response is almost always overwhelming: "We *get* it, already! Now, what do we *do* about it?"

So why would we need a second edition if the case has been made and we are collectively ready to do what it takes to bring substantive change to the way we care for and guide children and adolescents into productive adulthood? If society is ready to reengage our young by altering, sometimes radically, the systems and structures that serve them, why do we need to do more research, look at new and fresh data, ask deeper and more penetrating questions, challenge long-held assumptions, and be dragged into a more profound sense of fear for our kids? It is for one simple reason, and in the first edition I barely realized the implications of what *Hurt* had discovered and presented. The reason for *Hurt 2.0* is that those who control and define the systems and structures charged with nurturing and training up our young (and especially those who have the power associated with them) are either ignorant of how destructive life is for today's adolescents or unwilling to take the wide array of indicators seriously.

To me, both of these options are beyond regrettable: they are reprehensible.

For those who think I speak in hyperbole or who have encountered *Hurt* along the way (maybe even read it) but who somehow were able to discount the findings or ignore the implications, this edition is for you, as well as any newcomers who have never been exposed to these results and conclusions. *Hurt 2.0* uses the basic framework of the first edition, keeping in what has remained the same over the last few years. At the same time this edition takes on a whole series of new insights and data that have become relevant since the first edition was published. This edition goes point by point, paragraph by paragraph, and study by study in order to carefully assess what is going on with and inside today's kids.

Examples of some of the new materials and ideas examined for this edition include the following (and there are many, many more throughout *Hurt 2.0*):

- A CDC study states that 25 percent of fourteen- to nineteen-year-old adolescent girls have "at least one" of the more common sexually transmitted diseases (and this study was limited to those *reported* through CDC channels, so there is no knowing how widespread the danger is, and what the rates are when sexual activity ramps up in their twenties).
- In a Princeton and Cornell study on self-injury, one in five college freshmen girls and one in seven boys reported "self-injury" (a finding

based on self-reported data, which could mean it is much more serious than even these numbers—and this at our elite universities).

- MILF[1] was the sexually charged "word" of the day in the early 2000s; today those words are "cougar" and "sexting."[2]

- A campaign by developmental psychologist Jeffrey J. Arnett and others to remove the term *adolescent* from post-high school "emerging adults" so as not to "offend" those in their twenties and even thirties who are having a hard time settling into adult roles has created a ripple effect of recasting what term we use for the fourteen- to twenty-year-old former "midadolescent." Yet we see now three distinct stages of adolescence, given the classic understanding of the term, where early (eleven to fourteen years old) is marked by *concrete* cognition and psychosocial dynamism, late (twenty to as late as early thirties) employs *abstract* cognition and psychosocial dynamism, and the midadolescent is so engrossed in personal survival that his or her life and perspective can be described as *egocentric abstraction*.

- Yesterday's "helicopter parents," whose perceived overinvestment in their child's world and performance can result in overprotecting their children from consequences, have become "stealth bomber parents" who actually do more harm than good because their children learn how to adapt at the expense of their own developmental needs.

- In attempting to understand how midadolescents make sense of their daily lives, the first edition described them living in "layers." Based on new research theory and data, as well as our research team's observations and conclusions, *Hurt 2.0* uses the far more accurate image of multiple identities to describe the way midadolescents move from setting to setting, and even sometimes person to person. They live out of "multiple selves" (versus layers), and each of these selves has an interactive and causal relationship with the others.

These are but a sample of the new insights and perspectives offered in *Hurt 2.0*. This edition does not highlight specific changes from the first edition, but rather integrates new observations and studies from the last decade with the previous material. The response to the first edition has varied among different readers. For those "field workers" who serve and work with teenagers regularly—educators, adolescent counselors, social workers, urban youth and family specialists, youth ministry workers—*Hurt* has been almost universally embraced as giving a name and an explanation to what so many have experienced for a decade or more. In academic circles, regardless of the discipline, the reception to both the research and conclusions has ranged from lukewarm to negative by researchers and theorists, to the point of being dismissed by many academics. Some claim that the study and findings do not meet the criteria that rigorous scholarly study demands, and therefore, at times these results have generally not been invited to the conceptual table of adolescent health and well-being. Colleagues in various academic and pragmatic disciplines should realize that the research methods we have used provide the most academically credible and sound way of getting under the surface of what is actually happening inside the hearts and minds of this emerging population.

From our team's perspective, the traditional ways of studying young people—self-reports, wide-ranging general survey data sets, and focused interviews—obviously add to our understanding, which is why we have included much of this research in our citations and references. Even these methods of studying youth, however, fail to adequately describe and explain the complexities of the front edge of societal and developmental change, and, as a result, leaders often fail to recognize the significance of these changes for a young person growing up today. Few marriage and family therapists, clinical psychologists, educational administrators, and policy makers and influencers—to name just a few of those gatekeepers who hold the power to change our systemic response to the needs of the young—are even aware of these data and conclusions. In our opinion, it is vital that the way our adolescents view and experience reality be brought to the forefront of the national conversation, especially in light of the vast chasm between their per-spective and our cultural power systems. Our hope is that *Hurt 2.0* will present such an overwhelming case that dismissal on academic or technical grounds will be untenable.

I realized how important our collective dialogue about these issues is when on a panel with Dr. Christian Smith of the University of Notre Dame discussing his research from the National Study of Youth and Religion and book and film *Soul Searching* about the religious lives of contemporary adolescents.[3] We had watched the film prior to our discus-sion, and on stage he told the audience,

> One observation about the film, and this has struck me increasingly, but especially sitting right next to Chap today, is one theme that was not in the book (*Soul Searching*) hardly at all but was really in the movie, but it just came in through the process, was how teens are hurting. There was a lot of hurt in the movie, and that was not in the book. We did not write it into the movie, it just was there. There was actually more suicide talk in the movie that we edited out. I mean, we very carefully cut pieces out because we thought, this is just going to be a movie about suicide, so we cut it out.[4]

In developing a documentary that tries to get at the religious life of teenagers, something "struck" the filmmakers: today's kids are hurting. This is also what we saw in *Hurt*, and since the first edition, we believe the situation has gotten worse. More and more people are noticing, and perhaps it is time for all of us who study, serve, and make policy affecting the young to come together and address the issue of systemic abandonment, isolation, and most of all, hurt. For those who have read the first edition, the changes in *Hurt 2.0* should bring a depth and freshness to their understanding of the plight of today's teenagers. Our dream is that this edition will create the kind of stir among scholars, practitioners, parents, and, most of all, those in power over the systems and structures that guide how we work with and nurture the young that will lead us as a society to take the necessary steps to collectively reengage our young as they so desperately need and deserve.

preface to the first edition

"Why would anyone want to study us?"

This cynical sentiment from a seventeen-year-old high school junior struck me as a bit odd.

"I mean, what's the big deal about kids? Why would you get paid to write a book about us?"

Sharon had been in a class I had substitute taught, and the only thing I knew about her was that she seemed to have a cold cloud of gloom constantly hanging about her, like Seattle in November. She had been bugging me for some time about my motive for hanging around the school. My explanation of a sabbatical leave from my teaching job failed to satisfy her, as did my lighthearted quips about liking kids, and even my more detailed, serious explanation that I believed most adults had little understanding of where adolescents were coming from. Sharon simply thought there had to be an ulterior motive, an angle that would somehow serve me at the expense of her community of peers.

"Is this going to make you famous?"

I laughed out loud. "After writing some books that few actually read, I gave up on that kind of thing a long time ago."

"Then, why? Why are you doing this? Will it really matter to anyone?"

Her last question caught me off guard. What began as an idea for a sabbatical evolved into this book. I started with a desire to get to know students. I have spent my entire adult life attempting to care for what most adults refer to as "kids." But as the research objectives, methods, hypotheses, and scope of my interest took shape, and when a publisher became intrigued with the idea of a series devoted to the study of youth, family, and culture, I realized that this book had become far more than just several hundred hours of personal reflection on the state of contemporary middle adolescence. It had become a vital story that needed to be told. But the question has haunted me ever since: will this book matter to anyone?

Whether it will has ceased to be my concern, because I cannot force people to care about something; they must ultimately choose. I wrote this book for those who are willing to consider how life is different for today's high school students compared with past generations. This book will matter to anyone who chooses to take my findings seriously. Not every adult, or perhaps not even most, will agree with the discoveries I share and the conclusions I make. I offer, however, a detailed attempt to bring to light what the vast majority of adults have either ignored or missed. My goal is to raise the level of dialogue and ultimately the level of individual, corporate, and systemic commitment to the young of our communities.

As you read, I hope you will not lightly dismiss or easily disregard the observations contained here. I may not be right about everything. As with most ethnographic reports, this study is bound to be filled with theoretical holes and at times even missteps. But I have attempted an honest look at American teenagers from the inside perspective of their world. I have tested my conclusions with a wide variety of young people across the United States. They have affirmed that this is the most accurate and compassionate observation of their world they have ever received from an adult. Obviously, many others have gone before me, but I do not know of a single trained social scientist who has entered the adolescent world to gain a deeper understanding of today's postmodern teenagers.

For me, this project was more an exploration of a new world than an academic enterprise. The deeper I ventured into their world, the more I realized how much I had to learn. For me, this was Hillary's Everest, Cousteau's oceans, and Lewis and Clark's adventures. Like the handful of Europeans who headed over the western horizon to find an easier, more direct route to the East but found themselves in foreign and at times unrecognizable territory, I too had an unexpected adventure. I experienced a myriad of emotions over the course of the last two years, as I could not step away from the passions, the arrogance, and the groanings of the youth I came to love. May this book become an adventure of intrigue, concern, and compassion for you as well.

I started this project as an attempt to add to the research literature and scholarly understanding of what is happening in the developmental stage known as midadolescence (which spans roughly ages fourteen to twenty). As a result of spending hundreds of hours observing and interacting with students, I came away with far more. I realized that if I were going to speak and write about breaking the cycle of abandonment that our young experience so that they can somehow experience the kind of life we as adults so earnestly strive for, I had to be changed.

I could no longer live as I had. I had to find a way to care for the young people in my community. I was reminded that I am a steward of the most precious resource any society can ever have: its young. I am still in my late forties, a typical husband and father with a job, a mortgage, and a hidden need to figure out life for myself. But I have found a way to flesh out my desire to make a difference by having dinner with three high school boys every week.

May this book challenge you, disturb you, and cause you to be a champion for those who are desperate for the advocacy of an adult community who cares.

My High School Adventure

I had just started substitute teaching as a central part of my research project on the state of contemporary adolescence. Soon after telling a few high school students that I was there to listen to them, to try to understand them, and to write a book for adults about what life is like for teenagers today, one vocal junior became the spokesman for about a dozen others.

"Tell them our story," he remarked. "Tell them the truth—that nobody cares, that nobody listens, that teachers and coaches and cops and parents don't even know who we are. Tell them that and see if anybody listens. Ha! Not a chance!"

Although most were enamored by the idea of "being in a book," this remark was typical of a deeper skepticism I sensed in many students as I began a study of high school life. For more than six months I spent nearly every day with high school students as a participant-observer in their world. I wanted to get close and to listen to them, to develop enough trust for them to let me in to places that few adults are allowed. I wanted to discern their complex, contradictory worldview and watch how they navigate the multilayered expectations and relationships that control their landscape.

As a practitioner who works directly with adolescents, as well as an academically trained professor of youth, family, and culture, I had found that the literature about young people (from both religious and secular sources) provided conflicting data at best and was usually too generic and stereotypical to offer caring adults the level of information that could help them to connect authentically and deeply with students in a rapidly changing world. I sensed a vital need for an academically based research project that studied the world of contemporary adolescents. After years of hanging around the fringes of the adolescent world and reading books such as Patricia Hersch's *A Tribe Apart*, I knew that the only way to be invited in was to log the time and to build trusting relationships with students on their turf.

This study applies accepted social science research methodology to the reality of life for the middle adolescent in contemporary American society. The goal is to follow in the footsteps of some of the courageous pioneers, such as Hersch, who have reported on the world of today's young by applying a standard and quality of research methodology that scholars, academics, and even practitioners who care about and interface with adolescents have to engage.[1]

The Method

I decided to function as a participant-observer at a public high school in north Los Angeles County.[2] I chose Crescenta Valley High School because it is a nationally recognized Blue Ribbon School for excellence in academic achievement; has a widely diverse ethnic population (including many newly arrived immigrant students); has historically strong and diverse sports, music, and drama programs; and has a mean population that is socioeconomically middle class with an extremely wide economic divergence. In addition, the coprincipals were supportive of my noninvasive research methods and were even interested in interacting with and learning from the study in order to improve the academic experience for each student in the school.

In attempting to understand more fully what life is like for middle adolescents, I decided to conduct an ethnographic study (which basically meant becoming a part of their world) instead of relying on either objectified quantitative instruments such as written questionnaires, which would greatly limit the scope of the inquiry, or less personal qualitative methodologies such as phone surveys, which depend heavily on small sample interviews and controlled environment settings. Participant-observation research methodology allows for and even encourages new and fresh insights and avoids a priori conceptual or theoretical limitations in a changing sociocultural environment. A tenet of qualitative research methodology is the conviction that "social research is an interactive rather than controlling process."[3] Therefore, ethnography, a form of more deeply involved qualitative research, is a useful tool in attempting to grasp the world of a specific population in a changing environment. Although this type of research has some obvious limitations, such as the researcher's own historical, socioeconomic, gender, and ethnic biases,[4] a social scientist can gain a great deal of insight when he or she is welcomed as a participant in a relatively closed system and is allowed to record his or her experiences as an observer.[5]

Even though I sought to have an open mind and to learn from the world of the students instead of from my experience, training, and literature exposure, I had to concede that I carried into the study a powerful set of preconceptions. It was impossible for me to be completely value- and theory-free. I acknowledge this limitation in both the methodology and the research conclusions.

There is a helpful aspect, however, to a highly informed and dedicated investigator applying knowledge and experience to a qualitative sociological methodology. I am, and was when I began, intimately acquainted with the diverse and sometimes contradictory views of both the academic and popular literature on adolescence and adolescent development. I was also aware of the emergence of midadolescence as an accepted substage of the adolescent process. If I had not known that in the last ten to fifteen years scholars had accepted the existence of three stages of adolescence (early, middle, and late) instead of the historically understood two (early and late), I might have inadvertently ascribed attributes to the high school students in this study in a way that could have skewed my results and therefore affected my conclusions. My prior experience in the field of adolescent studies prepared me to enter this population.

Why Not the Different and the Fringe

Even a cursory glance at the table of contents reveals that this book spends little time on specific issues that divide, segment, or separate students. Certainly an argument can be made that economic, ethnic, or personal history can significantly impact an adolescent's view and experience of life. After months of consideration, I chose to focus on the more clearly observable, broad-stroke issues facing the vast majority of American high school students, even those who have been oppressed and marginalized by class distinctions and racial inequities. In focusing on sexuality, busyness, athletics, school, family, and the like, I hope to give readers the opportunity to enter the halls, locker rooms, and classrooms of the campus. What I intentionally left out were the sociological differences among races, between the poor and the wealthy, and even between genders. I did this to look at the larger whole, of which all midadolescents are a part, to discover a baseline from which to spawn further discussion and investigation. What I record here is an accurate portrayal of high school life for most students.

In addition to these intentional omissions, I also chose to leave out significant detail regarding some of the deeper, more complex issues that many midadolescents from all walks of life face. Issues such as drug use, eating disorders, physical and other kinds of abuse, date rape, sexual addiction, and cutting (a form of self-mutilation that is becoming more and more common), to name a few, are only alluded to in this book. By not highlighting them I am not saying they are unimportant compared to the more global issues I offer, nor am I asserting that students who face such issues do not warrant a close look. I did not discuss these issues (or in some cases only lightly touched on them) for two reasons. First, I believe these situations and behaviors make sense only when studied and discussed in light of the more sweeping issues presented in this book. Wrestling with "fringe" issues (and students) without an elementary grasp of the overall midadolescent social and cultural landscape could produce superficial and incomplete assumptions and conclusions regarding these issues.

Second, I did not focus on these destructive and painful behaviors and issues because most students between fourteen and twenty years of age touch at least the edges of them at some point in their journey. By its very nature adolescence is a time of great change. Students who enter high school as Goths[6] may become Punks,[7] then druggies, and finally all-league varsity soccer players. This constantly shifting identity formation and experimentation involves various aspects of fringe elements or behaviors, making identifying and categorizing each behavior an extremely difficult, thorny, and even academically suspect enterprise. As soon as you think you understand what is going on with a specific population, group, or even individual student, that population, group, or student takes off in a different direction.[8] Therefore, I chose to leave the discussion of these fringe elements, behaviors, and issues to others.

A Conclusion and a Beginning

Adolescence is a hard thing to describe. It is even harder to define. For the vast majority of adults, it is hard to understand. Most of us want to take the easy route of claiming that it hasn't changed since we were in high school. Others say it really doesn't matter if adults understand kids, as long as the young live up to adult values of respect, commitment, and hard work. Still others fall into the category of "If you can't understand them, join them!"[9] After years of study and conversations with countless adults, there is a gnawing, nagging reality that even though we may want to be committed to being a light to our young, we have no idea who or what we are dealing with.

This book is an attempt to peer into the foreign and seemingly hostile world of midadolescents. My intent is to try to understand them in order to care about them more effectively. This book may disturb you, make you mad (at me as well as the culture), frustrate you, or even cause you to disagree vehemently. As the researcher and author of this study, I find any and all of these reactions welcome. For too many years, even decades, adult society has pushed aside and blamed the young for their "rebellious" bent and for their seeming indifference to societal rules, norms, and values. As you embark on this journey, I ask you to consider who or what has created the catalyst for the rebellious and cavalier arrogance of the younger generation over the last fifty years. Could it be that the source has finally been identified? Is it possible that what we as adults see as a rebellious generation is really a uniquely vulnerable population living out the necessary reaction to being set to sea rudderless, adrift without a compass? Welcome to *Hurt: Inside the World of Today's Teenagers.*

acknowledgments

L ike any book, this one is a product of numerous people. I had the privilege of working alongside many who contributed to this book, and I gratefully acknowledge their contribution. First, thank you to the many people who worked on the original research for the first edition, especially Amy Jacober and Mark Maines. I was also given the gift of numerous editors, most of them graduate students, but Emrys, Jim, and Margaret worked many long hours and gave invaluable insight into refining the first edition.

For the second edition, twelve grad students gave many hours compiling research that strengthened, challenged, and updated the issues presented in this book. *Hurt 2.0* would not have happened without them, so thank you to Luke Brooks, Paul Ching, Chris Dart, Chad DeKay, Greg Dolmage, Erik Fuller, Alison Kilgore, Lee Mullins, Keeban Nam, Virgie Pickering, Angela Williams, and Dan Zomerlei. I believe that this second edition takes these issues and not only updates what is going on in the lives of adolescents but also is now an even better and more helpful guide to understanding our kids. There are two people who drove this effort to the next level, and it is important to note that I could never have accomplished this revision without either of them. I am so grateful that Kristie Berglund and Jesse Oakes committed to this project and led the way to making this extensive revision a reality. Where this book makes sense and works, much of the credit goes to these friends. If there are any errors, omissions, or even a leap or two in logic, the blame goes solely to me.

I was greatly helped by the administration, faculty, and staff at Crescenta Valley High School. I am fully aware that this is one of the best schools in the country, and to be embraced for my work among you was a true gift.

I especially want to thank the high school students at Crescenta Valley and in other places where I have had the privilege of walking with them and hearing their stories. Your openness and gut-wrenching honesty made this far more than a study or even a book. You changed me. I will never again be able to lump high school students into a huge, stereotypical mass, because now I see each one as a unique, valuable person who matters. Thank you, each one of you, for allowing me to see inside your world. I only hope I did you justice in this work.

Thank you also to my family (Dee, Chap, Rob, and Katie) for putting up with my moods and struggles while getting this study into book form. You have, as usual, been a source of strength to me. I am blessed and a better man, husband, father, and advocate of kids because of each of you.

Lastly, to my students and colleagues at Fuller Theological Seminary, you teach me to keep pushing the envelope regarding what it means to care for those we are called to serve. May this project cause the world to be stirred to the point of taking our young seriously, and may it begin with us.

introduction to the youth, family, and culture series

While this book is written as a general academic book for readers from a wide variety of life experiences and perspectives, this is the first book in a series dedicated to the preparation and vocational strengthening of those who are committed to the spiritual development of adolescents from a faith perspective. The series title—Youth, Family, and Culture—frames the broad categories for studying and caring for the needs of the young. The hope is that those who care about the specific needs of adolescents will be encouraged to examine the environment of those they are seeking to understand and serve. For those in the faith community, the label "youth ministry" has historically been used to describe a Christian response to the particular needs of adolescents. This series, however, is more committed to helping readers think deeply about issues such as family relationships, changes in development, social setting, and the nature and influence of the culture in which young people live and think than it is to providing programmatic, highly contextual, or event-centered pragmatic models or guidelines. The series seeks to cause readers to think differently about the complex and multifaceted challenges faced in ministry to postmodern adolescents.

Hurt: Inside the World of Today's Teenagers is the first book in this series. For the college or graduate student, parent, counselor, or educator who does not share the religious worldview of the author or the series, this book provides a qualitative analysis of the state of contemporary adolescence. For those who come to this book with a commitment to serving the young from a faith conviction, *Hurt 2.0* offers in broad strokes insight into their hidden social setting.

part 1

the changing adolescent world

The smiles are genuine, and the flashes of joy are real. There is no doubt that much of life on the surface of the adolescent landscape is light, carefree, and straightforward. This is a time when life can feel like it is full of possibilities and when no barrier seems insurmountable. This is the place where students happily run at the lunch bell, where cheerleaders giggle in packs, and where athletes saunter without a care in the world. On the surface of their world, high school students seem no different from their parents or even their grandparents. The games bring excitement. There are dances and parties to attend, plays to put on, and homework to get done. In the majority of high schools, college is on the mind of many students, and the future seems basically bright and welcoming.

But there is another side to this idyllic picture. The surface of the adolescent landscape is where internal fears, loneliness, and insecurities must be held in check, where friendships are generally shallow, and where performance and image are the name of the game. Beneath the superficial and all-too-often cosmetic layer of high school life, there are dark, lonely corners where the neon light of sanitized conformity seldom penetrates. Just below the sheen of coerced normality are the stress and strain of personal survival in a hostile world.

There are two different perspectives on the nature of the adolescent landscape, depending on one's viewpoint and on the angle from which one looks at the evidence. Adults believe either that contemporary adolescents are highly nurtured, motivated, and functioning or that they are in dire straits. In this discussion, there is rarely a middle ground.

How is it that we are so divided concerning the state of our young? Asking a vocal advocate of either perspective to answer this question can invite scorn to the point of ridicule.[1] Perhaps the solution lies not in trying to seek compromise between the perspectives but in attempting to reconcile the apparently contradictory data. While recognizing the complexities of the debate, affirming the evidence of well-done empirical research, and intuitively sensing that all is not well with contemporary midadolescents, I sought to find a way to hold these perspectives in tension. Somewhere in the middle of the study an explanation for the conflicting views began to dawn on me: both perspectives are valid and real, yet on different levels. In most settings, for example, adolescents appear genuinely happy, carefree, and seemingly healthy. What the vast majority of high school students confided, however, was a far different story. After months of reflection on and study of the perspectives concerning the adolescent landscape, I concluded that midadolescence is a new, understudied element of the adolescent process and journey. Unlike at any other stage of life, midadolescence is a world of multiple selves.[2] Midadolescents are not able to compartmentalize their lives while operating out of a personal sense of self. Society has let go of personal and individual commitment to the young. Therefore, during midadolescence, they find themselves forced to function out of multiple selves. To survive, a young person must learn how to be a child, a student, an athlete, and a friend, while also continuing the ever-lengthening process of determining who he or she is. In other words, we have allowed a new stage of life known as midadolescence to emerge, and this new stage carries with it new and at times very difficult challenges.

Adolescents have the ability to apply abstract thought and reflective action within a given realm, or "self," of life. But once a midadolescent has moved on from a self—be it a relationship, a role, an expectation, or an activity—he or she creates a different, almost totally unique conceptualization process in the new self and then applies abstract thought and processing in that context as well. This has always been true of adolescents who have the ability to actualize abstract and nuanced thought processes. But what is new is the lack of ability to construct bridges between one self and another. The inability to see contradictions as contradictions and the ability to easily rationalize seemingly irreconcilable beliefs, attitudes, or values are but two of many markers that may be pointing to an emerging phase of adolescent development and may provide a key indicator of the essence of midadolescence.

In some ways, I am diving into waters that go beyond the scope of my academic training and expertise, yet I am also aware that few have allowed themselves to ask whether changes in culture may have an effect on the cognitive (and therefore moral and even spiritual) development of an adolescent. This is for others to discuss, debate, and research, but I am certain that something is going on, something that has changed the very nature of adolescence.

Part 1 lays the foundation for the premise of this book: adolescents have been cut off for far too long from the adults who have the power and experience to escort them into the greater society. Adolescents have been abandoned. They have, therefore, created their own world, a world that is designed to protect them from the destructive forces and wiles of the adult community. May this section open your eyes to the world beneath.

the changing face of adolescence

These kids are no different from when I was a kid. They are just more indulged today. And they have more options—from sports to money to the internet. Kids today are just a more spoiled breed of us when we were young.

high school teacher

This assessment was volunteered by a veteran teacher I had gotten to know over the course of my time on the high school campus. Occasionally, he would ask me how my research was going. On one occasion, he made this definitive declaration. Once he said it, and because of the way he said it, I knew it would not be easy to convince him that, indeed, things had changed—and changed a great deal.

Through numerous conversations since, and by immersing myself in literature related to the study of adolescence from a variety of disciplines, I have become aware that many adults have a similar view of adolescents. The tune of accepted folk wisdom goes something like this: "Kids (i.e., adolescents) have always been kids and have always been a part of the social landscape. Things may change on the surface, but teenagers have always been with us and have always pushed the extremes of adult society. They are basically the same now as they were thousands of years ago. Only the styles have changed." This perception is regularly supported in articles, stories, media reports, and books about the young. Even the term *kids* can mean many things.[1] It can refer to any age group from pre-elementary school children to those in their mid to late twenties (such as when a new teacher confided in me, "I'm as much a kid as the guys in my class!"). When referring to the young, adults rarely attempt to distinguish between those who are just leaving the psychosocial and relational confines of childhood and entering that strange and wholly different experience known as early adolescence, and those who are in graduate school living off their parents and "trying to figure out what to do with my life." It is all too easy in our culture not to ask the question, what is the difference between adolescents today and teenagers of the past? Instead, we fall back on the caricature that kids are kids, and they have always been kids. But is this true?

At times, adults attempt to reach back into antiquity to add credence to this characterization. Socrates, for example, is often erroneously credited with this comment on how the young of his day were viewed: "Our youth love luxury. They have bad manners, contempt for authority; they show disrespect for their elders, and love to chatter in places of exercise. Children are now tyrants, not the servants of their household. They no longer rise when their elders enter the room. They contradict their parents, chatter before company, gobble up their food, and tyrannize their teachers."[2]

Augustine, bishop of Hippo in North Africa (fourth century AD), is known for his philandering and "adolescent" lifestyle prior to his conversion to Christianity. Augustine himself described his teenage years in his *Confessions*: "I had a period of leisure, living at home with my parents and not doing any work at all, the brambles of lust grew up right over my head."[3]

These and a handful of other similar quotations have been cited to add credibility to the notion that young people throughout history have always been basically the same. The attempt is to show that adolescents of antiquity were essentially the same as adolescents of the 1940s and the early 2000s, and that the issues facing adolescents and their responses to them are universal. Indeed, Eddie Haskell, the prototypical deceiving and conniving adolescent of the late-1950s and early-1960s television show *Leave It to Beaver*, is but one example from the past of a teenager who would be no different today. Add to that James Dean (*Rebel without a Cause*) in the 1950s, Arthur Fonzarelli (The Fonz from *Happy Days*) in the 1970s, and even the rebellion showcased in the movie *The Breakfast Club* in the 1980s, and it is easy to see that in the minds of adults, adolescence has not changed much over the decades or even the centuries. It is for this reason that today's teenagers—particularly with all the time they spend creating and maintaining profiles on social networking websites—are often deemed to be "all about me, me, me," even though research has revealed that such activities certainly "need not imply narcissistic self-absorption" but are more likely an extension of peer-group relationships.[4]

This book contends that adolescence is a fundamentally different thing than it was even thirty years ago. There is, in fact, nearly universal support for the idea that adolescence as we know it was a cultural invention of Western society that was first noticed around 1900.[5] Numerous anecdotal narratives across time and cultures depict characteristics of what we call adolescence. The examples often cited (such as the ones above), however, represent extremely unusual exceptions to the record of civilization. Citing these and other examples from antiquity to assert that the adolescent experience in contemporary American culture is equivalent to the experience of teenagers in ancient Greece is participation in a reductionism that is dangerous at best. For example, Socrates's argument, mentioned above, is not even true to the original text[6] and, moreover, was not concerned with the young but with the excesses of the entire society. In more recent decades, media depictions of rebellious and insolent youth have offered a clear distinction between the "good" kids and those who lived on the fringes of the youth culture rather than the mainstream, like Eddie Haskell in *Leave It to Beaver* and *Happy Days'* The Fonz. Yet society's view of teenagers has been subtly shifting over the last several decades to where many adults view teenagers in general as insolent, difficult, and arrogant. Even while this perception has gained momentum, there still is this fundamental perspective that kids have always been the way we now see them.

Throughout time and in every society, the dominant culture has seen the young as its most sacred treasure. Because of this, the human life span has historically been understood as having only two primary stages: childhood and adulthood. Children were viewed as a precious and nurtured resource and as such were guided into their place in the world by those responsible to care for them in their family and community. Once a child had completed the rituals, rites of passage, and training experiences necessary to be accepted into interdependent relationships within the adult community, he or she was fully assimilated as an adult member of that community. This process, called the *rite of passage* by Arnold van Gennep in 1908,[7] had three elements: separation from the old status; transition, usually with a specified ritual; and incorporation into the adult community. For over a century, formalized processes of incorporating the young into adulthood have been devalued, especially in the United States.[8]

First labeled and identified around the beginning of the twentieth century,[9] the span between childhood and adulthood, beginning with puberty and ending with the assuming of full adult responsibilities or even economic independence,[10] was approximately three years. The average age of menarche, the most common measurable marker for the beginning of adolescence in a society, was, prior to 1900, fourteen years, and a person began to assume an adult role in society as young as sixteen. Many accepted developmental theories, created primarily in the mid-twentieth century, tend to view the adolescent journey as a relatively stable, predictable, and orderly, though sometimes difficult, process.[11] For the past two or three decades, however, researchers and theorists attempting to understand human development more fully have challenged many of these orderly themes and stages of development. Postmodern culture has also tossed a proverbial wrench into the gears of developmental theory. In particular, variables such as shifts in cultural values and structure; changes in the family system; new research into peer relations, gender, and ethnic uniqueness; and new ways of thinking about morality, character, and ethics have become increasingly important in describing the nature of adolescence. Some researchers believe that culture has changed so quickly that the developmental, societal, and relational needs of children have been neglected in recent decades and that by the time children reach adolescence they have been left on their own to attempt to navigate the path toward adulthood.[12]

Adolescence—What Is It?

Many adults not only struggle with the notion of changing adolescence but also have a hard time describing what an adolescent is. I have experimented with defining an adolescent in a variety of settings with adults, and with few exceptions, when a group of adults are asked to vote on whether teenagers are big, more sophisticated children or inexperienced young adults, they will invariably be split fifty-fifty, generally with parents of older adolescents voting the former and parents of young children the latter. Society has not provided much help, for the inherent ambiguity and relative imprecision of the term *adolescent* causes us to fall back on more easily measured and therefore identifiable terms such as *teenager* and *pre-teen* or even blatantly generic terms such as *youth*.[13] Adolescence has been relegated to an amorphous transitionary phase of life. Most people see those in this general age range as being "sort of adults and sort of kids."[14]

This foggy view of the period of adolescence has given rise to much adult ambivalence and even to systemic neglect. We simply have not agreed on who or what we are dealing with, and it is therefore easier to turn a blind eye to the unique needs of this population. In spite of the rhetoric and wishful thinking that adolescent life has not changed all that much, the vast majority of adults believe that there is something different going on in the world of today's adolescents. In hundreds of casual and formal conversations I have had with adults, when it comes to nailing down what is truly happening with young people in our society, nearly everyone agreed that the rapid and in many ways severe changes in the last few decades have created new challenges, issues, and dilemmas for adolescents. But what those challenges and issues are and how they impact adolescents remain unclear. On top of this, many adults are not clear about the most fundamental question of all: Are adolescents big children (a view that brings with it a more or less clear set of assumptions) or little adults (a view that moves us into another set of assumptions and practices)? Or are they a blend of both? As Frederick Buechner puts it, "The opaque glance and the pimples. The fancy new nakedness they're all dressed up in with no place to go. The eyes full of secrets they have a strong hunch everybody is on to. The shadowed brow. Being not quite a child and not quite a grown-up either is hard work, and they look it. Living in two worlds at once is no picnic."[15]

While we may implicitly affirm that adolescence is an in-between-but-not-quite place, this view may not tell the whole story. Developmental theorists have acknowledged for decades what the general populace has yet to comprehend, much less embrace: Adolescence is not a blend of both child and adult, nor is it an expanded phase of either. Adolescence is a unique phase of life that must be understood and dealt with on its own merits.

A generally accepted definition of adolescence has been summarized by developmental psychologist John Santrock. He calls adolescence "the period of life between childhood and adulthood. . . . [The process] lasts from roughly 10–13 years of age and ends at 18–22 years of age. [However,] defining when adolescence ends is not an easy task. It has been said that adolescence begins in biology and ends in culture."[16] Santrock offers as tight a definition as the phenomenon allows, for the entire adolescent experience fluctuates constantly and deviates greatly according to such variables as culture, locale, and even familial stability and makeup. A standard academic definition of adolescence comes down to "two main components—separateness and self-assertion."[17] Other scholars add to this drive for uniqueness ("separateness") and quest for personal autonomy ("self-assertion") a desire to move toward the discovery of community, belonging, and interdependence.[18] Adolescence, then, is a psychosocial, independent search for a unique identity or separateness,[19] with the end goals being a certain knowledge of who one is in relation to others, a willingness to take responsibility for who one is becoming, and a realized commitment to live with others in community.

Another important factor in understanding the nature of adolescence has to do with brain development. A recent radio report noted a significant aspect of this: "The nerve cells that connect teenagers' frontal lobes with the rest of their brains are sluggish. Teenagers don't have as much of the fatty coating called myelin, or 'white matter' that adults have in this area."[20] Neurologist Frances Jensen contends that teenagers "often seem so maddeningly self-centered" simply because that's the particular developmental phase their brains are in: "They aren't yet at that place where they're thinking about—or capable, necessarily, of thinking about the effects of their behavior on other people. That requires insight"—which, as the report goes on to state, "requires . . . a fully connected frontal lobe."[21] Particularly because it is still in such a crucial state of development, the teenage brain is "tuned to be responsive to everything in their environment" and is "wired to form new connections" in response. This is valuable information for us to consider as we reflect on the way teens are often regarded. Joseph Allen and Claudia Worrell Allen note, "It seems we humans have a strong, persistent bias to attribute behavior to innate qualities of individuals even when the objective evidence that their environment is shaping their actions is overwhelming. . . . This bias is at its most persistent and most dangerous when applied to groups that lack the social status or verbal skill needed to articulate just how much they are affected by their environments. Groups like adolescents."[22]

Some pressing questions arise from these observations. First of all, what is the difference between the ways kids' brains are being formed today and how they were formed in previous generations? How have shifting environmental factors affected the development of our teens' brains? As we did not have MRIs forty years ago, it is impossible to answer these questions definitively. However, calling attention to research conducted by Bogdan Draganski and his colleagues in 2004 on the dramatic way the human brain is influenced by its environment—even to the point where the simple act of learning to juggle can quickly change the structure of the brain—Allen and Allen rightly wonder, "If a few weeks of juggling practice can change the brain, what can years of passivity and overprotection do?"[23]

The Timing and Duration of Adolescence

To understand adolescence, it is important to define its parameters—where it begins and ends and what it involves. Using Santrock's definition—that adolescence ends when culture affirms one's entrance into the mainstream of adulthood—we can say that adolescence is the journey from biological adulthood to societal adulthood. This is the process sometimes referred to as "second individuation."[24] The emerging adolescent, embarking on a new journey in development, seeks to assert his or her distinctiveness and move toward an internal locus of control, while at the same time remaining relationally connected as an ongoing member of the family system and the community.[25] While there is no standardized definition of the term, *individuation* has, for many, become the central issue of the adolescent process and therefore the overall motivating task of adolescence.

As noted above, the oft-cited beginning point of adolescence is puberty. There is debate, however, over when the exact physiological changes of puberty begin, and this is even harder to determine for boys than for girls. It is relatively accepted that the age of puberty for girls has been slowly dropping, from fourteen-and-a-half years old a century ago to as early as twelve years old today. The American Medical Association, the U.S. Centers for Disease Control, and the majority of social scientists report this as demonstrable fact.[26]

When culture affirms that someone has individuated in terms of identity, is willing to take responsibility for his or her life and choices, and has entered interdependently into the community and adult relationships, that person is said to be an adult. This, then, defines the end point or completion of adolescence. Interestingly, almost no social scientist or developmental theorist uses legal age as a reference point for the end of adolescence. Because the process is psychosocial, chronological factors such as readiness for marriage, driving, smoking cigarettes, voting, or drinking alcohol are not considerations when defining the end point of adolescence.

The process is about how one sees oneself and thereby relates to others. Nearly everyone today who ventures to define when adolescence ends states that it is somewhere in the middle to late twenties. According to a recent study by the MacArthur Foundation Research Network on Transitions to Adulthood, "people between 20 and 34 are taking longer to finish their educations, establish themselves in careers, marry, have children and become financially independent."[27] Allen and Allen assert that "twenty-five is becoming the new fifteen,"[28] and Robert Epstein laments that "for the first time in human history, we have artificially extended childhood well past puberty. . . . Somewhere along the line, we lost sight of—and buried—the potential of our teens."[29] While proposed responses to this issue may differ significantly,[30] the phenomenon of extended adolescence itself is widely acknowledged.

This ambiguity bumps up against everyday life when decisions have to be made regarding when a person is an adult or a still-developing adolescent. Unfortunately, at times governmental agencies and systems do not seem capable of or even interested in wading through the complex issues that emerge when someone clearly is a midadolescent, behaves like a midadolescent, and yet participates in behaviors that have adult consequences. This is but one stark example of what we all must ultimately face as we consider the changing adolescent. There are countless other examples, many of which I experienced and are in this book, that demonstrate the need for adults to wrestle with the facts of our changing culture when it comes to caring for the young.

What about Now?

"When I was in high school . . ."

Throughout this study, I must have heard this preamble several dozen times. I did look for ways to stoke the fires of critique and dismay buried beneath the sheen of adult compassion for the young, but it rarely took much effort to get adults going on a critically laced, negative comparison between today's adolescents and themselves. Inevitably and without much prodding, the focus would turn from what I was seeing to what they were convinced of, as evidenced by the following comments:

- "That's interesting. Well, I think it's easier for kids today. They're spoiled; that's the problem!"
- "Well, if you ask me, kids today are just lazy—too much to do, too many choices."
- "There's no respect anymore, and kids don't seem to care about anybody but themselves."
- "Teenagers have never had it easier—they've got more money than we did, more freedoms, more options, and yet they are more defiant and more arrogant than we were."
- "Teenagers have always been rebellious. But when I was in high school, there were only some who lived on the edge. The rest of us were basically pretty good and normal—we did our homework, listened to our parents, and cared about our school. I think the biggest thing with this generation of kids is that most are like the fringe used to be."

Although academics argue over whether empirically verifiable statistics can help us to understand what is going on in the world of adolescents, when pressed, most adults intuitively recognize that the world is different from when most of them were in high school. I have presented my findings and observations in numerous settings, and as those in attendance reflected on the overwhelming evidence, rarely did anyone reject outright the premise that things have indeed changed, and changed significantly. Along with this admission, however, consistently emerged an attempt to rationalize or at least explain away the severity and the impact of the changes. Almost always something or someone was to blame for the changes: the media, parents, the educational system, Vietnam, post–cold war society, a lack of religious conviction, a loss of family values, or a myriad of other demonizing forces. But there was never a doubt that change had indeed occurred and that today's adolescents are clearly a different breed.

What Has Happened in the World of Adolescents?

Within the span of a few short decades, adolescence changed from a relatively brief two-to-three-year period to a five-year process with two distinct stages: early and late adolescence. The reasons for this change are beyond the scope of this book, but somewhere in the late 1960s, a massive social upheaval occurred that altered the social landscape of all segments of American society. There are different labels for the changes that took place and several opposing theories regarding why it happened, but for the purposes of this study, I will simply affirm that this was a watershed time for our culture in how it affected adolescence as a stage of the life span.[31]

The culturewide social shift that took place during this time influenced the young both directly and indirectly, and it has significant implications for our understanding of the adolescent landscape. The evolving changes of the twentieth century directly affected how social systems, structures, organizations, and institutions nurture the young, and they indirectly influenced the developmental processes relating to the psyche and inner security of adolescents.

External Impact of a Changing Culture

During the early and middle decades of the twentieth century, especially during the 1950s and 1960s, adolescents enjoyed a newly affirmed status in the dominant culture. There was, at least in terms of popular rhetoric, an identifiable "subculture," sometimes referred to as the "teenage culture." Society was still orderly, especially compared to today's standards, and yet teenagers were increasingly granted a certified cultural niche that was generally embraced by the adult culture. Certain elements of this trend, of course, were not wholly endorsed: James Dean (*Rebel without a Cause*), Elvis Presley, long hair, and even the Beatles still caused a stir with many adults. But for the most part, these were relatively minor distractions as the "teenager" became a vibrant, exciting aspect of American life and culture.

The turbulent 1960s saw a marked increase in social unrest and upheaval. The decade began with an escalation of the cold war that nearly erupted in a global nuclear exchange. In just a few years, three popular and powerful American leaders were gunned down, displaying our vulnerability and shattering our sense of social cohesion, control, and power. First, John F. Kennedy was assassinated, then Martin Luther King Jr., followed almost immediately by the likely next president, Robert Kennedy. The Vietnam War became decisively polarizing, primarily along age lines. The ugliness of personal and institutional racism and the resultant fight for civil rights showed the underbelly of an American national narrative that was painful for everyone. These were dark and frightening days for all Americans, and a tremendous sense of confusion, societal insecurity, and cultural instability spilled into nearly every institution, social structure, and relationship in the nation. The fights over hair length and music were but symptoms of a much more sweeping social movement: the idyllic American image of post–World War II days was being ripped apart, and there was little to replace it.

Out of this chaos came political scandal, a national recession, and ultimately a country trying to take a collective deep breath from all the upheaval. By the middle of the 1970s, we had settled into a rhythm marked by a societal philosophy that conveyed that it was up to each person to make sense of the social fragmentation, its mantra being "Live and let live." We had embarked on a path where the rules, norms, and values of society were left up to the individual. The 1980s came to be known as the "me" decade, in which the only thing that truly mattered was recapturing the American ideal of radical individualism and independence. The 1990s followed with the collapse of what we thought was our last identifiable enemy, the Soviet Union, thus removing the last remaining reason for a national metanarrative. We experienced a powerfully expanding economy, which created a greater number of jobs

What is teenage life to me? That's a good question. If I said what teenage life is to me in one word, it would have to be "hard." No one really gets you, and you don't even really get yourself. You're just starting to figure yourself out, who you are and why you are here.

high school student

and opportunities for a wide range of people but also threw us once again into a catatonic state of false security and independent arrogance. The media took a prominent place in our daily lives, its adolescent-oriented messages focusing on the temporary pursuits of leisure, comfort, and living for the moment.[32]

During this time, the biggest change affecting adolescents was the shift in focus for adult systems and institutions. Until the late 1960s, adult-led organizations and structures were primarily focused on caring for the individual and corporate needs of adolescents. Youth sports, activities, education, and even religious movements saw each young person as a gift to be cared for and cherished. But as society began to unravel, adults found themselves trying to find their own safe place, a haven of security and rest. No longer was there energy and health available for giving to others. Instead, adults waged a fight for emotional and relational survival, and this in turn spilled over into the developmental longings of adolescents.[33]

For youth-directed organizations, institutions, and systems, the shift in focus was not immediate; in fact, it evolved over several decades. But as society in general moved from being a relatively stable and cohesive adult community intent on caring for the needs of the young to a free-for-all of independent and fragmented adults seeking their own survival, individual adolescents found themselves in a deepening hole of systemic rejection. This rejection, or abandonment, of adolescents is the root of the fragmentation and calloused distancing that are the hallmarks of the adolescent culture. The evidence for and the eventual consequences of this trend are the basis of this book.

Internal Impact of a Changing Culture

Virtually every theory and scholar of human development recognizes the importance of a stable familial environment on the developmental health of a child and adolescent. From Mary Ainsworth and John Bowlby's work on childhood attachments[34] and Margaret Mahler's work on childhood separation-individuation[35] to Peter Blos's "second" separation-individuation[36] and William Damon's youth charter,[37] a great deal of research, scholarly investigation, and resultant intervention strategies have gone into trying to understand and address the psychosocial needs of children and adolescents. Yet the cultural changes that occurred during the 1960s and 1970s also had a powerful implicit and internal impact on development that, like a social earthquake, caused so much foundational damage that historically dependable developmental theories and assumptions must be revisited.

One of the most underreported but striking aspects of these years occurred within the structure of the family itself. David Elkind, in his book *Ties That Stress: The New Family Imbalance,* argues that during the post–World War II era of American family life, men enjoyed stable, routinized family lives; children and adolescents were nurtured and cared for; and women experienced a disproportionate burden of expectations, roles, and responsibilities. As the culture virtually dismantled previously rigid guidelines for family life, a new family imbalance occurred as men and women attempted to redefine their roles and relationships within the family system. The consequences of this imbalance began to fall to the child/adolescent, who was left to fend for himself or herself as parents sought to find their own way in life.[38]

Since the late 1960s and 70s, two powerful shifts occurred, changing the way adolescents perceive the familial reality and influencing how they see themselves. The first shift was the way in which the definition of family was radically altered from the long-held definition of "two or more persons related by birth, marriage or adoption who reside in the same household"[39] to the current definition of a free-flowing, organic "commitment" between people who love each other. This is exemplified in a Tufts University course for undergraduates titled "Family and Intimate Relationships," in which family is "defined broadly as those with whom one shares resources and values and to whom one has a long-term commitment."[40] The second shift involved how we view the institution of the family itself. We moved from a culture with a divorce rate that affected 2 percent of the married population in 1940 (264,000)[41] to a society in which 43 percent of first-time marriages end in separation or divorce within fifteen years of marriage, as of 2002.[42] Recent statistics show that in 2008, 67 percent of children ages zero to seventeen lived with two married parents, down from 77 percent in 1980.[43]

I observed this new ratio firsthand while attending a dance competition in Orlando with my daughter. Of the thirteen girls on the team, all from the high school where this study took place, more than half came from divorced families. Of the parents who attended, one forty-year-old mother brought her sixty-seven-year-old live-in boyfriend, and a fifty-six-year-old father was accompanied by his thirty-one-year-old girlfriend, while his ex-wife brought her live-in boyfriend. It is indeed a new day when it comes to what the word *family* means.

For the adolescent who is trying to hold on to something, at times anything, that is stable and safe, societal mores and parental choices concerning divorce, adult sexuality, and the trend for unmarried parents to cohabitate while children are in the home has had a noticeable impact. In the course of my study, I found that for many kids this effect has been powerfully destructive, and the pain and betrayal they experience are real. The reshaped definition of family has been used to affirm and legitimize even the most casual of liaisons, and this change represents a monumental shift in social history. The adolescent is left to discern how to handle the conflicting messages related to home, stable relationships, and internal security—all while trying to figure out how to survive lengthened adolescence. This only adds to the aloneness most young people feel.

The Emergence of Midadolescence

Beginning in 1904 with G. Stanley Hall's two-volume *Adolescence*, and throughout the last hundred years of focused attention and research on adolescence, the almost universally accepted concept of adolescence held that it involved two stages: early and late adolescence. During this time, studies and theories generally dealt with adolescence as a unit, but occasionally they would focus on or highlight one stage or the other. For most of the twentieth century, since adolescence lasted a relatively stable three to five years, this was an appropriate framework in which to study the phenomenon. As the average age of menarche began to drop, however, and as adolescents began to delay entrance into adulthood (for reasons to be discussed later), adolescence began to lengthen. Until approximately 1960 or 1970, for example, the average age of menarche was thirteen years, and most people met the test of individuation by the time they graduated from high school. Thus, adolescence was a five-year process. Junior-high-aged students were described in academic literature as early adolescents, and high school students were late adolescents.

A shift began as early as 1980 with the emergence of an entirely new stage in the adolescent process. Early adolescents were still defined as junior-high-aged students, but several studies included children as young as ten years old, considering them adolescents.[44] Late adolescents were still studied, but many of these studies focused on college-aged students or even graduate students and young adults.[45] The newly appointed stage known as *midadolescence* emerged as a distinct phase in the 1990s,[46] but little work has been done to define precisely the differences among these stages. The fact that social science has affirmed this new stage is remarkable because historical theories of development do not provide the necessary theoretical framework for studying this middle stage. An e-newsletter from the American Counseling Association defines midadolescence as follows:

> Midadolescence generally corresponds to grades 9 through 12 and ages 15 through 18. Many of the developmental changes of early adolescence are

extended and refined during midadolescence. This period also presents new challenges and changes for high school students. . . . As students move through high school, they are progressively faced with important decisions regarding future schooling, career paths, and related options. This is both exciting and stressful for many adolescents. The exhilaration of new opportunities and freedoms is often coupled with a sense of isolation and vulnerability ("What if I make the wrong choice?"). Adolescents "face leaving the world that they have always known and stepping out on their own" (Wallbridge & Osachuk, 1995). Increased privileges, such as driving a car and scheduling one's own time, also represent increased responsibilities. Freedom and responsibility represent two sides of a developmental coin that can become a major source of conflict between high school students and their caregivers.[47]

While to those who spend time with midadolescents the information may seem obvious, the very fact that these kinds of unique characteristics are being discussed in academic circles is a new turn in adolescent literature. The authors recognize that midadolescence is a difficult time. The "exhilaration of new opportunities and freedoms . . . often coupled with a sense of isolation and vulnerability" mentioned above is but one of the paradoxical issues facing midadolescents in contemporary society. Dozens of other conflicting elements are unique to the modern midadolescent. This book is intended to cast some light on at least a few of these.

There are three major reasons why this is such a crucial new area of study. First, most of the newfound freedoms that accompany midadolescence were originally designed for late adolescence. The freedom that comes with the privilege to drive, for example, presents an opportunity to get away from the perceived confines of parental authority, to spend additional time with peers, and to find new avenues of discovery, adventure, and even risk. This freedom, however, used to be reserved for a late adolescent, one who was close to completing the adolescent journey and who, therefore, was better equipped to handle the consequences of the freedoms. A midadolescent, in contrast to a late adolescent, retains the residue of self-centered childhood and may not have the developmental acumen to make the kind of choices that make driving, to use this one example, safe. Without knowing the issues related to lengthened adolescence and the developmental reasons behind the newly apparent lack of driving responsibility, state governments across the United States have either raised the driving age or severely curtailed the initial freedoms a driver's license offers.

Second, because today adolescence lasts up to fifteen years, a midadolescent has a more difficult time than did previous high-school-aged students seeing college and career as the hope of a secure and fulfilling

When it comes to high school life, most adults say, "I understand" or "I know, I was in high school once," but that was once and this is now. It's much harder to live life now than ever. You have one true friend, the one who is always there for you and the one who is there for you when you cry. All your other friends are just there. They listen and are fun to be around, but you can't always trust all your friends because some will betray you. Most of my friends are sixteen, seventeen, eighteen years old and have had to go to their friend's funeral because they overdosed on drugs or alcohol. Three students died last year at my school because of drugs and alcohol. Two years ago there was a count of seventeen girls pregnant.

high school student

future. In this study, for example, the attitude students had toward the future was "What's in it for me?" rather than "How am I going to make a difference in the world?" Thus, while appeals to the future may be motivating factors for some midadolescents, for the vast majority they can easily become one more adult mantra and therefore something to be dismissed.

Third, it has generally been assumed that high-school-aged students have the capacity for abstract thinking. What I noticed during this study, however, is that midadolescents' ability to engage in abstract thought is limited to the immediate context of a discussion. I observed a nearly universal inability to integrate the multiple selves of their lives with any sense of abstract cohesion. In other words, the most significant difference between midadolescents and late adolescents is that late adolescents can cogently discuss multifaceted concepts that cut across social and relational lines in a way that allows for the implications of that discussion to intersect with any level or relationship. Midadolescents, on the other hand, are fully capable of penetrating and insightful dialogue regarding a variety of topics and issues, but when it comes to applying the conclusions reached during these discussions to a relationship or social reality, especially in a different social context, they cannot see the connection. For example, students would go into great detail regarding the love they had for a parent and what that meant in terms of how they treated that parent. Yet a short time later, they would make arrangements with a friend to deceive that same parent in order to do something that, if the parent found out about it, would cause great pain and heartache. When I pointed out this incompatibility to the student, almost always the response ranged from a blank stare, to rationalization, defensiveness, argumentation, and ultimately retreat so as not to have to face such a discussion.

I had glimpsed elements of these three midadolescent distinctives, and I had a hunch that this was just the tip of the iceberg of understanding this population. I chose, therefore, to attempt to get close enough to see for myself what was going on in their world. This book is concerned with one thing: to understand and describe what the adolescent world looks like through the eyes of those who live it.

Why This Book?

I wrote this book because I believe that adults understand very little of the inside life of the American teenager, especially the midadolescent. Now, after a few years of living with midadolescents and looking through the lens of their life experience, I am more convinced than ever that adults need to be more astute students of the kids we are mandated by society to nurture.

Here is a summary of the basic issues that drive this book:

- Most adults intuitively believe that things are different for today's adolescents, but they hold on to rhetoric and attitudes that support the fantasy that little has changed.
- Academics and social science researchers are divided over what is different, but little work has been done to see inside the hidden lives of midadolescents.
- As I studied students and culture, I came to believe that we as a society have allowed the institutions and systems originally designed to nurture children and adolescents to lose their missional mandate. In other words, society has systemically abandoned the young.
- Young people are desperate for an adult who cares. Certainly, some adolescents have been so wounded that rebuilding trust may appear almost insurmountable. Yet those who serve them with tenderness and respect will testify that even the hardest young soul cries out for someone who authentically cares.

This is not a how-to book but rather a wake-up call to help every adult recognize and struggle with what our choices as adults have done to the children of our society. The majority of this book will explore the issues resulting from feelings of abandonment among adolescents and reflect on what has occurred as a result. A few solutions are offered in the final chapter, but these are somewhat obvious. We as adults need to roll up our sleeves and invest in the lives of individual young people.

abandonment—the defining issue for contemporary adolescents

The adolescent community is a creation by default, an amorphous grouping of young people that constitutes the world in which adolescents spend
their time.

Patricia Hersch, *A Tribe Apart*

Part of my melancholy is just the loss of childhood. I can almost remember
the day I realized nobody could really take care of me or protect me, that
awareness of mortality and being on my own. Nothing's been the same
since.

singer Lucinda Williams[1]

did not conduct this study in a vacuum. My career calling has kept
me in close relationship with adolescents since my own graduation
in the early 1970s.[2] Further, as an actively involved parent of three
high school students, I have seen multiple sides of adolescents. Because
of this background, I began my study with the misguided belief that I
possessed a fairly thorough understanding of young people. As prepared
as I may have been, however, I was not as ready as I had thought. My
middle son, a high school junior at the time, sensed my apparent comfort
and offered a meaningful warning: "I know you think you know a lot

about kids, Dad, but you had better be ready for a shock. I don't think you really get it! I don't think any adult gets it!"

Out of what I would later recognize as naïveté at best or blatant academic and professional hubris at worst, I was, in fact, ill prepared for what I encountered in the world of the middle adolescent. I had known a great number of students over the years and had built close relationships with many of them, but when I approached students seeking to understand the complexities and nuances of their world, my simplistic views were quickly challenged, if not outrightly dismantled. I had expected a few surprises in penetrating the walls and secret places of their society and community, but what I now understand is that my history and training had given me an incomplete and therefore distorted picture of their world. In many cases, I had been able to get close to the students I had known over the years, but during this study, I recognized that each of those relationships had been rooted in my terms and created on my turf. The people I had known were in reality only conjured presentations. In effect, those relationships were based wholly on my social and worldview contexts rather than theirs or even a mutual context. I had failed to recognize that each young person exists in a social setting vastly different from my own. Therefore, as painful as this admission may be, I missed truly knowing most of them. I now believe this is true of almost every adult, including those who work with adolescents on a daily basis. The world of young people is different, period. It is fragmented, complex, and multilayered, and therefore, their worldview, lexicon, value system, and even the framework used to decipher and navigate the extraordinary complexity of adolescence has changed.

The State of Contemporary Adolescence: The Academic Debate

Pulitzer Prize–winning author Ron Powers[3] made quite a stir in March 2002 with the publication of an article in the *Atlantic* in which he made the observation that "the inconvenience of children, the downright menace of children—has become a dominant theme of life."[4] His article and subsequent interview on *60 Minutes II* focused on the increasing culture of disenfranchisement of the young and the resulting violence perpetrated by adolescents, especially in his home state of Vermont. His intent was to encourage adults to sit up and take notice regarding the condition of our young.

There are those, however, who believe that Powers's view was skewed by a few isolated events and that he ignored the overwhelming evidence that suggests precisely the opposite—that adolescents are in far better shape than they have been in years. University of California, Santa Cruz, sociologist Mike Males, for example, is one of the most vocal scholars arguing against Powers and others who claim that life is changing for the worse for today's young. Males not only disagrees with Powers but also attempts to dismiss his perspective when he states, for example, that today's young "are doing better than ever."[5] Males says that those who claim that youth are "in trouble" suffer from "ephebiphobia—extreme fear of youth," and that the popular writers and pundits who perpetuate the view that adolescents are in trouble are creating a "full-blown media panic."[6] An increasing wave of reports describing arrogantly delinquent and dangerously violent new adolescents has spawned what Males believes is a false fear that we as a society have abandoned and neglected our young. Focusing primarily on the media attention given to Powers and his book on violence and youth, Males attempted to discredit Powers and whoever else tended to agree with him. He asserted that today's adolescents are healthier, happier, and more nurtured than ever before. Indeed, on paper, his use of a wide variety of empirical data clearly refuted Powers and those who follow him.

This ongoing debate between those who believe that the young of our culture are in trouble and those who are optimistic about the state of teenagers is usually waged in battlegrounds characterized by the protected confines of academic literature. In such cases, empirical data (i.e., quantitative studies and hard numbers) are often seen as proof of legitimacy on both sides of the debate. Because Males's studies cite "objective data," for example, many scholars and academics tend to side with his view. His argument echoes the disdain some researchers express toward those who perpetuate unproven yet sensational "findings" or "alarming trends" that are regularly reported in the press. Frustrated with what is seen as a "popular"[7] view of today's adolescent struggles, many in the academic world believe there is substantial evidence that today's young are flourishing and that they are "resilient."[8] Males is one of the few social scientists to receive a public hearing in the media, for he has the ability and the commitment both to engage in primary research and to interpret academic findings and conclusions in a way that the average person can understand. Popular literature may be fueled by violent or other sensational events such as those Powers relies on[9] or by stories of darkness or loss of innocence, such as that of the nine-year-old girl who was recently arrested for prostitution, claiming that she "wanted to make money."[10] Yet, neither academic nor popular literature would go so far as to say that as a society life is as stable as it has ever been, especially as it relates to developing adolescents. In fact, esteemed psychologist Robert Epstein contends that the systems and structures we have erected to serve our young have actually done them great damage by holding them back, what he terms *infantilization*.[11]

Perhaps the most interesting question has not yet been introduced into the debate. Does the type of research most academic studies rely on (i.e., historical theories, quantitative studies, and survey research) actually tell us all we need to know in order to understand the reality of the inner lives of today's adolescents? The apparent contradictions and differing viewpoints actually represent different angles of the same adolescent experience. As young people attempt to navigate the increasing complexity of life, they are both incredibly resilient and deeply wounded. The culture itself is no longer as attentive to the needs of children and adolescents as it once was, and therefore, the young work hard at finding out how to make it on their own. This, however, is an almost impossible task. As David Elkind argues, "identity formation requires a kind of envelope of adult standards, values and beliefs that the adolescent can confront and challenge in order to construct and test out her own standards, values and beliefs. . . . Today, however, adults have fewer standards, values and beliefs and hold on to them less firmly than was true in the past. The adolescent must therefore struggle to find an identity without the benefit of this supportive adult envelope."[12]

On the surface, the adolescent world appears to be relatively stable and healthy. Yet beneath the calm waters presented by positive empirical data there is turmoil that is difficult, painful, lonely, and even harmful to our young. Even among those who argue that adolescents are basically fine, virtually no one would question the need young people, and especially adolescents, have for adults who are available, who care, and who come to them without a hidden or self-centered agenda. The fact is that adolescents need adults to become adults, and when adults are

> I can't ever find someone to talk to who knows how I am feeling. My parents always say that they know how I feel and that they have been there, but times have changed. They don't know what I'm going through. So I am forced to keep my feelings bottled up inside. Sometimes I just crack. I get onto everyone I am around. I hate it. I wish I could find someone to talk to who knows me and understands me.
>
> **high school student**

not present and involved in their lives, they are forced to figure out how to survive life on their own. As Patricia Hersch notes, "The more we leave kids alone, don't engage, the more they circle around on the same adolescent logic that has caused dangerous situations to escalate."[13]

In this study, I found that a far wider relational and social chasm exists between adults and adolescents than I had previously considered. The data and observations from this study, especially when triangulated[14] with academic and popular literature and with feedback from middle adolescents across socioeconomic and ethno-geographic lines, do not allow me to respond with casual academic indifference or cavalier theoretical dismissal. There is simply too much cumulative weight that points to a disturbing trend: the way midadolescents have been forced to design their own world and separate social system has created perhaps the most serious and yet understudied social crisis of our time. We hear such statements so often that it is easy to turn a skeptical or even deaf ear, but my hope is that the evidence emerging from this study will prove too convincing for even the most dubious readers to ignore.

The Hurried Child and a Culture of Abandonment

Tufts University professor David Elkind wrote the first edition of *The Hurried Child* in 1981, then followed up with a revised version in 1988 and again in 2001. In both revisions, Elkind emphasized his understanding of how things had changed for young people.[15] In the 1988 edition, he wrote that in earlier books he was attempting "to further document how our changed treatment of adolescents and of young children was making life harder rather than easier for them."[16]

In the 2001 edition, he stated:

Many of the problems that I described in the preface to the second edition have only gotten worse. The concept of child competence, which drove much of the hurrying of childhood in previous decades, is very much alive today. Parents are under more pressure than ever to overschedule their children and have them engage in organized sports and other activities that may be age-inappropriate. Unhappily, the overtesting of children in public schools has become more extensive than it was even a decade ago. In some communities even kindergarteners are given standardized tests. Media pressures to turn children into consumers have also grown exponentially.[17]

Based on my observations during the course of this study, I agree with Elkind's theoretical assessment that as a culture we tend to "hurry" our children. However, I prefer to use the label *abandoned* rather than *hurried*. As Ron Powers and many others note, adolescents have a longing that parents, teachers, and other adults have ceased as a community to fulfill. The reasons are many and varied, but this concept of the systemic abandonment of adolescents as a people group seems to capture the widest range of descriptors used by careful observers of adolescents and adolescents themselves.

Numerous articles and books have noted the prevalence of this systemic abandonment of adolescents. In *Ties That Stress: The New Family Imbalance,* for example, Elkind states, "Like all those whose needs are not being met over the long term, postmodern children and adolescents are feeling victimized. They believe that they must suppress their own needs for security and protection to accommodate their parents' and the society's expectations that they be independent and autonomous. Like modern mothers, postmodern young people either turn their anger on themselves (for letting themselves be used) or at the world around them."[18]

Gen-X authors William Mahedy and Janet Bernardi, coauthors of *A Generation Alone: Xers Making a Place in the World,* detail their generation's rebellious nature and summarize their experience by stating that "we know that no one really needs us."[19] They are, in actuality, describing a societywide slide in focus, nurture, and care of the young.

This concept of systemic abandonment became a major theme in Hersch's groundbreaking study, *A Tribe Apart,* in which she concluded, "The adolescents of the nineties are more isolated and more unsupervised than any other generation."[20] Over the course of this study, I not only came to agree with these assertions but also experienced firsthand their stark reality. "A tribe apart" is more than just the title of a book; it is a vivid and intensely accurate description of modern middle adolescents. The young have not arrogantly turned their backs on the adult world. Rather, they have been forced by a personal sense of abandonment to band together and create their own world—separate, semisecret, and vastly different from the world around them.

Abandonment by External Systems

As has been noted, the concept of adolescence as a social construct, or definition of a unique life stage, has been recognized for just over a century. Prior to this, the transition from childhood to adulthood was seen less as a process and more as an event, marked in many cultures by significant ritual and celebration. It is as though the mere act of naming the stage caused a change in the way we thought about and acted toward our young. Prior to the official recognition of adolescence, for example, only 10 percent of the population attended high school. Today, more than 90 percent does. Within two decades of naming adolescence, public

I could stare in the mirror for hours and find no connection between my thoughts and the face staring back at me. He seems more like a poorly casted actor whose eyes show his disdain for his role. And yet he smiles. He leads an exceptional life with above average grades and social skills. I just wish my real life were more like the person radiating from his smile. Other people seem like actors and actresses in the same sick drama, almost unreal to me. I have to remind myself when I speak to them that it is the actor they see and not an image more fairly representative of my thoughts. I feel like a renegade separating myself from my intended role, and yet my misery seeks no company. I consider myself too humane to invite stable minds into my thoughts, like enticing the healthy into a leprosy colony. I therefore suffer in silence, longing to be understood but refusing to share such a nightmare with the unknowing. It is a lonely place in the mind of an unwilling actor.

high school student

high school, or secondary school, became a common experience in the United States.[21] Over the next several years, innovative programs began to spring up across the country. Youth sports, music, dance, drama, and even religious youth programs provided opportunities for teens. These were originally designed and structured with a common goal: to nurture emerging adolescents by providing systems, structures, and activities to help them grow into adulthood by means of the smoothest, most productive transition possible.

Consider how this new support worked in the middle decades of the twentieth century. Educators, for instance, may have required homework, but rarely did it place an overly weighty burden on students' schedules. Rather, it was a way to encourage students to spend time assimilating the information they had received in class. Girls and boys were taught dance and social skills in social settings. They also had opportunities to experience music, drama, and fine art both within and outside the school context. While these and other nurturing structures and movements were beneficial in many ways, a subtle change soon took place. These structures eventually distanced adults from the specific needs of adolescents.

Fast forward to today's environment, by the time adolescents enter high school, nearly every one has been subjected to a decade or more of adult-driven and adult-controlled programs, systems, and institutions that are primarily concerned with adults' agendas, needs, and dreams. Take these examples as evidence of how far we have drifted in our commitment to the young:

- Families with eight- and nine-year-old boys pay hundreds if not thousands of dollars to spend Thanksgiving weekend traveling so that their boys can "have the opportunity of a lifetime" to play in a contrived, skillfully marketed, mythical peewee football "national championship."

- An eight-year-old who loves to dance is no longer allowed to attend a class she loved for its fun, free, raucous, hour-and-a-half adventure in tights. Her dancing now consists of up to six (or more) hours of training, repetition, and practice per week, culminating in something called a "dance competition," a phrase that was formerly an artistic oxymoron.

- Parental fistfights erupt during a seven-year-olds' tee ball game in what I was later told is "an intense competitive atmosphere" because it is, "after all, competitive tee ball!"

- A high school junior who arrives home from school promptly at 5:30 after volleyball practice begins a four- to six-hour nightly ordeal called homework—on an average night. She has dinner over a textbook, which allows her to avoid conversation with her mom, and falls asleep exhausted at midnight, only to rise the next morning at 5:30 for band practice before her 7:00 AP calculus class.

What is interesting is that many adults will highlight these and other activities as proof of their commitment to the young. "I drive my kid to all of these activities. I sacrificed my own life, work, avocation, and enjoyment in order to take the kids to soccer games, concerts, and competitions." This statement is in and of itself yet another subtle form of abandonment.[22] As Madeline Levine has observed, "Achievement pressure often comes from parents who are overinvolved in how well their children perform and inadequately involved in monitoring these same children in other areas. We can be overinvolved in the wrong things, and uninvolved in the right things, both at the same time."[23] This kind of misplaced involvement, says Levine, is "startling and unproductive,"[24] putting adolescents in a place where they are so micromanaged on the outside that they are "inadvertently deprived of the opportunity to develop an inside."[25]

We have evolved to the point where we believe driving is support, being active is love, and providing any and every opportunity is selfless nurture. We are a culture that has forgotten how to be together. We have lost the ability to spend unstructured down time. Rather than being with children in creative activities at home or setting them free to enjoy semisupervised activities such as "play," we as a culture have looked to outside organizations and structured agendas to fill their time and dictate their lives. The problem is not simply organized activities or sports. It is the cumulative effect that children experience as they grow up in today's social structure. Sports, music, dance, drama, Scouts, and even faith-related programs are all guilty of ignoring the developmental needs of each individual young person in favor of the organization's goals. Add to this the increasing amount of homework being assigned to students at younger and younger ages. The systemic pressure on American children is immense. Too many of us actually enjoy the athletic, cultural, or artistic babysitting service provided by those organizations. Even with the best of intentions, the way we raise, train, and even parent our children today exhibits attitudes and behaviors that are simply subtle forms of parental abandonment.

The shift has taken place not only in how our systems react to the demands of a particular enterprise but also in the focus of those in charge. In general, the good of the unique individual has been supplanted by a commitment to the good of the _____ (fill in the blank: team, school, community, class, or organization). Today, even very young children learn that they are only as valuable as their ability to contribute. Rarely are youth activities, especially group activities such as sports and dance, safe places that allow children to explore latent potential, develop appreciation for a sport or activity, or even simply enjoy being involved. Perhaps a "slow" five-year-old (relative to other five-year-olds) will always be "slower" than his or her peers, but does that mean the child should be denied the enjoyment, encouragement, and full participation in a sport? This is just one setting among dozens in which, from an early age, children learn that there are some who are special—pretty, smart, athletic—and some who are not. By the time these students reach middle adolescence, they show signs of the rejection they have been subjected to throughout their lives. As one community leader of youth sports told me, "They have to learn this lesson sometime—that they either are or aren't an athlete. It is better to find out when they are young." I wondered, "Better for whom?"

The voices are few that encourage society to focus on the individual adolescent when it comes to the creation of systems and structures.[26] While youth mentoring programs have arisen in part as a response to this unfortunate state of affairs, little research has been done on their effectiveness.[27] Statistics have, however, demonstrated the negative impact resulting from mentors who don't keep their commitments to their kids, such as "drops in self-worth and perceived scholastic competence" and "increases in alcohol use."[28] All of this underscores the need for adults to be highly committed to each individual kid, no matter how difficult or delicate the relationship may seem.[29] In general, there is a tremendous momentum of self-protection and self-promotion for institutions and organizations (and even individuals), and this makes it increasingly difficult for even the best teacher, coach, or youth worker to "waste" the time it takes to walk alongside an individual adolescent, much less create an environment in which each one is uniquely nurtured and led. A child who seems relatively slower, distracted, insecure, or otherwise handicapped (according to the dictates of the organization) has little chance of being considered anything other than one needy but incompetent face among many.

One day when I was working with a teacher in preparation for substituting in her class, she illustrated this perfectly, if unintentionally: "My morning class has three or four great kids," she said, "but the afternoon class is full of average kids, and are they ever a pain." This comment not only struck me as odd but also deeply disturbed me. Although she had been a teacher for only five or six years, she had already reached a point of hanging an "average" label on several fourteen- and fifteen-year-olds she did not like or approve of. She obviously had never considered (or had simply stopped caring about) the sad fact that many of these kids came from difficult family settings, were not recognized athletically, could not sing or draw or write, and had been consistently reminded of such things since they were young.

Some children and adolescents rise to the top early, whether through a unique skill, a quick wit or tongue, or an attractive look, style, or quality. Some learn how to cope with abandonment by adopting a countercultural style or persona. They discover, again often at a very young age, that they do not have the ability to receive attention in a positive way, yet they have an inner desire to be noticed. Both extremes, the achievers and the challenging youth, are known by teachers and the administration and are therefore given the greatest amount of energy and attention. The fact that teachers I talked to knew well those who were the stars as well as those who were the troublemakers led me to the first stark observation I made during this study: there is a third category. The "middle" student, who has not, for a variety of reasons, taken the steps necessary to be unusually liked and coddled or to fight and rebel, is an almost unnoticed person. There are far more of these middle students than there are students in either of the other two categories. The sharp and attractive and the rebellious and countercultural make up only 20 percent of the population, and yet they receive 80 percent of adults' attention.

I've always been prone to episodes of extreme loneliness and longing for a place where I could feel safe enough to let down my defenses. Because I was an extremely outgoing and energetic little girl/adolescent, no one would ever guess how alone I really felt. I was the girl who was always surrounding herself with people from all "groups," as teenagers love to place people in, but something has always felt like it was missing. Every so often this "hole" pops up in the pit of my stomach, and it can stay anywhere from a couple hours to a couple days. I have never been able to pinpoint exactly where the emptiness begins, as hard as I may try. I have many friends and acquaintances, and my home life is more than I could ask for. I just wish sometimes I could find somewhere to belong.

high school student

This observation led to another that was even more startling: those who were noticed intuitively knew that they were noticed because of something they produced, displayed, or created. I tried to find and talk to the "cream of the crop," the sharpest students, to see if they were indeed what they appeared to be. I wanted to know if they were playacting to gain attention. The closer I got to those who occupied the upper tier, the more I realized that these kids wore their uniqueness—intelligence, athleticism, wittiness, or respectability—like a cloak. Underneath the surface, even for the top students, there is a great fear of being found out and losing everything they have worked so hard to attain. "I have to get the grades and play sports," one senior male student confided. "I have nothing else." (This from a student held in the highest esteem by the faculty, carrying a 4.0 grade point average, a starter in a major sport, and well liked and respected by everyone on campus.) Indeed, some of these bright and talented students even seek other—sometimes harmful—ways of standing out from the crowd. Cultural trends researcher Walt Mueller quotes an email sent to him by a student:

I come from an upper-middle-class home. I'm a straight-A student, class president, and an overachiever in every way. I don't really know why I am anorexic, but I think it's partly because I thought that if I got really sick, people would pay attention to me more and like me. I know my parents love me, but they think I am so bright and capable that I don't need help or attention anymore. I just want people to realize I do not have a perfect life, and I am lonely.[30]

No adolescent is immune from the need to "play at" various roles to survive this phase of life.[31] As Paul Willis observes, "For young people, passing through adolescence means that they are in one way or another marginalized."[32] In American culture, this marginalization begins at an early age in nearly every system originally designed to serve, nurture, guide, and protect the young. A careful look at such systems—such as the classroom[33] or athletics[34]—reveals that a shift has occurred over the past forty to fifty years. Organizations, structures, and institutions that were originally concerned with children's care, welfare, and development have become less interested in individual nurture and development and more interested in institutional perpetuation (or the competitive, even pathological, needs of the adult in charge). Today's adolescents have indeed been abandoned.

Perhaps you are not yet convinced. Many reviewers who read early drafts of this chapter, primarily graduate students but professional adults as well, could see my general perspective but were not wholly convinced of the pervasiveness of this assertion. One in particular encouraged me to offer "oodles of quotes and scenarios" that would convince readers by their sheer volume. I have chosen to take a slightly different tack. I am starting with the assumption that midadolescents are where they are because of systemic societal abandonment. Throughout the book, I present the specifics of how this plays out in various areas of life. At this point, I am not concerned that you buy the notion of abandonment but that you are open to the possibility.

Abandonment by Internal Systems and Relationships

The notion of systemic abandonment is not limited to those external systems originally designed to nurture, protect, and help shape a unique adolescent. Another form of abandonment, perhaps more subtle yet far more insidious, has occurred that has had a devastating effect on the adolescent psyche and landscape. Adolescents have suffered the loss of the safe relationships and intimate settings that served as the primary nurturing community for those traveling the path from child to adult. The most obvious example of this is in the family. The postmodern family is often so concerned about the needs, struggles, and issues of parents that the emotional and developmental needs of the children go largely unmet.[35] Add to this trend the rarity of extended family available to the vast majority of adolescents, the deemphasizing of the importance of marriage, and the lack of healthy relationships with adults as friends and mentors, and it is easy to see why today's adolescent faces an internal crisis of unprecedented scope.

The loss of meaningful relationships with adults has been the most devastating to developing adolescents.[36] Because midadolescents have not had enough life experience to understand fully the accompanying sense of loneliness and isolation they feel, few could articulate their experience specifically as "loss" in my study. But the reality of the experience oozed out of nearly every student. And in discussions with midadolescents across the country, not one disagreed with this bleak assessment.[37] When feeling safe enough to admit it, every student I talked to acknowledged that loneliness is a central experience. In decrying the panic in the lives of young girls in the midst of contemporary culture, Mary Pipher provides a wake-up call with her poignant summation of how parents so easily miss what is happening with their children: "To paraphrase a Stevie Smith poem about swimming in the sea, 'they are not waving, they are drowning.' And just when they most need help, they are unable to take their parent's hands."[38] They feel this way about all adults who they perceive are not there for them.

The Consequences of Abandonment

During the course of this study, I was invited to be a panelist for the city of Glendale, California. I was one of four people administering the final interview with the top three candidates for the position of youth outreach coordinator, a position aimed at serving teenagers who were at risk for getting into trouble. I had one question that was designed to tell me how well these candidates understood the world of adolescents: "Describe for us an at-risk kid." Each candidate was extremely well qualified. Two had master's degrees, and the third had an experience-rich résumé. When we got to my question, not one of them hesitated or even blinked. Each was emphatic, and each responded identically: "Why, all of them! Every single young person who has grown up in America is only one major event or catastrophe away from falling over the edge into what most would call at-risk."

Chris Frappier, an investigator with Vermont's state public defender's office, recently spoke out against what has happened to adolescents in a culture of abandonment:

> So our kids, our children, who feel lost, disenfranchised—they join [gangs]! And why not? . . . I mean, look at the communities in this state that wage

war on their youth. You've got Vergennes kicking kids out of the park. You've got Woodstock banning skateboarding. . . . What I'm seeing in recent years is the total and complete alienation of youth. And it is not coming from them; it is coming from the adults who aren't bothering to reach out to them. And it is terrifying.[39]

Many people who work directly with a broad spectrum of adolescents have come to similar conclusions.

But it is not only these practitioners who have come to such conclusions. There is also evidence—empirical, verifiable, and quantifiable data—that points to the notion that adolescence today is more difficult, complex, and treacherous than in previous generations. The increasing duration of the adolescent journey, a cultural psychosocial invention,[40] makes the consequences of this systemic abandonment all the more apparent. In a major study of one thousand children and adolescents, for example, the majority reported that the time they spent with parents was often hurried. Even those who did not feel this way lacked evidence of the depth and substance of the child-parent interchange that is essential for healthy adolescent development.[41]

This situation is exacerbated when an adolescent is a member of a conflicted family system. The greater the self-absorption of the parents with their own problems and struggles, the less aware they are of their children's social and developmental needs. When there is conflict in a family system, parents are more likely to rely on a limited (or misguided) perception of their children's maturity, which in turn leads parents to depend on their adolescent children for guidance and support—a circumstance that greatly increases the pressure on adolescents. They are forced not only to deal with the pain and fear associated with losing the stability of the most significant system in their lives but also to engage in parental conflict in a way that short-circuits their ability to meet their own needs arising from the crisis.[42] Research has consistently shown that parental conflict forces children to sacrifice their own developmental needs to meet the needs of their parents—needs that they are, needless to say, ill equipped to meet. In fact, they are often pushed into taking mediating roles when things get tough. Young children are even forced to take sides in parental conflict or to offer advice to a struggling parent.[43] This abdication of parental responsibility has devastating consequences for children who must prematurely look after their own needs.

In their book *Generation on Hold*, James E. Côté and Anton L. Allahar speak about adults who are "excessively self-interested" and note that "as the identity of adult members becomes ambiguous, they are less able to guide the young through the self-discovery process that is an integral part of forming an identity. Consequently, they may feel alienated from

I was two when my dad walked out on me and my mom. Sure, I saw him a lot, but it hurt. I never saw him again after fourth grade. He stopped calling and writing. My mom remarried the summer after fifth grade. I hated him. In sixth grade I lost my virginity. I just wanted to be loved by a guy. I hated my life, but when I had sex I felt like I was cared about and loved. I slept with three guys. Then in seventh I started to do drugs and drink. I would go to parties and stay out late. My mom kicked my stepdad out, so I was happy. School started. I was smoking and drinking a little here and there. I didn't really feel loved or cared about. I felt dead inside. I picked up cutting. When I saw myself bleed, I just felt so alive. To feel the pain was the best feeling I could feel. My mom found out, so I stopped because I had to see a counselor. A few months later I stopped eating. I had to be perfect. I was the worst daughter. I had bad grades. I had a bad attitude. My dad wasn't around. I felt like I was worthless. I wasn't good enough for him. I feel like my life is worthless. I just want to die half the time. I want to feel like I'm worth something, loved, and cared for. Where do I find that?

high school student

their juniors, and be less likely to welcome them into adult society. This ambivalence could precipitate a crisis among the young."[44] Similarly, Carla Barnhill, writing in *Books & Culture* on "How Good Parents Give Up on Their Teens," describes the natural push and pull that goes on between parents and their children. She details how parents who do not maintain their rightful and necessary role of supervisor and authority create stress for children when it comes to understanding themselves. When even their souls are a commodity to be shopped out to someone else, it's not surprising that teenagers feel their parents are too busy for them or unsure of their ability to parent. Teenagers can smell fear. As soon as they've sensed they've gained control, as soon as they believe that adults are afraid to challenge them, it's human nature for them to push until they find the boundary. They may complain about the limits parents set on them, but several studies, including one from the National Center on Addiction and Substance Abuse at Columbia University, show that teens desperately need and want the sense of control and safety that healthy boundaries provide.[45]

Adolescents notice when they do not get to spend enough time with parents and other adults. In facilitating a parent/youth event for a community group in Seattle last fall, I asked students to compile a list of what they wanted adults to know about them. One of the most telling statements they recorded was how they perceived time with significant adults: "We spend no time with adults from junior high on—maybe fifteen minutes every other day is the best we ever get." It is as though adults don't understand that time spent with significant adults, especially parents, provides the most important environment for healthy adolescent development. But even in the best families, spending time together is a struggle. As Hersch states, "'In all societies since the beginning of time, adolescents have learned to become adults by observing, imitating and interacting with grown-ups around them,' write Mihaly Csikzentmihalyi and Reed Larson in *Being Adolescent*. 'It is therefore startling how little time [modern] teenagers spend in the company of adults.' In their study Csikzentmihalyi and Larson found that adolescents spent only 4.8 percent of their time with their parents and only 2 percent with adults who were not their parents."[46]

There are at least two consequences of parental and adult abandonment. First, the adolescent journey is lengthened, because no one is available to help move the developmental process along.[47] Joseph Allen and Claudia Worrell Allen observe that "the extension of adolescence has expanded so boundlessly that many teens no longer have any realistic sense of what they're ultimately preparing for, or even that they are preparing for something."[48] This applies even to those youth who appear to be healthy and successful but who nonetheless "wake up in their mid-twenties clueless about how to get a job, manage money, cook, or live on their own."[49] Second, adolescents know that they are essentially on their own, for "aloneness is the enduring result of abandonment."[50]

Surprise! Adolescents Want Adults

Contrary to what most adults may think, middle adolescents want significant relationships with adults who care about them.[51] When asked about this in various settings—one-on-one, in informal groups, or even in a large convention setting—students confirmed this assertion, and most seemed almost eager to have an adult friend. The difficulty comes when they attempt to reconcile this need with their perception of the lack of trustworthiness in adults. When I spent time with a group of teachers, one (who was nearing retirement) said, "They have got to learn to come halfway! I am sick of trying to build trust with kids and then have them reject my overtures." That comment strikes at the heart of the issue of kids relating to adults—they want and need adults, but because many (or even some) of the adults they have known over the years have participated in abandoning them, they have little trust in any adult (and for most midadolescents, this includes their parents, at least for a season). A middle adolescent, then, simply will not come halfway—why should they risk more disappointment? An adult who wants to connect but who demands that midadolescents come halfway only serves to confirm the mistrust they feel and deepen the divide between adolescents and adults. To the midadolescent, this attitude is yet another confirmation of abandonment.

Due to the midadolescent's recognition that for most of his or her life the norm has been a lack of authentic concern and care at almost every turn, few are able to easily trust an adult who does reach out. While some people may claim that the way we treat adolescents in this culture is similar to how adolescents have generally been treated over the ages and across cultures,[52] both my observations and those of others who have studied the adolescent world up close offer a vastly different view. Systemic abandonment has created an environment in which midadolescents believe they are truly on their own. As a result, they go underground; they pull away from the adult world. This causes a uniquely ordered society, a world beneath, a world in which rules, expectations, a value system, and even social norms are created to maintain an environment in which the middle adolescent can achieve the single most important goal of this stage of life: survival.

If adults cannot be trusted to be authentic, committed, and selfless advocates, then the only alternative available to adolescents is to flee. With early adolescents, families still hold the greatest possible hope of providing the care, protection, and support that kids need. But with the development of abstract thought in later adolescence comes the heightened ability to recognize the complexity of the world and to be able to read mixed motives and inauthentic or inconsistent treatment from adults and adult institutions. Middle adolescents band together to create their own world where they hold the keys to dealing with their perception of abandonment and their need for relational stability, protection, social guidance, and belonging. As Hersch describes it, "Their dependence on each other fulfills the universal human longing for community, and inadvertently cements the notion of a tribe apart. More than a group of peers, it becomes in isolation a society with its own values, ethics, rules, worldview, rites of passage, worries, joys, and momentum. It becomes teacher, advisor, entertainer, challenger, nurturer, inspirer, and sometimes destroyer."[53]

When I was able to get close enough, to be trusted enough, to get a glimpse of life in this world, I did not hear a few voices crying out. I heard an overwhelming chorus of longing to be cared for and to be taken seriously. The collective adolescent society may appear impenetrable and may even be a powerful social force to be reckoned with, but beyond the perceived hostility that surrounds the midadolescent is a fragile soul hidden behind a sophisticated layer of defense and protection. Even the most "solid" students confessed that life is far darker, far more violent, far more difficult, and far more tiring than adults, including their parents, realize.

Conclusion and Musings

"They have no clue, Dr. Clark."

This comment about adults in general came from a beautiful junior in high school who maintains a 4.0 grade point average, is an all-league volleyball player, and is one of the more well-liked and respected students on campus.

"But you seem like you are managing it all pretty well."

"Yeah," she said, "I'm pretty good at it, huh?"

What she meant was, "I'm good at playing the game, maintaining the show, and somehow surviving the obstacles."

My conclusions in this chapter may sound depressing, and it may seem far too sweeping an assessment to make, for many middle adolescents are able to overcome the general condition of the whole and do rather well dancing between adapting to the expectations of the adult world and maintaining the relational integrity necessary to connect to the world beneath. This said, many young people are one step away from the abyss of isolation and despair. One articulate junior reminded me of this with a poem.

> You come into the world alone,
> You go out into the world alone,
> In life you have no friends.

In sum, systemic abandonment by institutions and adults who are in positions originally designed to care for adolescents has created a culture of isolation.[54] It is into this world of retreat we must go, determined to listen, to see, and ultimately to understand the circumstances that adult abandonment has helped to foster. By the time children, even the successful ones, reach high school and middle adolescence, they are aware of the fact that for most of their lives they have been pushed, prodded, and molded to become a person whose value rests in his or her ability to serve someone else's agenda. Whether they experience it from a coach, a schoolteacher, a parent, a music teacher, or a Sunday school counselor, midadolescents intuitively believe that nearly every adult they have encountered has been subtly out to get something from them. When this awareness begins to take root during middle adolescence, it leads to frustration, anger, and a sense of betrayal. These feelings drive the experience defining middle adolescence and create the perceived need for the world beneath.

In Alexander Wolff's surprisingly critical front-page story on youth sports in *Sports Illustrated*, he subtly inserted the following line into his conclusion: "To answer the question of whether we believe high school to be a precious interval in a young life or some Scholastic Fantastic stopover on the way to the Show is to learn a lot about who we are."[55] This poignant and insightful statement was so cleverly woven into the fabric of his article that its power may have easily been missed, but Wolff's challenge to look in the mirror when trying to understand our young bears repeating. High school life in America left behind the idea of being "a precious interval in a young life" long ago. Unfortunately, few adults have taken the time or had the courage to look closely at what we left behind. Middle adolescents understand their abandonment and therefore spend their youthful energy attempting to find a safe place from which to live out one of the most difficult and challenging developmental periods they will ever face.

The late football coach Abe Lemons once remarked, "You don't coach seniors. You just tolerate them."[56] From a midadolescent's perspective, far too many adults treat them in much the same way. Yet there are exceptions. I have witnessed adults who are bucking the trend of societal abandonment. Put simply, this is my hope—that more adults, especially adults who are in positions to turn the tide of abandonment, would strive to change the systems and structures that have caused collective anguish for our young. As we work together, we can make a difference.

3

the world beneath

One of the more common comments I heard as I shared my research with others was, "Is it really that much different now than when I was in high school?" (which typically ranged from ten to thirty-five years ago). This comment usually revealed a subconscious yet nevertheless cognitive debate concerning the changing world as it affects not only adolescents but the rest of us as well. In many ways we want life to remain, if not static, at least somehow related to the world in which we grew up. But there is so much that reveals the opposite, and the conversation that followed such comments almost always headed in this direction: We think it is or at least should be pretty much the same for teenagers today as it was in the 1970s, but when we honestly look at the daily realities of the world today's young are growing up in, we must admit that, as much as things may look the same, the world is very different.

Many researchers who study adolescence have concluded that far more research is needed to allow for a deeper and more penetrating psychosocial glimpse into the culture and life of the high school student community. Jeffrey Lashbrook, for example, while describing the difficulty of understanding this population using quantitative methods, suggested, "Videotaping peer interactions in a natural setting would be ideal, since it would offer a record of both verbal and nonverbal cues."[1] This suggestion and others like it reflect researchers' view that what we know about adolescents is minimal at best, is often discovered via artificial methods, and is most likely limited to an individual issue (such as smoking or sexuality). Those who yearn for a larger data pool from which to draw in attempting to grasp the sociological reality of the adolescent experience see the need for a closer, firsthand look. In this study, therefore, I sought to become a part of the landscape so that the adolescents being studied were free to live their lives without filters (see the appendix for a more complete explanation of the study).

Another issue frequently raised regarding the study of adolescence is the concern that a researcher could do damage to an already fragile group by either trivializing its experience[2] or reducing the complexity of the midadolescent experience to stereotypes and labels.[3] As I have mentioned, what I observed was tested by both the academic literature and informal discussion groups.

I came to two conclusions within the first few weeks of this study. First, the vast majority of adults simply do not comprehend the complex and different world in which nearly all midadolescents dwell. Second, most adults fear and in many cases are basically repulsed by what they see in the adolescent world. The first conclusion was articulated by Patricia Hersch in *A Tribe Apart*. She states, "Adolescents today inhabit a world largely unknown to adults."[4] The second conclusion was not limited to my observation but has been evidenced in other literature as well. In a 1999 survey by Public Agenda that asked adults what they thought of American teenagers, the words that came to mind were *rude* and *wild*.[5] Both conclusions confirm the need to find out how abandonment and adult attitudes have affected adolescents.

A World Beneath

I did not approach my study believing that I would discover an overriding framework within which to organize the data and conclusions, but that is what happened. I discovered that midadolescents have responded to systemic abandonment by creating a separate and highly structured social system, what I call the *world beneath*.[6] The world beneath is a broader concept than the notion of a youth culture or a generation gap. This world has been evolving over several decades, but within the last several years, it has shifted from a rather innocuous and at times innocent withdrawal to a unique and defended social system. Whereas midadolescents of the past formed "treehouses"—esoteric but largely conspicuous expressions of separation—the world beneath today's adolescent landscape is much more like an underground society: sophisticated, pervasive, and not meant to be seen. It is not unlike the social system of any culturally oppressed subgroup: while its members know they must live in the majority world, they also have a distinctively different world that is reserved just for them,

People think I have the "perfect" life. I wear the right clothes, I hang with the "cool crowd," my family has money. But the funny thing is, they don't know that I cry myself to sleep every night because my dad's expectations are impossible. I struggle with keeping up with school work. I come from a divorced home. They never see the real me. I have to put on a mask. I deal with the struggles of beer and alcohol. They don't know.

high school student

where few "outsiders" are welcome.[7] It has its own rules of relating, moral code, and defensive strategies that are well known to midadolescents and are tightly held secrets of their community.

The separation of youth from the world of adults began perhaps as early as the first few decades of the twentieth century. During World War II and throughout the 1950s, there was a distinct flavor to the younger generation. Rock 'n' roll, teen films, and adolescent dress and style were introduced as markers of this newly developing subculture. As previously discussed, the 1960s was the decade of change in many areas of American life. Our naïveté and carefree life of post–World War II culture were shattered by political assassinations, the civil rights movement, the Vietnam War, and the newly highlighted drug culture. By the late 1970s and early 1980s, we were well on our way to a we/they relationship between the adult world and the adolescent community.

During the early and middle part of the century, adolescents forged a unique path in the landscape of the adult world. In the 1960s, only a vocal and visible handful attempted to live as if the adult world's rules and norms did not apply to them. As the years wore on and the abandonment of the young increased, however, adolescents went completely underground and created the world beneath.[8] The contributing factors are varied and complex, but the foundational reason behind the separation between the adult world and the world of adolescents is that society has abdicated its responsibility to nurture the young into adulthood. The blame for this separation cannot be placed solely or even primarily at the feet of the typical enemies of traditional society: Hollywood, television, technology, the Industrial Revolution, music, or even parents. For years, adults have blamed adolescents for their rebellion against society and have, by neglect, pushed adolescents away. The formation of a separate culture for reasons of protection and safety is hardly a new phenomenon. Throughout human history, oppressed people groups have often created private subcultures in response to marginalization at the hands of those in power. What is new is that our own young people—by and large—have become marginalized by a neglectful adult culture.

Three major issues are related to the world beneath. First, adolescents intuitively believe they have no choice but to create their own world; to survive, they have to band together and burrow beneath the surface to create a safe place. Second, because midadolescents sense an emotional and relational starvation, the most important thing in their lives is a relationally focused home where they know they are welcome. Third, midadolescents have an amazing ability to band together in a way that satisfies their longing to connect with others as they try to navigate the challenging and at times harrowing journey of adolescence.

Like the farmer in *Field of Dreams* who felt he had no choice but to build the baseball field at the bidding of a persistent yet elusive voice, every adolescent hears an equally compelling internal voice calling him or her to build the world and social setting he or she so desperately wants.[9] The notion of social capital, that individuals must receive vital relational and social resources to understand who they are and where they fit, is now viewed by many as a central element of adolescent development.[10] As midadolescents become more aware of their surroundings, they develop a heightened sense of the world around them. As they enter this stage of development, they begin to recognize the abandonment discussed in the previous chapters. Many cannot describe this awareness, but when given the opportunity to reflect on their experiences, they put the essential impression of abandonment on center stage. In light of the culture of abandonment, in which adolescents perceive little adult social capital directed their way, it is no wonder that they feel the need to create the world beneath. As Robert Putnam put it in *Bowling Alone*, "The absence of positive norms, community associations, and informal adult friendship and kin networks leaves kids to their own devices. It is in such settings that youths are most likely to act on shortsighted or self-destructive impulses. It is in such settings too that youths are most prone to create their own social capital in the form of gangs or neighborhood 'crews.'"[11]

Every parent who has gone through this period knows that midadolescents have an insatiable appetite for peer relationships. When abstract thought begins to emerge (at roughly fifteen years of age), adolescents have an intuitive awareness that the process of becoming an adult necessitates finding oneself in the context of peer relationships. What is new to this stage is that because midadolescents believe they have been taken advantage of for most of their lives by those in authority (and are not yet developmentally able to distinguish the good teacher/coach/Sunday school

Waking up and still being tired
Trying to sleep and still being wired
All of the hectic time in between
Portrays the mind-boggling life of a teen.

Being forced to make many decisions at school
Wondering if our peers will consider us cool
Facing the pressure of continuous stress
Made of never-ending homework and responsible tests.

Falling in love and feeling pure bliss
Only to have your heart ripped apart and someone to miss
Knowing if your parents keep treating you this way
There's no way you'll make it through another day.

high school student

teacher from the bad), they experience to a greater intensity the need to build deep, intimate, and powerful peer relationships to survive. Because of this intensity, the drive to build a reservoir of social capital will not be denied, regardless of the source. Thus, extremely potent emotions come with peer relationship development and maintenance.[12]

In an article dealing with the difficulty of being an adolescent in contemporary culture, especially in terms of sexuality and the media, John Chapin borrows from Anne Rice's novel *Belinda*, in which she uses a character named Belinda to describe what it is like to have reached physical adulthood and yet not be prepared or equipped for adulthood:

> I had my first period when I was nine. . . . I was wearing a C-cup bra by the time I was thirteen. The first boy I ever slept with was shaving every day at fifteen; we could have made babies together. . . . But what is a kid here? . . . You can't legally smoke, drink, start a career, get married . . . all this for years and years after you're a physical adult. All you can do is play 'til you're twenty-one. . . . We're all criminals. . . . To be an American kid, you have to be a bad person. . . . Everybody's an outcast. Everybody's a faker.[13]

This was typical of the kind of talk I heard throughout my study. Few midadolescents have the developmental ability to reflect on why they feel cut off, alone, and anxious, but just like Belinda, they feel the effects.

As William Mahedy and Janet Bernardi put it, "Young people who have been abandoned and left to themselves are understandably wary and tentative, trusting little and withholding commitment."[14] And because their need for social bonds is so heightened, they can think of little else but the quality and experience of their friendships and romantic possibilities (which are linked at this stage to the same developmental need).[15]

In the midst of this driving need to create places of safety and belonging, even as they intuitively feel the results of being abandoned, they are what literature refers to as "resilient."[16] An external optimism characterizes them, such that they feel they are okay, that they can take care of themselves, and that they do not need anybody. As one teacher remarked, "I don't know why I keep hitting my head against the wall. Maybe the kids are right when they tell me that I don't know them or understand them and that they are fine without me. Sometimes I just don't know anymore why I even bother." Many adults have felt this same frustration. Because of the multiple forces and agendas squeezing them, many teenagers exhibit a callous and indifferent spirit. They often act as if they believe that adults are unnecessary. Yet this is never the whole story, for at their core each one is crying out for an adult who cares. By the time adolescents have entered the middle stage of the process, they have so little trust that they are reticent even to allow an adult to glimpse how badly they desire an adult who cares.

A year or two before I began this study, I was invited to attend a lecture by a world-renowned developmental psychologist. One of the points of his lecture was to sell the notion of "kids' resiliency," which he viewed as an important component of healthy adolescent development. When this speaker-researcher was asked about this in the context of divorce, he stated simply that "kids for the most part get over divorce, for divorce is episodic and kids are generally resilient." On a superficial reading of the available evidence, he was technically correct, for data affirm that adolescents have a powerful capacity for surviving and even thriving in extremely difficult circumstances.[17] He called divorce, then, "episodic," a singular episode that, in his opinion, a young person can and usually does move on from in relative wholeness.

But divorce, or any other expression of abandonment, is episodic only in that most young people generally learn how to find a way through the pain, even though the hurt runs deep. While it is fairly clear that adolescents are resilient, traumatic events are permanent reminders of abandonment that can cause significant psychological suffering many years down the road. Being resilient to trauma is similar to "getting over" the loss of an arm. The consequences of a ripped-apart family system remain a constant source of brokenness throughout one's life. In this same way, while abandonment may be experienced due to episodic events scattered over time, and while adolescents may learn how to rebound, the cumulative results of this perceived abandonment still weigh heavily on them.[18]

A Complex Social Reality

In tunneling beneath the observable adult landscape and creating the world beneath, the primary preoccupation of midadolescents is to find a place of relational safety. As society allowed for the erosion of consistent and coherent rules, norms, rites, and rituals that nurtured the young from childhood to adulthood, midadolescents were forced (or believed they were forced) to create their own.[19] In every human there is a driving need to fit in with others and to find one's sense of place in a social grouping. This search for a larger story, or what some call a *metanarrative*, coupled with the desire to be with others who make one feel comfortable, is what drives the adolescent need to create a unique world without adults. The world beneath is concerned with one major feature: safety.

In my study, I was amazed by midadolescents as they sought to create their own sense of place in a complex and intricately structured social hierarchy and setting. As freshmen went about the task of determining where and how they fit, even apart from the process of developing their primary friendships (which is discussed in chapter 4), they were drawn in and enveloped by the web that had been spun by those who had gone before. The entry into this world, therefore, is a fait accompli by virtue of their being thrust into the midadolescent social setting of the school. The environment is in many ways sophisticated and tightly controlled, for it accommodates the constant ebb and flow of the release of graduates and the assimilation of incoming freshmen.

One of the most striking discoveries I encountered was the degree of adeptness required to function in the varied social settings of midadolescence. As Chapin notes, "Models of adolescent development differ in the number of tasks they posit and the labels attached to them. However, most agree that the central work of adolescence includes developing a positive body image, beginning to achieve economic and emotional independence, more completely defining sex roles, developing relationships with the opposite sex, preparing for future occupational and family roles, and developing civic competence."[20] This list, however, barely scratches the surface of the variety of tasks assigned to adolescents in contemporary culture. It does not include, for example, the necessity of determining how to navigate the multiple expectations of teachers, parents, and other adults while maintaining satisfying and fulfilling adolescent relationships. One needs to balance loyalty to family with creating a sense of family with peers. One also needs to learn how to

I feel like I live life in a painting—like all these false emotions and crazy colors stroked in an insane pattern form an "image" of me and who I am. I get so frustrated because this painting of me isn't really me at all. Not even my best friend, whom I confide in and depend on the most, or my boyfriend, whom I have given everything to, knows the true me. I want to wash away all these painful strokes, absurd colors, and false emotions. I want to be cleansed of all the fake things that make me. But the fear of rejection always seems to be greater, it always overcomes the yearning for change.

Everyday I live my life for other people and not myself. I can never rest and just be me. I have to be the cheerleader or the honor roll student or the football player's woman. I can never just be me. All the drinking, parties, football games, even a walk down the halls of my high school seem like an endless drama.

Don't get me wrong. I love my friends and my boyfriend and I really love high school life sometimes . . . but sometimes I wish I could just be me!

high school student

please a parent, coach, teacher, or other youth influencer while dealing with an internal sense of abandonment. These are but a sampling of the multiple contexts of life within which every midadolescent must live. Each of these contexts presents its own unique challenges, making the world of midadolescents a highly volatile, at times hostile, place. The world beneath provides for midadolescents the respite they need to survive the aggressive anonymity of the high school world.

This line of thought led me to another startling observation, namely, that today's midadolescents have been forced to live according to the multiple selves that define them. As Susan Harter and her colleagues report, adolescents develop a "proliferation of selves that vary as a function of the social context. These include self with father, mother, close friend, romantic partner, peers, as well as the self in the role of student, on the job, and as athlete. . . . A critical developmental task of adolescence, therefore, is the construction of multiple selves in different roles and relationships."[21] This

necessity for multiple selves, a far more complex developmental requirement than for any previous generation, causes midadolescents to seem
almost schizophrenic to adults who can see life only through the lens of a
single (or dominant) self who plays many different roles. As midadolescents
bounce from self to self, the ability to handle each situation and setting
requires a heightened capacity for integrated abstract thought. Over the
course of this study, I became convinced that the defining developmental
characteristic of midadolescence, then, is the ability to draw on abstract
and complex processes of thinking and logic within each layer. Interestingly enough, however, midadolescents are not yet able to integrate such
thinking across the many layers in which they live.[22]

I came to this conclusion after observing numerous contradictions
within sharp and clever students. For example, I listened to a sophomore
girl (a self-proclaimed active church attendee) convince me that she
loved her parents more than anyone else and that she would never do
anything to hurt them. Yet almost immediately afterward she engaged in
a profanity-laced conversation with a friend as she described her sexual
relationship with a boy she had met the previous weekend. I was clearly
within earshot of this discussion, yet she seemed oblivious to my presence. When she turned back to me a few minutes later, I admitted to her
that I had overheard a bit of her conversation. I asked her, "How would
your parents feel if they had heard you?"

She simply smiled. "What they don't know won't hurt them."

"Would you lie to your parents if they guessed anything?"

"Of course. Well, not lie, exactly, but I know that they would be mad
at me, and so I would make sure that they would not find out the truth."

This winsome, attractive, and deceptive young woman did not see
the contradiction between her behavior and her attitude. She lived her
life in multiple selves and, in this case at least, did not see a conceptual
bridge between them.

Adults who acknowledge that adolescents operate in multiple layers
tend to think that this is their way of attempting to create a more coherent sense of identity as they grow up. Such adults also often implicitly
believe that adolescents simply move from setting to setting trying on
different selves as they move through their day. What I observed, however,
tells a substantially different story. The home base of a midadolescent
is the world beneath. Therefore, any entry into a layer of living that is
ordered and controlled by an adult (or even under the influence of an
adult-controlled system, such as a student-led and -run endeavor like
the school yearbook, student government, etc.) is a temporary excursion
into potentially hostile territory and is, therefore, basically not safe.
An adolescent will move back as quickly as possible into the world of
adolescents, where he or she feels included.

Today's midadolescents have discovered that they must adapt to the expectations of those who control the world in which they live. They have become adept, therefore, at making adults believe that the selves they see are in reality the entire package. This was incredibly discouraging in my work with midadolescents. The person I cared for, taught, counseled, and even befriended was not the true, authentic, unfiltered self that friends saw. What parent of a contemporary midadolescent has not heard, "You don't even know me. The only people who know me are my friends!" For midadolescents, living in multiple selves is pretense and accommodation while the world beneath is reality.

Not only did I observe midadolescents living in multiple selves, but I was also struck by the consistent and bald-faced self-centeredness of the community. It makes sense, of course. If adolescence is the process of trying to discern who one is and ultimately take responsibility for one's life (*individuation*), then the process itself forces the midadolescent to be self-focused. As adolescents recognize that for much of their lives they have been under the authority of an adult agenda that they perceive holds little regard for them, they feel the need to flee and create their own world away from adult control. Hersch states, "The adult agenda is not about what might work better for adolescents. It's all about let's control the kids, keep them in check. That is the attitude that turns kids away."[23] In this turning away, they burrow beneath the surface of the adult world, which they perceive as a threat to, or at least a roadblock in, their personal journey. They see this distancing from adults as the only option for happiness, security, and safety. In light of internally perceived abandonment, then, midadolescents live in a constant state of reactivity.

As the study progressed, an obvious question was, is this world beneath limited to the dominant culture, represented by the European-American middle and upper-middle classes? As much as I sought to distinguish ethnic differences in response to abandonment, I saw few differences, with the exception of newly arrived Korean immigrant students. I observed that Latino, African-American, Armenian, and Asian students who had been even moderately assimilated into the dominant culture experienced and responded to the issue of abandonment in ways similar to those of European-American students. Studies have shown that while ethnic adolescents tend to reject their parents' rules and norms, just as those in the dominant culture do, they do not reject identification with their ethnicity.[24] In the world beneath, all students are looking for a safe place, even when in that world there remain ethnic and socioeconomic subgroups.

As has been noted, many researchers believe that, despite compelling evidence to the contrary, "the picture of adolescence today is largely a very positive one. Most adolescents in fact succeed in school, are attached to their families and their communities, and emerge from the teen years without experiencing serious problems such as substance abuse or involvement with violence."[25] My study confirmed that on several levels this is indeed the case. Most midadolescents are basically healthy and solid young people who are simply trying to make sense of a life made almost unbearably difficult by adult society. There are several wonderful things to be said about the state of contemporary adolescence, for a spark of creativity, resilience, inner strength, and determination resides at the core of the human person.

But I cannot affirm that "the picture of adolescence today is largely a very positive one." I instead prefer the image of the vaudevillian plate spinner who is skilled at getting several plates to spin at once and even making it look easy at times. But the performer and the audience both know that the plate spinner is one small event, decision, or experience away from having the entire show fall to pieces. There are many good things going on in the world beneath, but the plates are spinning at an alarming speed, and the energy it takes to keep them on their poles is taking its toll on the hearts and psyches of midadolescents. As Madeline Levine writes, "Not only are many of these kids expected to perform at the highest levels; they are also expected to make it look easy. Heavily dependent on their 'public' success for a sense of self, many of these youngsters have little in the way of authentic purpose in their lives, leaving a void where conscience, generosity, and connection should be."[26]

The Outer Shell and the Inner Reality

The most visible mark of the world beneath is the callousness that most adolescents wear like a defiant badge of honor when adults try to penetrate their world. Adults often mistake this air of callousness for a genuine hardness and indifference, thus increasing the distance between them. Whether this callousness arises from a general defensiveness or in an effort to claim power and collective identity in a world perceived as hostile, adults often perceive this shell as an indication of a separate and resistant youth culture.[27] Adults are, frankly, afraid of most adolescents and therefore too intimidated to see how deep the layers of hardness go. This is most often misinterpreted by adolescents as a lack of care and concern for them, and thus the cycle continues.

I, however, did not observe a culture of calculated defiance emerging from midadolescents. What I encountered was a reaction perceived as necessary by a specific age group that sees itself as abandoned and therefore on its own. The apparent callousness and indifference I experienced seemed to be a test for any adult who tried to come too close. Midadolescents generally do not trust adults with the intimate reality of their lives. These fragile young people are not pretending to be callous; rather, they are wearing their toughness like a shield to protect them from further disappointment. This, however, is an exhausting and never-ending game, for even midadolescents know that many adults really do care and are worthy of trust. For most, however, the risk is too great. And yet they are so tired of keeping up the pretense.

One of my graduate students who read the first draft of this chapter asked at this point, "Is this pure speculation, these last few sentences? They are poetic, but are they substantiated?" The last few paragraphs represent my strong impressions as I reflected on the idea and state of the world beneath. I offer the following example in response. It is anecdotal, to be sure, but it is nonetheless representative of the kinds of things I heard and saw as I was let into the world of midadolescents. This poem by a junior is but one of nearly one hundred serious poems students composed and gave to me.

Step into the Dark
Step into the dark where no one can see
Step into the dark where all you see is me
Step into the dark where there is suffering and pain
Step into the dark where not a single person knows your name
Step into the dark where the only color is black
Step into the dark where love is a mystery
Step into the dark where real men don't come back
Step into the dark where no one leaves tracks
Step into the dark where hell is a block away
Step into the dark where you might brighten my day

John M.

The world beneath exists because midadolescents believe that few if any adults genuinely care about them. Writing specifically about the plight of contemporary young women, Mary Pipher, in *Reviving Ophelia*, asserts that "girls are having more trouble now than they had thirty years ago. . . . Something new is happening. Adolescence has always been hard, but it's harder now because of cultural changes in the last decade. . . . There is an African saying, 'It takes a village to raise a child.' Most girls no longer have a village."[28] Certainly, this applies to boys as well, and it is most acute in midadolescence, when the ability to reflect and think abstractly reveals a discouraging truth: adult society has contributed to the state of our young by not swiftly and decisively putting a stop to any and all forms of abandonment. We have stood by and allowed a small group of teachers to belittle, authorities to ridicule, coaches to discourage, and parents to neglect and abuse. The young respond by

When I reach down into my inner being trying to grasp hold of who I am, many times I find myself digging into an empty abyss. I'm not saying I feel my life is insignificant. Rather, I feel life is a competition, one that forces me to be someone I'm not. In high school, everyone hides behind masks of insecurity trying desperately to be cool, leaving the search for true friends a long and bumpy road.

high school student

creating the world beneath as the only satisfying option for survival in an unsympathetic world. Hersch puts it well: "Aloneness makes adolescents a tribe apart."[29]

Today's adolescents are, as a lot, indescribably lonely. They cling to their friends in the world beneath because they feel they have no other choice. There are certainly notable exceptions in every corner of an adolescent's experiences—at least a few good teachers, a caring and kind coach, a present parent. But the irresistible conclusion is this: as adolescence has lengthened and midadolescence has become more amorphous and its members more set apart, young people have begun to wonder if anyone truly cares about them. Friends care, but only insofar as they are able to maintain the norms of their peer group. Many adults care, but it takes a great deal of effort to undo what one Sunday school teacher, Little League coach, or piano teacher said or did so long ago. And so for now, they keep their collective chin up and make the best of the world beneath.

Conclusion and Musings

As I said earlier in this chapter, I had the privilege with so many teens to sit on the steps of their secret world. I saw encouraging and positive things coming out of that world. I saw genuine kindness and loyalty. I heard lofty dreams and honest stories. I saw great potential; sincere desire to make a difference; flashes of goodness, creativity, and light.

Yet I also witnessed palpable darkness. I heard vicious and vile conversations. I saw new levels of vulgarity that I found astonishing. I saw tremendous pain masked by obnoxious defiance, an insatiable selfishness, and indescribable cruelty. Even with all the good, the world beneath is filled with dark corners and hidden crevices. We as adults have a long way to go to penetrate the layers of protection that keep us from being one more disappointment in a world filled with them. But I am convinced that we are welcome to visit the borders of this mysterious and separate world, but only if we are willing to become students of our young.

Considering the complexity of the world beneath the surface, adults and adult systems have no choice but to attend to the developmental needs and nurturance of midadolescents. The most discouraging and even offensive obstacle to doing so is the myth that our young are doing fine, a view unfortunately promoted in many books and articles.[30] The first step, then, is for adults—especially those holding positions of power in institutions and systems that interact with adolescents—to repent of neglect and insensitivity. We must see the young as our kids, not someone else's problem—not the schools', the parents', the government's, or the media's. We must recognize that we have abandoned our young for decades and that it will take years to correct our indifference. We have no choice. As William Mahedy and Janet Bernardi argue, "No society that alienates its youth and sets them adrift can continue to exist, for it is already in a state of collapse."[31]

The most vital things those close to individual midadolescents can do are to, first, understand their world, and second, provide boundaries for them in a way that will keep them from making seriously negative choices even as they attempt to navigate this difficult developmental phase of life. Again, Mary Pipher puts it well: "When teenagers temporarily lose their heads, which most do, they need an adult to help them recover."[32] This help is at its best when an adult or, better yet, a community of adults seeks to truly understand what life is like for contemporary adolescents and then lovingly surrounds them with support, nurture, and authentic care.[33] It is by recognizing that today's adolescents have felt forced to create their own separate, distinct, and private world—the world beneath—that we as adults can begin to unravel and rebuild what has been lost as we have abandoned our young. To begin to change the current state of adolescence, we need to understand the specific implications and consequences of the world beneath.

part 2

the landscape of the world beneath

It is undeniable that children and adolescents have never been more taken care of, even pampered, than they are today. In many ways, the optimism occasionally reported in academic literature and popular media is indeed accurate. Many middle adolescents enjoy their home life, find security and comfort in their peer relationships, and approach life as a grand challenge to be conquered. When and where these perspectives and attitudes are evident, today's adolescents look and sound much like adolescents from the past several decades, indeed, much like their parents. In light of such cases, pundits remind us that today's kids are doing better than ever.

But adolescents have also been marred by the same adults who at times pamper them. As shown, this abandonment has caused them to dive underneath the observable surface of the adult world, even while adapting to the shifting and often oppressive expectations of our external and performance-driven culture.

Part 1 presented the theory, explanation, and background for what has happened in the world of adolescents over the past thirty-five years. Part 2 talks about the specific results. While the first three chapters focused on the abstract (e.g., the changing adolescent, abandonment, and the world beneath), we now head into the specifics of how this all plays out in the lives of midadolescents. How midadolescents make decisions about issues such as ethics, sex, busyness and stress, family, alcohol, gaming, and internet use are all affected by living in the world beneath. For the sake of all of us, come and see what life is like for today's midadolescent.

peers

My parents don't know me, my teachers don't know me, even my coach doesn't know me. The only people who really know me are my friends.

high school student

Kyle, a junior on the football team, and I were in the midst of a conversation about his life, his parents, and his friends. Kyle was among the most fortunate of the midadolescents I knew. His parents were married, they seemed to like each other, and the family was as stable as any. He was cared for, and his parents were supportive and active in his life.

The longer we talked (this had been the fifth or sixth occasion we had spent time one-on-one), the more he allowed me to glimpse the tougher aspects of his life. When he talked about his father, a "man's man" who seemed to be "more into my football than I am," the incongruity he felt in the relationship was clear. Kyle loved and even liked his dad, but he sensed somewhere inside that, while his father loved him, at times he was more interested in his accomplishments than in him. Kyle was not observably scarred, but he saw his dad as a relatively distant yet powerful force who ultimately wanted success for his son. When it came to his mom, Kyle said she was great and "of course" he loved her. Then Kyle made the statement, "My parents don't know me. . . . The only people who really know me are my friends." Studies have demonstrated that

Kyle is not alone in these sentiments: adolescents feel free to be more authentic with their peers than with anyone else. Susan Harter and her colleagues report that perceived relational support is associated with true self-behavior and high self-esteem and that for adolescents "the least false self-behavior is reported in relationships with close friends."[1]

In chapter 2, I made the claim that nearly every adult system, structure, organization, and institution has systemically abandoned adolescents. In early adolescence, children do not have the cognitive ability to recognize this, and because they are closer to childhood than to adulthood, they have a greater connection with the relationships and institutions that provided safety during childhood. The early adolescent will show signs of entering a new psychosocial phase, called the second separation-individuation[2] (the first is the developmental shift from infant to toddler), but because he or she does not have the cognitive ability to identify the source of the offending system or individual, he or she turns to a parent and the family system to ease the as-yet-unidentified pain.

During midadolescence this changes. The shift from early to midadolescence occurs when the ability to apply abstract thought begins to take shape. At roughly fourteen or fifteen years of age, adolescents begin to reflect on how they have been treated for much of their life, and it slowly dawns on them that they have been abandoned by those who—either explicitly or implicitly—were once there for them. When I encouraged adolescents to talk about past disappointments, to bring these feelings to the surface, and to examine past and present systems and institutions that impacted them, the emotions expressed ranged from disappointment or mild sarcasm to outright bitterness and hostility.

The Reason for Clusters: Kids Need a Safe Place

Changes have taken place across all segments of society, not the least of which is the high school sociological landscape. In the 1950s, a large pool of homogeneous adolescents jockeyed for a closer link to the inner circle of the popular students.[3] Today, high schools are populated by smaller groupings of friends, or clusters, who navigate as a unit the complex network of social interdependence with a loyalty similar to that of a family. Nearly two decades before my study, Donald Posterski recognized the emerging new social order of clusters.

> A friendship cluster is more than just a circle of relationships. It is heart and soul of being young today. It is a place to belong. There is no formal membership. You are either in or you are not. Being in means you share many things: interests, experiences, intimate thoughts, problems, and

You were right when you said we need a safe place. And I do want to be known for who I am. But I also want to know other people, and I want them to trust me so much that they could tell me anything. That's very important to me—that I can be there for my friends no matter what.

high school student

triumphs of the day. Being in means you tune in to the same music, wear each other's sweaters, and generally just enjoy each other.[4]

Today, the cluster is a family with a set of respected and controlled expectations, loyalties, and values. Sometimes the flag for a cluster is a similar interest, but what gives a cluster its power is a common, almost tribalistic bond and unifying social narrative (a grand story that gives meaning and cohesiveness to the cluster and defines who is in and who is not). This bond is the hallmark of the social group that nearly all mid-adolescents will rely on throughout their high school life.

The inability during midadolescence to balance disappointment over specific events, people, or institutions by separating the good from the bad drives the intense need for a safe place. Midadolescents gather in like-minded groups to protect themselves from the forces they perceive as alien to them. This is the main reason clusters have replaced cliques in today's adolescent social economy: adolescents believe they have no alternative.

Clusters: The Social Self-Defense Mechanism of the Midadolescent

One of the most clearly observable aspects of middle adolescent life is the structure of their social world and the operational expectations of their peer relationships. A social hierarchy organizes their relationships, both friendships and romantic relationships. Students also arrange their daily tasks according to this socializing structure. From what hallway to walk down between classes, to where to see friends, to whom to go to the homecoming dance with, the parameters of day-to-day experiences flow directly from the phenomenon labeled clustering.[5]

During the early 1990s, as I was making the vocational move from direct work with adolescents to an academic arena, the ideas postulated by Posterski and several others rang true for me, but I did not have a comprehensive framework that allowed me to understand fully this changing social system. Over the next ten years, I relied on research on peer relationships from around the world to help me grasp the complex changes going on in the world of adolescent peer relationships. I became convinced that something new was happening in the way adolescent friendships were formed and operated. Friendships and popularity as described in the media seemed to match my own experience from the 1970s and early 1980s, but it was evident that neither most adults nor the media—print, film, and television—was accurately portraying the radically changed nature of adolescent life and relationships.

While an increasing body of literature looks at peer relationships in adolescence, most focus on a single issue, such as drug or alcohol use, risk behavior, or sexuality.[6] These issues are integral to adolescent life and are therefore included in this book.[7] Unfortunately, far too little is known about the unique characteristics of peer friendships when applied solely to midadolescents. Yet it is during this period that peer relations take on an extremely significant role in the life of an adolescent.

Peer Cluster Theory

The construct known as peer cluster theory has been discussed for several years, albeit rarely, in adolescent academic literature.[8] Yet it remains difficult to study adolescent peer relationships. An obvious reason is that researchers face difficulty getting inside the sociologically defined and psychosocially arranged relationship groupings, or clusters. Research literature, therefore, is filled with conflicting accounts and conclusions. For example, in a chapter in *Readings on Adolescence and Emerging Adulthood*,[9] one of the most prestigious contemporary compilations on adolescent life and development, the authors dispute ethnographic and participant-observation findings that describe the increasing concreteness of adolescent peer groups (a precursor to fully developed clusters), despite the findings of more recent, solidly researched articles.[10] They appeal instead to classically palatable theoretical and empirical research. The problem is that the studies and reports used in the chapter to soften (and in some ways even discredit) the recent findings were written in the 1970s and 1980s.[11] Thus, even in the most current academic textbook on adolescent development, the issue of peer relationships is mired in theories at least twenty years old.

In all fairness, because the adolescent landscape is changing at such a rapid rate, it is extremely difficult for studies and theories regarding peer relationships during adolescence to keep pace in any meaningful

For the most part, my family has been a sort of unstable part of my life. Between divorces and tempers, I don't feel like I can depend on my family as my rock here on earth. That's where my friends come in. Sure, a lot of friends come and go, but I've been fortunate enough to develop amazing relationships with a select few—a few who aren't afraid to risk hurting my feelings so as not to let me get into things I shouldn't be getting into, a few with whom I can be completely real without fear of ridicule, friends who could sit there and listen to my problems for hours just because they care and know that I wouldn't hesitate to do the same thing. Don't get me wrong, I love my blood-related family, but my friends are really more my family than my family.

high school student

way. There is, however, an alternative way to pull together divergent research and conflicting data. Typically, social science begins an inquiry into human activity with observation and open-ended research to try to get an accurate picture before attempting to test results, conclusions, and hypotheses. After the parameters and basic elements of a targeted population and area of study have been framed, instruments and methodologies are designed to test both the original assumptions and the resultant conclusions and hypotheses. This is generally referred to as the process of developing grounded theory, the most basic and unbiased form of research methodology.[12]

The current process for interpreting information regarding adolescents, however, especially when attempting to understand them as a population, has not typically followed this method. Those who study adolescents have tended to reverse this process, starting with theories of development, performing narrowly framed empirical studies, and then forming generalized conclusions. This reversal of scholarly inquiry has created assumptions about adolescents that may have led to a theoretical framework that is neither helpful nor accurate. Theories, constructs, and data must be reassessed in light of fresh, unbiased qualitative and grounded research.

Based on the research I had encountered, I came to the present study prepared to witness elements of clustering and to attempt to describe and discern the power and impact of clustering on the social reality of middle adolescence. What I discovered as I lived among the students at the high school was far more powerful and pervasive than I had expected. Not only did I come to see clusters as the social order of the day, but I also observed firsthand the almost complete dismantlement of the social system and structure that I had experienced in high school in the early 1970s.

As we seek to understand how adolescents experience, define, and order their world, four aspects of clusters are especially significant: the reason clusters emerged, the distinguishing characteristics of clusters, how clusters are chosen and identified, and the protocol for members of one cluster relating to members of another.

The Why of Clusters

Generally, peer relationships have been seen as a normal part of the adolescent process. Traditional theories of development affirm that the shift from familial allegiance and intimacy to peer affiliation and commitment is a normal process during adolescence.[13] Few would argue against the necessity for intimate peer relationships during adolescence, for they are important for social skill development.[14] Other related theories of development involve important dimensions of peer relationships such as differentiation from parents[15] and the development of communally negotiated moral and value structures.[16] As contemporary theorists and researchers attempt to describe and codify the changes in adolescent development, they recognize that relationships are a, if not the, vital issue. Daniel Lapsley and Jason Edgerton, for example, have noted that "the press toward individuation requires the young adult to shed parental dependencies," but—importantly—"this should not come at the expense of close family ties. Rather, the goal of individuation is relational autonomy, whereby independence and self-governance are affirmed within the context of continuous, mutually validating relationships."[17] Jeffrey Lashbrook reports that the social bonds that are developed during adolescence are essential for two reasons: they address the need to belong, and they provide a cohesive unit that serves as glue for society.[18] An even more significant driving force for clustering today is the need to find a safe place.

There have been those who believe that adolescent peer relationships are not altogether positive for healthy adolescent development. As early as 1979, Urie Bronfenbrenner argued that the gravitation toward peer relationships during adolescence has a negative side.[19] While stable, intimate, and satisfying relationships with peers assist adolescents in a variety of crucial developmental tasks, argued Bronfenbrenner, adolescents may tend to distance themselves from their families as they gravitate toward their peers. This is all the more true thirty years later, as the forces encouraging the culturewide abandonment of adolescents are growing more powerful.[20] Many now see that parents have gradually pushed aside their children to the point that they have no choice but to form intimate associations with peers in order to replace what has been lost at home. This is the thesis of David Elkind's *Ties That Stress*[21] and *The Hurried Child*.[22] It is also the conclusion of an important study on peer relationships by Maja Dekovic and Wim Meeus, in which they state that "adolescents turn to peers for companionship and emotional support not because they are inevitably attracted to peers, but because they are pushed in that direction by inattentive and unconcerned parents."[23] In fact, Madeline Levine has argued that even "well-meaning parents" add to this by "pressuring their children, emphasizing external measures of success, being overly critical, and being alternately emotionally unavailable or intrusive."[24] As previously shown, not only parents but also society has created the catalyst for clustering.[25]

Midadolescents believe their only choice is to find a relational place where they are not in danger of being ignored, used, or pushed aside. The cluster, then, is not simply a developmental means to the end of preparation for adulthood. It is far more basic. The need for affiliation, support, and security during midadolescence is fertile ground for intensely powerful peer relationships. Because they have a need to discover social bonds that are meaningful and supportive, adolescents' primary motivating factor is their immediate social structure. As Denis Jarvinen and John Nicholls found, "Satisfaction in peer relationships [is] associated with communal goals and beliefs that represent social interaction as an end rather than those agentic goals and beliefs about the causes of success that make social transaction a means to an end."[26] In short, clusters develop because midadolescents know they have no choice but to find a safe, supportive community, and in a culture of abandonment, the peer group seems to be the only option they have.[27]

The What of Clusters

A cluster, while not in adolescents' vocabulary, is a group of adolescents who identify themselves as a defined relational unit. Adolescents describe such a grouping as their "friends." The word *friend* has been used for centuries to describe everything from a casual acquaintance to an intimate soul mate. In today's adolescent world, the word *friend* represents something much different from what it meant in the late 1970s.

The following list of distinguishing characteristics of clusters represents my observations of adolescent relationships as expressed on a local high school campus.

- Size: Clusters can contain as few as four or five and as many as eight or ten (and rarely, more) members.
- Gender: Clusters are almost always gender specific. Often a male cluster will align itself with a female cluster (see "The 'So What?' of Clusters" below), and they will spend a great deal of time together.
- Timing: Typically, a significant mark of the move into midadolescence is affiliation with a cluster. In most cases, this happens sometime during the latter months of the freshman year and is often solidified by the end of the sophomore year. Once the cluster attachment begins to give way to the psychosocial broadening experience of college or the military, there is usually a shift into late adolescence, marked by a willingness to explore new relationships and alliances. For those who stay in town to work or go to a local college and remain regularly devoted to their cluster, the power of the cluster can cause them to remain in midadolescence for several years.
- Loyalty and commitment: A cluster is familial in that once it is formed, there is a strong implicit agreement to remain loyal and intimately and regularly connected to the members of the cluster. In their 2005 study, Ricardo D. Stanton-Salazar and Stephanie Urso Spina found that "the principle of mutual trust also assumes a key role in adolescent friendships—specifically, the expectation that friends will not reveal confidences, will not break promises, and will not sabotage other vital ties in the peer network."[28] Because a cluster is formed out of an internal need for safety and belonging, loyalty to those with whom one has chosen to align oneself has the highest value.[29]
- Rules and norms: While a cluster is being developed, a subtle, almost imperceptible negotiation goes on among the members. The necessary rules, norms, values, and even narratives of the cluster that serve to bind the members together are all worked out prior to the cluster's ultimate formation. After these have been negotiated and established (again, almost never through explicit dialogue or reflection), the members of the cluster tend to subordinate their own personal convictions, loyalties, and norms to the will of the collective whole. While midadolescents may believe that their parents continue to influence "beliefs about control over social conventional and prudential issues," Christopher Daddis has shown that "close

In ninth grade, I felt that having a lot of friends and being accepted were the most important things. I even conformed to their desires and dyed my hair pink, dressed somewhat punkish, and went to parties with rock music, smoking, and other activities. After a while, I realized that this was not me. It wasn't until eleventh grade that I broke away from that destructive group of friends and chose to hang out with others. My group of friends wasn't as big, but at least they were more like me.

high school student

friends were the most relevant in the construction of boundaries regarding personal and multifaceted issues."[30] This subordination of the individual's personal convictions to the will of the cluster is also demonstrated by the numerous studies conducted regarding peer influence on adolescent drug and alcohol use and aggressive or nonaggressive behaviors.[31]

The How of Clusters

There has been scant quantitative research addressing why teenagers choose the friends they do, especially during midadolescence, when clustering takes place. Even less research has asked how they go about the process of choosing their friends. What evidence there is has shown that contemporary adolescents choose friends who are similar to themselves.[32] As Kathryn Urberg and her colleagues state, "Adolescents are choosing new friends who are as similar to them as are their existing friends, and . . . the similarities often predate the friendship."[33] This basic assertion is helpful in confirming what I observed on the high school campus. As emerging midadolescents begin to realize that they need friends in order to have a home base from which to navigate the psychosocial journey they are on, they see the path of least resistance as the most important factor in determining their friendship cluster. Most students remain close to their natural affinity groups even while they search for friendships that could go beyond mere acquaintance or activity-based friendship.

Every person enters the adolescent phase of life shaped by three forces: genetic makeup (what some call *nature* and others refer to as the *created self*), familial and parental influences (often referred to as *environment*), and an internal determination of how to integrate the two.[34] When children begin the process of embarking on the individualized journey of adolescence, they come to this phase of life with a fairly well-developed sense of self, or what is sometimes called self-concept.[35] By this point (at eleven or twelve years of age), family setting, social environment, and the millions of messages from every experience have created inside the child an internalized picture of who he or she is, especially in how the child sees himself or herself as a social being. Relying on John Bowlby and Mary Ainsworth,[36] some believe the adolescent self-concept[37] is formed according to the degree of attachment with the mother (or primary caretaker). But there is evidence that this is but one of several factors that influence the development of self-concept. Certainly, infant and child attachment are highly significant, but the stability of the familial environment, including the perceived stability of the relationship between the mother and the father (even if they are no longer married but remain cordial and emotionally safe), and the child's experience of growing up are also important elements in the development of self-concept. Once formed, this self-concept creates the soil from which the natural process of cluster development occurs. B. Bradford Brown and his colleagues affirm the importance of familial influence in determining adolescent self-concept and its relationship to peer clustering. "The evidence . . . indicating that parents influence many behaviors by which adolescents are assigned to crowds, seems to favor a conceptual model in which parents play a significant but indirect role in adolescent peer group affiliations. . . . [S]pecific parenting behaviors are significantly associated with specific adolescent characteristics, which in turn predict the peer group with which the adolescent is associated."[38]

Some researchers assert that parents play a significant role in cluster formation. They make the assumption, however, that parental behaviors get passed on from parent to child and that these behaviors then predict the peer group.[39] While this view is one possible explanation as to how parents influence adolescent peer relationships, an equally plausible explanation is that what gets passed on from parents to children is less dependent on specific behaviors than on a psychosocially internalized self-concept. In my observation of cluster formation, the common draw for students seemed to be less about behaviors or even activities and more about a sense of comfort and safety. As students navigate ninth grade, an almost ritualized courtship process takes place as friendships and groups are tested. Once relationships begin to solidify and a cluster begins to form, the attraction that formed the basis of the cluster becomes easier to observe.

While students did not express their parents' involvement in their choice of group, and many suggested that their parents were against their choice of friends, a preference common to the members of a group was present that made the mutual attraction of the group understandable. This sense of self, which became the marker of the group, was not formed by the group itself but was what drew the individuals together. The unifying concept had been developed long before the group formed. Maja Dekovic and Wim Meeus demonstrate a similar observation in their assertion that "the quality of the parent-child relationship affects the adolescent's self-concept, which in turn affects the adolescent's integration into the world of peers."[40] Self-concept gives shape to an adolescent's still-forming worldview. This personal worldview and the accompanying sense of self, which is the center of that worldview, are the basic criteria on which clusters are based.

This hypothesis held up as I observed both the formation of clusters and the clusters themselves in action. As has been mentioned, when an adolescent achieves a sense of reflective personhood in the process of becoming an independent, unique individual, he or she shifts from early adolescence to middle adolescence. In middle adolescence, friendships are perceived as indispensable to survival. There is, therefore, an observable difference between the way incoming freshmen relate to their peers and the way juniors and seniors relate to their peers. The first several months of the freshman year are a time of recognizing the new realities of middle adolescence.

Here is a sample of comments made by freshmen during the first few months of high school:

- "My friends from junior high are different now. It's like everybody is changing."
- "I'm not the same person I was last year. And my friends, well, they just don't seem to do it for me, you know?"
- "I don't feel as close to my friends as I did last year. We promised we'd stay close, but now we're kinda drifting apart."

These comments reflect the view that the transition from junior high to high school is a transitional shift from one stage of adolescence to another.[41] The difference between today and twenty or more years ago is that adolescence has lengthened, creating three stages of adolescence instead of two. The shift, therefore, is between early and middle adolescence. This remains a dramatic and sometimes traumatic experience for adolescents (and their parents).

This transition between stages of adolescence sets the stage for the drive toward clustering and provides the setting in which clustering takes place. As young people enter high school and ultimately begin to recognize that life is going to be different for them from this point forward, they look at their friends in new ways. In contemporary culture, the psychosocial marker of adolescence is a recognition within a child that he or she must begin to separate from his or her family and the role he or she played in that system in order to continue on a unique journey to becoming a unique person. Adolescence is a fifteen-year psychosocial journey of self-discovery and self-acceptance, and the middle adolescent recognizes that walking the "tightrope of adolescence"[42] is a long and at times treacherous experience. No matter where adolescents are on that fifteen-year tightrope, they remain squarely situated between reliance on and connection with their family, on the one hand, and reliance on and connection with a welcoming, embracing community of peers, on the other. For middle adolescents, the emotional and relational antidote to this no-man's-land is found in the protection of intimate peer relationships. During this time, friends attain heightened significance as the only support system believed to be both authentically committed and readily available.

In my observation, students' choice of cluster, based on their self-concept, became a permanent defining expression of how they viewed themselves when compared to other students. If, for example, a student attempts to build a deep and meaningful friendship of mutual support with someone who holds a higher degree of self-concept, that student will constantly feel inferior to that friend, thus negating the reason for clustering in the first place. If, however, a student attempts to build a cluster with someone who has a lower self-concept, then that person will feel as though he or she is being socially and emotionally dragged down by the other person. While this all takes place with little or no verbal or even reflective deliberation, that does not mean it is an unintentional process. I repeatedly observed the dedicated and proactive search for a safe social place, as located in the potential of a cluster. This dance of cluster formation is a highly complex process of relational exploration and negotiation.

As I began this study, I was not prepared for the necessity and power of clusters. The middle adolescent, especially early in the process of cluster formation, depends heavily on a cluster for rules, norms, and expectations. This is a time of rethinking previously held commitments and assumptions. The primary concern of the vast majority of adolescents is finding common ground with their newly aligned cluster. Previously held convictions are latently present, but pleasing the cluster is more important.

This all takes place beneath the conscious awareness of the adolescent. I had thought that in many cases kids—especially those who join clusters in which other members seem to possess a higher social status—were acutely aware of a certain sacrifice they would have been making in order to join.[43] What I observed, however, was that clusters are more primally negotiated according to who will make one feel the most welcome and safe with the least amount of work and stress, even though this central criterion is rarely verbalized. Once the choice of cluster has been settled, there may be some overlap and movement from cluster to cluster, but this too seems to be the exception rather than the rule.

The "So What?" of Clusters

Clusters comprise the building blocks of adolescent society. Thick walls develop around various clusters as they create social and operational rules and norms. Each cluster, then, functions as an independent unit with its own approved behaviors, which continually reinforce the predetermined values of the cluster.[44] Yet some clusters' members have self-concepts similar to those in other clusters, and they create a bond of friendship that can be described as a community of clusters, or a "cousin cluster."[45] At the same time, individuals within clusters may develop a hostile view toward those in clusters with different social views. I observed definite rules and boundaries between cousin clusters evidenced by such things as where students hung out before school, whom they sat with at lunch, which hallways they walked down, whom they talked to in class, and even what events they attended. The majority of the time, clusters set up an extremely subtle but clearly delineated "demilitarized zone," and all parties tacitly understand that they will not get involved with one another. On high school campuses across the United States, there is an undercurrent of stratification and even an implied threat of violence (if only emotional violence) between various clusters and cousin clusters.[46]

Some students can overcome the social barriers that separate students from different clusters by "being friends" in a specific and ordered context

> I may seem like I would fit in, but I'm not too popular. I try to fit in as best as I can. I think that I do a pretty good job. I just don't know what I did not to fit in. It may just be a stage in my life, but I never feel in the right place. This makes me feel so depressed, but I never show it. I always come off as a happy person to those I meet.
>
> high school student

(such as on a sports team). In fact, since the first edition of this book, I have increasingly recognized a phenomenon that I did not observe or note in my original study: the *shadow cluster*. In subsequent focus groups and in dialogue with those who spend a great deal of time with adolescents, I have sought to differentiate between the uniqueness and characteristics of the cluster as described in this chapter and those of other secondary peer groups. I have argued that the vast majority of adolescents rely on their primary cluster as their main nonfamilial social entity, which then serves as the most powerful fallback system in their lives. Yet if midadolescents find themselves needing a mutually self-protective group when their cluster is unavailable, a shadow cluster may act as a temporary friendship group, and therefore *in that setting* carry the same weight and impact as the primary cluster. These shadow clusters may even be somewhat permanent when located in a given fixed system, such as on a team or in a youth group or student government setting. What is important to note, however, is that the shadow cluster will rarely if ever trump the interests, values, or convictions of the primary cluster when disassociated from the shadow cluster's setting or environment.

Conclusion and Musings

For some time leading up to this study, I had been aware of the subtle shift in high school social structure from a network of relatively homogeneous social relationships to the stratification of clustering. What I recognized early on, however, is how much this phenomenon affects the student community. In effect, on almost every high school campus, there is no such thing as a "student community."

The striking thing is that the systems that are present to serve midadolescents are typically locked into servicing a more or less cohesive adolescent community. Schools assume the presence of a student community, thus the perpetuation of identity formed in classes (as in freshman, sophomore, etc.). Coaches rely on students' willingness and ability to work as a team. Even the church tries to bring together young people from a wide variety of schools and clusters into what they call fellowship. These and countless other programmatic assumptions may have a noble intent, and in some cases may even appear to the adults in charge to be somewhat workable, but they do not take the changing youth culture and relational shift seriously. As a result, young people are once again offered up on the altar of an adult agenda at the cost of their personal sense of safety. In other words, today's teenagers are thrown together in false relationships by adults who think kids connect with one another just like they used to. Teens will perform as necessary to fulfill the roles they have been cast to play, but for many, how they appear on the outside stands in stark contrast to the driving sense of place and home they crave on the inside.

Clusters are not necessarily bad; they are just different from what most adults have experienced. Those who work with the young can take great strides forward in caring for them by understanding how they organize their social relationships and working with these arrangements. Peer groups are powerful and extremely important. Adults in positions of nurture and influence would do well to remember that these are not their parents' cliques. They are, instead, a short-term but nonetheless real family for many adolescents. Adults would do well to honor what is important to them and to find ways to invest in the other members of the cluster. I have found that once an adult is "in" with a member of a cluster, he or she is "in" with everyone else in short order.

Finally, the rhetoric of intense loyalty and commitment to their friends that adolescents often use masks a deeper sense of dis-ease. Even while operating in intimate and exclusive social relationships, they are still lonely. Somehow the cluster is not all it is advertised to be (but few kids can admit this). Should we confront this incongruity head-on? No. We would make a greater difference in individuals' lives if we were simply there for them, without an agenda or a list of critiques. The quest for a safe place is what drives the cluster phenomenon in the first place. Perhaps a few adults can come alongside an adolescent and provide a safety net without disparaging or discouraging other support systems, especially his or her friends.

5

school

Instead of fostering in its students traits of honesty, integrity, cooperation, and respect, the school may be promoting deception, hostility, and anxiety.

Denise Clark Pope, *Doing School*

could not believe what I was hearing, and even as the researcher in me was desperately trying to remember each word being said, the adolescent advocate (and parent) in me was ready to go to war! Before me stood a teacher who had been in the classroom for more than a decade and who was describing the students in each class I was going to substitute teach for her. Her flippant, callous description of several students was so disrespectful and arrogant that I literally had a hard time maintaining a pretense of support for her. I knew some of those she was describing, and although I could understand in many cases why she was annoyed or even disappointed in behavior and classroom performance, she was going so far as to dismiss their ability to produce anything of value.

This sentiment is also illustrated well in the 2008 French film *The Class*, which depicts a year in the life of the teachers and students at an inner-city high school in Paris, primarily from the perspective of teacher François Marin. In one scene, a colleague of Marin's rants to his fellow teachers, "I'm sick of these clowns. Sick of them. I can't take any more. They're nothing; they know nothing. They look right through you when you try to teach them. . . . I'm not going to help them. They're so basic, so insincere, always looking for trouble. Go ahead guys. Stay in your crap neighborhood—you'll be here all your lives and it serves you right!"[1]

I have been working among teenagers for three decades, most of that time in and around the public school setting. I have heard countless stories of unfeeling and unfair teachers. Through the years, I have attempted to take a more or less neutral stance when students (or their parents) have been negative toward their teachers, and I have even tried when appropriate to help them see a teacher's perspective. The experience I had during this study, however, opened my eyes to what young people have been saying for decades—sure, there are a handful of great teachers and a few more good ones, but many teachers have apparently given up on the reason they entered education as a vocation in the first place. As with any occupation, public school teachers are a mixed bag—a few are outstanding, some are good, some are not so good, and several need to be either retrained or removed.

The school in which I lived among students is by any standard a great public high school. The coprincipals were willing to allow me to do my research and also invited me to work with them in making the school a healthier environment for their students. The leadership of the school was helpful, open, and honest.

As I got closer to the front lines of the school personnel, specifically the counselors, teachers, and coaches, I felt from some an authentic welcoming spirit. The reception I received from others, however, was somewhat guarded. I sensed from some a clear message that I was an alien on their turf, and I was being watched. My impression is that, especially in a midsized or large public high school, most counselors and teachers are so overwhelmed with the demands of their job, so fed up with the constant criticism they receive (generally but not exclusively from parents), and so discouraged by the hordes of students who do not seem to care much about anything, that they have responded by creating a nearly impenetrable "bubble" around themselves as they go about their daily activities and duties. High school public education is a tough calling. Yet it is also a high calling, one that demands flexibility, openness, constant retooling, and the kind of temperament and psychological health that can handle student, parental, and administrative critique as well as a lack of motivation and even disrespect from midadolescents.

As made clear previously, this study is not intended as a defense or apologetic for the adults involved in public high school institutions. Were this the case, I would be the first to praise and defend the efforts of those who are willing to serve our young in the public school arena. For the purposes of this study, however, I chose not to allow myself to consider "their side," for I was most interested in what was happening in the world of the midadolescent.[2]

The Public High School in America

The public high school has become an immortal icon in American pop culture. Prom, homecoming, football players and games, the lunchroom, fast cars, pop quizzes, cheerleaders, school plays, nerds/geeks/freaks, letterman's jackets, dances, parties, and the yearbook all bring back a flood of memories for every adult. High school has been the mainstay of many songs, novels, television shows, and films. Usually, the high school experience is portrayed as the most glamorous and exciting time in one's life. As much as adults and the media have tried to maintain the cultural myth of the thrill of high school, to a great many contemporary students, it is anything but one continuous adventure. One student from my study, upon hearing from a teacher that high school is the best time in one's life, said, "Great! If this is the best it's ever going to get, I might as well kill myself now!"

I encourage those who are over thirty-five and who hold any illusion that the high school they went to is similar to the one today's students attend to visit the school, walk the halls, and listen to the students talk to one another at lunch or during breaks. Unless you have stayed in close touch with the changing adolescent culture, you will most certainly be struck by the fact that the world you inhabited and the experiences you had are but a distant memory.

The intent of this chapter is to discuss just how different the school of today is compared to that of the past and how the changes have affected midadolescents both as individuals and as a population. This chapter examines the school environment from two viewpoints, that of teachers and that of students. It is not directly concerned with the adults who run schools but with how the concept of societal abandonment has affected midadolescents as they function in the high school environment. It has been shown that school-based influences play a role in the healthy development of children and adolescents,[3] and therefore, the attitudes and behaviors of teachers[4] will be discussed alongside the attitudes and behaviors of students.

View of the Teachers

Teachers are like everybody else—it is nearly impossible to speak about them as a group without ruffling a great many feathers along the way. I have narrowed this discussion of the attitudes and behaviors of teachers to three basic issues that directly impact the lives and development of most midadolescents. (1) Most teachers believe that learning for its own sake should be enough to motivate students. (2) Far too many teachers pigeonhole students to the detriment of their developmental health and progress. (3) Teachers feel overburdened and overwhelmed, and the consequences of this spill over into their teaching.

First, I observed an underlying conflict between students and teachers as soon as I entered the classroom. Teachers seem to hold fast to the perspective that learning is (or at least should be) a pleasurable experience[5] and that the ultimate goal of learning (and thus teaching) is the joy of learning. To midadolescents, however, the only pleasurable experiences that register in their developing worldview are those that bring instant and immediately recognizable benefits. Research has consistently documented that teachers who are passionate about their subjects are more effective teachers.[6] Likewise, a teacher who genuinely likes students has a greater likelihood of encouraging students to be better students.[7] As Michael Nakkula and Michael Sadowski demonstrate in their recent book *Adolescents at School: Perspectives on Youth, Identity, and Education*, the teacher who has a passion for both the subject matter and students is by far the most effective at helping students to excel. They write, "For the vast majority of youth, school is the single context within which the combination of skill and relationship development occurs on a regular basis, day in and day out. . . . Good teachers teach their subject matter well; great teachers engage students in the learning tasks of the moment and instill in them the desire to keep learning long after graduation."[8]

If a student can perceive a direct benefit from a specific area of study, then he or she is more likely to be engaged and even excited about that subject matter. I encountered a small but honest handful of students who were able to find something they could latch on to in some of the more traditional disciplines such as chemistry, algebra, or English literature. I also discovered another group of students, exponentially larger than the first, who found room in their curriculum for what they already enjoyed, such as sports, drama, music, student government, and forensics. That said, the overwhelming majority of students, even those who were deemed smart by their teachers, could not find anything "pleasurable" about the academic element of the high school experience. "School is okay—if only I didn't have to study" was a common mantra. As harsh as it may sound, this kind of sentiment was common across the spectrum of midadolescents.

Teachers' implicit attitude that learning should be pleasurable is enough to drive an almost instant wedge between them and the students they are attempting to teach. I could sense that students believed most teachers were disappointed in and critical of them as a group because of this bias. Students wanted teachers to appreciate them and not to hold anything against them, even though they did not want to be there. Few teachers I talked to, however, were able (or willing) to see this. Midadolescents are an extraordinarily perceptive lot, and they can smell inauthenticity, judgment, and dismissive critique a mile away. For many students, this is where the rub starts, and, sadly, it begins the day class convenes.

My second observation was that many teachers pigeonhole students, thus hindering students' ability to grow and develop. While there are obviously many effective, caring, and dedicated teachers in American public high schools, I encountered far too many who boxed, categorized, labeled, and dismissed their midadolescent students. Sociologist Elliott Currie found this as well in his study of middle-class youth: "The bottom line was that the schools functioned less as actively nurturing institutions, committed to building the competence and intellectual capacity of all their students, than as instruments for sorting and categorizing them—sifting the good from the bad, the promising from the 'losers,' the troublesome from the 'OK.'"[9] Some schools may actually do more harm than good when it comes to the care of midadolescents.

A case in point was the annual banquet for one of the varsity sports teams at the high school where I did my initial study.[10] Each year the coach stands in front of the students and their parents and summons each student-athlete to the podium to receive his letter. This particular coach is one of the more well-known teachers/coaches in the school and has a reputation for being gruff. He chose, instead of writing down his comments to ensure that every athlete was affirmed, thanked, and encouraged for his participation in the sport, to make up his comments on the fly as the boys' names were called. Those who were talented or well liked by this coach received a glowing acknowledgment of their contributions. Those who did not play much, however, or who for one reason or another did not turn the eye of the coach, heard either almost nothing as they walked forward or, worse, heard disparaging—even degrading—comments about their lack of performance, playing time, or physical skill. Year after year this painful ritual continues. When I asked other coaches and parents about it, the most common response was, "Oh, that's just how Coach is. He doesn't mean to hurt anybody; he just tells it like it is." This last year I even heard the rationale, "He is great. He doesn't pull any punches. These kids have to learn how to handle the truth!" This ritual can be so uplifting for the favored young men and yet so permanently painful in the lives of the others.

As a rule, many teachers are far more willing to get to know and invest in "good kids," "talented kids," or "smart kids" than in those they do not feel contribute to their own agenda. With these teachers, midadolescents recognize quickly that it is up to them to decide whether they want to play that game. The ones who are typically embraced are those who have chosen (whether the choice is conscious or not) to win the attention and affection of the teacher. They have decided that their midadolescent experience will be more satisfying and productive if they convince teachers that they are worthy of their engagement. For so many kids, relationships with teachers have become little more than a game. During this phase of development, students live out their "school self" as they operate within the school's expectations and parameters of conduct. This includes the persona they reflect and the relationships they initiate with their teachers.[11]

For many teachers, the litmus test of a "good" young person is how much respect the student shows the teachers. One of the most common reasons given as to why teachers write off the majority of their students is the lack of respect they receive from many of them. As almost any teacher will tell you, respect from students is no longer an automatic expectation. It is a hard-earned benefit to be won. It is no wonder that many teachers disdain their students.

The issue of the lack of respect teachers feel, however, is not limited to students in the classroom. Most teachers feel underappreciated and even abused by their administration, district, and even state.[12] In a thoroughly researched report by Public Agenda, teachers said that "their views are generally ignored by decision makers, with 70% feeling left out of the loop in their district's decision-making process."[13] Along with budgetary woes, this was the leading source of complaint I heard consistently from teachers. From what I observed, it was one of the more significant factors in causing teachers to become discouraged. This discouragement is sometimes reflected in a negative attitude that spills over into the classroom and onto the individual psyches of the students they have committed themselves to serve.

Third, a significant number of teachers feel overwhelmed by the very task of teaching in the contemporary American public high school system. They also feel that when it comes to external support and recognition, a vital component of employee morale,[14] they are on their own. Researchers have suggested that the role of teachers today is more about the developmental trajectory of adolescents than about the observable or measurable behavior or academic achievement of a student at any particular time.[15] Many teachers recognize this expectation, and yet the demands of standardized testing, score-based evaluation systems, the disruption of behavior problems, and a host of other factors all converge, causing teachers to feel stretched beyond their ability to do and be everything demanded of them. Add to this situation the contemporary educational mind-set that teachers are one of the last remaining groups that truly understand and care for the young and that therefore teachers need to take on the lion's share of responsibility for rearing adolescents,[16] and it is little wonder that teachers are discouraged.

Teachers say they want more involvement from parents, and it is a fact that parents are less and less involved with high schools.[17] Over the course of this study, I found that most teachers do—publicly and privately—bemoan the lack of parental involvement in children's high school education, for they understand precisely what researchers Robert Crosnoe and Glen H. Elder observed, which is that "the linkage between emotional support from parents and adolescent academic performance is well-established. Warm and supportive relationships have been found to promote academic achievement and positive attitudes about education, whereas more distant or conflictual relationships can be tremendous stressors that disrupt proper functioning in school."[18] But I also witnessed several events and conversations in which parents who showed an interest in working with teachers were seen as a threat.

The parent-teacher relationship is one of the more complex and at times stressful relationships in the overall high school structure. Teachers believe that children are far more successful when their parents are involved with both the student and the school. At the same time, however, teachers regularly feel as though parents are more interested in defending their children and rationalizing their behavior and performance than in allowing teachers to offer their expertise. To many teachers, partnering with parents means inviting parents onto a team captained by the teacher for the training of children. In my experience, teachers are often apprehensive toward parents, and this fear can quickly communicate to a parent that the teacher is not interested in a parent's perspective, even if the teacher enthusiastically wants to connect with parents. Added to this dynamic are parents' fears that they have far less control over their child than they are supposed to have (and the school is often the perpetrator of this perception). These issues place a significant wedge between a parent and a high school teacher even before there is any interaction.[19]

In numerous conversations with teachers and administrators over the past several years, I found that the problem may lie with teachers being implicitly trained that they are the only societal institution left that has

The SOL (Standard of Learning) exams are the worst part of school. You can get straight A's all year long, but if you fail the SOLs, you have to take the class over. It's a lot of stress at times.

high school student

the education, training, and commitment to understand and nurture the young. This attitude, unfortunately, applies even to parents and families. Indeed, educators overwhelmingly report the necessity of the involvement and investment of parents in their children's education. Yet at the same time, they are regularly (and vocally) critical of parents' lack of commitment, meaning lack of commitment to the narrow perspective and focus of the educator.[20]

The study I conducted consistently showed that most parents are concerned about their children's education, but for many it is not the highest priority on the list of things that parents of midadolescents have to worry about in today's society. Parents have to worry about their kids' sexual behavior, the internet and the media, the impact of clustering and peers, and the constant temptation of substance use and abuse. A high school teacher sees students for less than an hour a day, and for the most part, that teacher's entire perception of them is based on the external roles, behavior, and academic performance shown during that hour. A teacher almost never knows anything about the dynamics of students' family systems, their friendships and internal struggles, or how other adults perceive them as they live in the multiple selves created by postmodern society. All too often a teacher makes a snap judgment, and students and their parents are forced to live under that label until the end of the semester.[21]

View of the Students

Getting students to talk about their feelings regarding school was the easiest aspect of this study. What was interesting was the consistent message that came from nearly every corner of the population. Certainly, as with every other element of this study, there were students who did not line up with the general trends. For example, students' approaches to school and academic performance ran the gamut: some students were serious about their studies (they were committed to getting the grades they needed to open future doors), some were trying to get by doing the minimum required of them to stay in school, and some did not seem to care at all. Four broad areas of consistency did, however, emerge: attitudes toward teachers and the respect they deserve, the motivation behind academic achievement, the prevalence and morality of cheating, and the high level of anxiety that the competitive environment of the classroom can produce.

In terms of respect for teachers, students believe that respect is something to be earned, not granted. In discussing respect for teachers with midadolescents, the widespread view was that teachers do not deserve respect simply because they are teachers. (This viewpoint was not limited to teachers; it applied to every adult.) A report covering twenty-five national surveys confirms this view, stating that "only 9% of surveyed Americans said [high school] students they see in public are respectful toward adults."[22] What I found especially intriguing was that most students believe that teachers do not even deserve the benefit of the doubt and that, instead, teachers must earn the respect of students by showing them respect first. Several scenes in *The Class* poignantly demonstrate this. For instance, at one point teacher François Marin attempts to communicate to his class that he is genuinely interested in their feelings and their view of life, and he is met with student reactions such as "you're only saying that to get us to talk and stuff." The students clearly do not believe he cares as much as he claims. Later, a student writes a short letter to Marin asserting, "I know you have it in for me, but I don't know why," and pleading for some respect. Clearly trust and respect are central concerns for these students, but they desire mutuality: trust and respect have to go both ways.[23]

The idea that people deserve respect and kindness unless they do something to break that code (and even then many still believe respect should always be granted) was previously an unchallenged value of our culture. Today, that rule does not apply, at least on high school campuses. Not only do midadolescent students not respect their teachers as teachers, but they actually enter a classroom prepared not to respect a teacher unless that teacher wins their respect. Ruben Garza concluded this very fact from his study of white and Latino high school students: "Culturally diverse students need a relationship with their teachers that is mutually respectful if they are to learn. They not only need to like their teachers, but also must sense that their teacher cares for them."[24] Similarly, Alison Cook-Sather found that "consistently, students argue that in order to feel engaged in their schooling, they need to enter and experience a positive classroom environment and they need to feel that teachers know them and want them to learn."[25]

The second interesting perspective I discovered during this study involved how students approach academic achievement, especially the motivation for academic achievement. Researchers have begun to look at the dark side of the pressures on the academic elite. David Brooks, senior editor of the *Weekly Standard*, writes,

> There is a dark side to the meritocratic system, however. One of the most destructive forces in American life today is the tyranny of the grade point average. Everyone argues about whether SATs are an unjust measure of student ability, but the GPA does far more harm. To get into top schools, students need to get straight A's or close. That means that students are

not rewarded for developing a passion for a subject and following their curiosity wherever it takes them. They are rewarded if they can carefully budget their mental energies and demonstrate proficiency across all academic disciplines. They are rewarded, as Joseph Epstein put it, for their ability to take whatever their teachers throw out at them, in whatever field, and return it back in their warm little mouths. Idiosyncrasy is punished. Students are rewarded for having a lukewarm enthusiasm for all fields in general and none in particular. They are rewarded for mastering the method of being a good student, not for their passion for the content of any particular area of learning. They are rewarded for their ability to mindlessly defer to their professors' wishes, and never strike out on their own or follow a contradictory path.[26]

Developmentally, of course, midadolescents are not prepared to recognize that education is a valuable gift not only for them but also for society at large. I found few students who could articulate anything other than their own personal drive and agenda to "get somewhere" when it came to academic achievement. The days of a high school student finding learning to be a pleasurable experience rather than a means to an end are all but gone. Yet academic literature continues to perpetuate the pleasurable experience of learning as an educational motivation.[27]

The motivating factor was the same for those who were high achievers as for those who did not seem to care very much: a student will do whatever it takes to navigate the complex and varied demands of midadolescence with as much self-protection and self-interest as necessary. As already mentioned, midadolescents live much of their lives in multiple selves, and they put on personae that enable them to survive as they move from one layer to the next. Students who believe that getting good grades helps them feel better about themselves do what they have to do to get the grades. For those whose primary strategies lie elsewhere, grades are less important. What seems to be nearly universal is that the high school system forces midadolescents, as one researcher put it, "to falsify their behavior."[28]

One exception to the idea that midadolescents do not care for school had to do with students' talk about college. The academically oriented (some would say "gifted") students talked about college as a goal, and those who were not as academically oriented did not. The issue of what college to attend (or whether to go to a junior college or even at all) seemed to bring with it a mixed cauldron of conflicting motivations and values, and very few students knew precisely what they wanted and why. Most students, in fact, especially until the middle of their junior year, maintained grades and relatively stable relationships with teachers simply because it suited their idea of how best to survive high school, not because it was a means to an end of a specific career goal or even college.

Third, cheating is so widespread on high school campuses that it is considered by many to be the norm. Cheating for midadolescents is a complex issue and will be addressed more fully in chapter 10.[29] The mixed messages from parents and the school itself, the lack of a clear and universal definition of academic dishonesty and cheating, and the widespread relativism of society have created an atmosphere in which even the definition of cheating is nebulous. Many midadolescents simply will do whatever they believe is necessary to fulfill the expectations of their parents and teachers, and cheating becomes the way they deem best to do that.[30]

Studies on cheating reveal that students have become adept at laying the problem at the feet of everybody but themselves.[31] In other words, to midadolescents, cheating is rarely considered a moral problem, but when it is, a student almost never sees himself or herself as the culprit. Rather, he or she is the unfortunate victim who had no other option. Today, two rigid ethical commitments crash into one another at both the high school and the college level: the traditional ethic of academic integrity and the contemporary adolescent perspective that cheating is an acceptable and even relatively moral option for the student who needs to perform. This is an even bigger problem when one realizes that it is not a few who cheat. In one way or another, everyone cheats (statistically anyway).[32]

The most frequent reason given by students for cheating was the injustice of teachers. If a teacher were fairer, the argument goes, then there would be little need to cheat.[33] In dozens of conversations with students regarding cheating, the closest I got to anyone recognizing that cheating was actually stealing and therefore a moral problem was when a girl told me about a boy who cheated off her tests regularly. He "didn't care at all about studying," and he was therefore taking advantage of her. Although I pushed as hard as I dared, she simply could not go beyond being personally "ripped off" to condemning the practice of cheating as an ethical problem. The fact that he cheated was not the problem. She was morally outraged because he had cheated off her.

Abandonment, along with the general neglect in other areas of adolescents' lives, affects midadolescents in the school arena by contributing to one of the most disturbing trends in their world: the acceptance of deceit to protect, defend, or push oneself forward.[34] To contemporary middle and late adolescents, truth has become little more than a strategic effort to define one's own version of reality in order to control one's environment.[35] As Denise Clark Pope points out, "Successful students learned to devise various strategies to stay ahead of their peers and to please those in power positions; unsuccessful students, for a variety of reasons, were not as adept at playing the survival game."[36] This "game" has produced a continuum of students, ranging from those who are proficient at

I go to a school that has a very arrogant attitude about itself. It's the number 1 school in the state of Louisiana, which, if you know anything about the public education system in Louisiana, doesn't mean a lot. The teachers are constantly nagging us about how we're the smartest 1 percent of the smartest 1 percent in either New Orleans or Louisiana—I can't quite remember; I try to block them out when they try to tell us we're geniuses. The principal obviously doesn't know us very well, because she swears we don't lie, cheat, steal, or do drugs. She's wrong. The only way for a lot of people to pass most tests is to cheat, because the tests are so hard. And the people who could pass if they studied decide they can outsmart their teachers, so they put all their time and effort into figuring out how to cheat and don't study at all.

high school student

conforming to what others expect them to be and do to those who have to figure out how to survive when they cannot live up to those expectations. Midadolescents learn to cope, indeed, to survive, without adults. They have become adept at saying and displaying what adults want to hear and see, and they have learned how to play a role that helps them to survive the expectations of adults.

Finally, students who care about grades and academic performance are experiencing an ever-increasing level of anxiety and stress over school. The source of this pressure has been debated for some time—parents, teachers, colleges, society at large—but that discussion is beyond the scope of this study. What I observed, however, is that the locus of the anxiety is within the psyches of those students who have, for whatever reason, made the decision to compete with others and to do as well in school as possible. For some it is a first-, one-point-five-,[37] or even second-generation ethnically driven cultural ethos.[38] Others who are exceptionally "book smart" push themselves by doing things such as taking the SAT "for fun" as early as the eighth grade. Then there are those who are simply trying to maintain an A or A- average to be accepted into the school they (or their parents) want.

Two elements that add to the stress level of these students are the increasing amount of homework required and the university-mandated need to be involved in as many activities as possible while in high school. The school in which I did this study expected each student to spend from forty-five minutes to an hour per day on homework for each class. Students are required to take five classes, meaning that each weeknight they need to spend over three hours doing homework.

Added to this academic requirement is the need to be involved in athletics (two or more hours per day) and in extracurricular activities and clubs (such as school-based Key Club, faith-based Young Life, or a church youth group). And on top of all this, there is often an expectation to put in volunteer hours.[39] Typically, then, a student who cares at all about being a "good student," doing homework, and pleasing teachers and parents, starts the day before 7:00 a.m., gets home after practice or a meeting at 5:00 or 6:00 p.m., does an hour of homework, grabs dinner before heading out to an activity, gets home at 9:30 or 10:00, and finishes homework around 1:00 a.m. The bulk of the students I observed, especially those who were active and involved, were often exhausted, harried, and frazzled. There seemed to be little apparent systemic consideration for what these schedules, expectations, and pressures do to the development and health of midadolescents.

Conclusion and Musings

As Denise Clark Pope points out, "The school world has been described as a place where, too often, students feel anonymous and powerless."[40] This was a central observation of this study. Most students had learned at an early age how to "play to" the expectations of the educational system in order to adapt to its demands. Some researchers put a positive spin on this, leaning on the construct of "social capital" to describe how adolescents navigate the complex process of growing up by relying on others to promote successful transitions. Stanford Center on Adolescence researchers Shirley Brice Heath and Milbrey McLaughlin exemplify this perception when they argue that adolescents must learn how to behave properly in a variety of contexts to achieve the kind of support they ultimately need to become successful adults.[41]

But this is a catch-22 for adolescents, both the successful students and those who do not appear to be successful by institutional criteria. The successful students are those who are able to play the game better than their lesser peers. They are not actually being nurtured and assimilated into the adult world by caring mentors; they are learning how to beat the system! Adolescents who lag behind academically often devise another strategy for beating the system, either out of fear of failure or distrust of the system itself. They fall into the category of "average" or "unsuccessful."

Most teachers are doing a good job under a rigid, politically driven, difficult system. The American public high school places many layers of expectations and demands on teachers, and often what we ask of them as a society is not fair. They are poorly paid, lack sufficient resources, could use additional training and encouragement, and are overloaded with the demands made on them by classroom size, the rigors of objectified test scores, and a difficult cultural world. They get little thanks and are constantly under the microscope of parents and administrators, and it is little wonder many are discouraged.

That said, this book is intended to open the eyes of adults who care about the state of midadolescents in American society. It is intended to advocate for those who have been bruised by what society has done through cultural neglect and systemic abandonment. I, therefore, am not writing as a defender of teachers but as an advocate of adolescents. I intend to be neither harsh nor unfair to those who have given their lives to educating our young. I do, however, believe that what happens on a high school campus in many ways hurts our young. Not a week went by without my being deeply disturbed and sometimes militantly agitated by the attitudes, behaviors, and policies of teachers and administrators in one of the best schools in the state of California. For this reason, I offer two conclusions.

First, we have hurt entire populations of adolescents because we have allowed our limited understanding and definition of "gifted" to be shaped by an extremely narrow view of human potential. One obvious problem is that the timing of development is different for each person. Development has a direct impact on such things as cognitive memory and recall (a central methodological commitment in American education, even though it has proven to be among the least effective ways to educate a developing adolescent).[42] Surviving, much less thriving, in early and middle adolescence requires the ability to focus for fifty minutes on one subject, run to the next class without getting in trouble for being late, and focus on an entirely different subject, all while navigating the complex relational dynamics of each class. Add to this the different styles and expectations of teachers, and a student who is even slightly behind developmentally is put at a severe disadvantage in the rigid, tightly controlled educational environment of the American high school.[43] At a certain level, all kids have the innate ability to learn, and many of those who fall through the cracks are far more intelligent than our systems recognize.[44] There is also strong evidence that both learning and intelligence are extremely complex processes and that there are multiple types of intelligences.[45] We need to recognize that young people are the most precious and fragile resources of our society. Each one has a unique potential[46] and needs and deserves a deliberate, proactive, and nurturing school environment.

Second, I agree with Mel Levine, developmental pediatrician and author of *A Mind at a Time*,[47] that we have fallen prey to the misconception that we can treat all students in the same age category the same way. We have also forgotten that each adolescent is by definition in a state of transition and growth and therefore needs individual attention in every aspect of his or her life, including education. This is a tall order indeed for a teacher who has five classes of thirty students each, but we do not have the luxury of thinking of students as "classes" or of putting them in boxes with labels such as "average," "gifted," and "obnoxious." Each young person has tremendous potential within the context of his or her unique giftedness and therefore deserves personal care, attention, and a system that seeks individual growth and development. I asked Scott, the 2002–2003 teacher of the year at the school where I did this study, what it takes to be a great teacher. He said, "The same thing it takes to be a great spouse, or parent, or coach, or leader in any setting. It's not mystical, and it sure isn't a secret. It is just caring enough for each person in front of you that they know they matter to you. To be a great teacher means I am allowed the privilege of being with great kids. They're the ones who deserve this award."

6

family

Twenty-five percent of the people polled in a recent national inquiry into American morality said that for $10 million they would abandon their entire family; a large number of people are evidently willing to do the same thing for free.

Stephanie Coontz, *The Way We Never Were*

Regardless of headlines labeling us "helicopter" dads and "soccer" moms, in many ways parents seem almost invisibly removed. Twenty-first century parent-managers, negotiating every single logistical challenge of their kids' crammed schedules became too frenetically busy to be a magnetic presence in the internal landscape of a child's world.

Ron Taffle, *Childhood Unbound*

By the third week of my study, I was beginning to realize that the world I was being allowed to see was far more complex and precarious than I had imagined. One stunning illustration came in a conversation with a junior named Jeremy. What Jeremy told me about his family seriously threw me.

"Okay, I'll tell you something I've never told an adult. In fact, I'll tell you something I've never told anybody. Three years ago my parents got divorced, and they decided to keep it a secret. They told me and my sister that we weren't allowed to tell anyone, not even our grandparents, or we would get in big trouble. So for three years we all have been living a lie. I haven't told my friends, my coaches, my teachers, nobody, and neither has my little sister. My parents hate each other, and they fight all the time, but they pretend to be happily married around everyone else. It sucks!"

As I was trying to hide my shock and anger over what this young boy was being forced to carry, a shy girl on my left began to bite her nails and squirm.

"Me, too," she said quietly.

"Excuse me?"

"Okay, I guess it doesn't matter anymore anyway. My parents did the same thing last year to us. I hate them! I hate them both!"

Then the bell rang, and they were gone.

This event was not only gut-wrenching but also decisively instructional for me. I knew that for this study to mean anything, I needed to probe into every corner and pursue every possible angle of new information. Frankly, it had never crossed my mind that adults could do what these parents had done to their children. Unfortunately, such selfishness reflects a growing trend of parents placing their own needs ahead of those of their children.

It is likely that I had overlooked hundreds of hints and markers of the dark side of family life and had been fooled by the sophisticated callousness many young people are forced to exhibit on a daily basis. There are obviously many solid, supportive parents and families in American society. Generally, their children are the strongest and healthiest adolescents and are able to find a relatively stable path through the issues presented in this book. But the depressing and eye-opening reality I encountered that day is that the brokenness in today's families is far more pervasive and destructive than I had ever imagined.

The Definition and Meaning of Family

The concept of the family has undergone intense and contentious change over the past twenty or so years. Today it is commonplace for popular television shows to depict "family" in a variety of nontraditional ways. The sitcom *Modern Family*, for instance, portrays three immediate families that are connected as extended family (a father and his two adult children): the father is remarried and has a young son the age of his grandchildren; the daughter is married and in a traditional family; and the homosexual son and his partner are raising an adopted daughter. Over time the idea of the family—what it is, who (or what) is included, and why it matters—has been slowly relegated to private opinion, creating a sociological and cultural divide.

I first encountered the battle over the definition of and the standards ordering the concept of the family in my doctoral studies. One well-respected professor told us that one of her more passionate academic goals was to change the definition of family in academic literature. She was dedicated to the ideological position that lesbians and gay men should have the right to raise children from birth and that therefore the more traditional understanding of the family (one man, one woman, and children) was an oppressive and outdated social construct that needed to be dismantled. I liked and admired this professor in many ways, but I believe she violated the most important command of academic integrity that she herself had drilled into us as PhD students: "Let the research lead you to conclusions about life, and do your best not to let your personal life or your pet perspectives taint your research conclusions." The academic and popular debates adults have waged over the definition, meaning, and impact of the family have taken a toll on the young. What has happened with the notion of and attitude toward the family is perhaps the most significant form of cultural abandonment midadolescents have endured.

Overwhelming data regarding the influence of parents on child and adolescent development reveal that the most important place of safety for a young person is a supportive dual-parent setting.[1] The kind of environment in which a child, especially during midadolescence, may ultimately be strengthened as he or she moves through the adolescent process is provided by a family with a relationally committed father and mother and a home that is a place of safety and security and where, even during conflict and rocky circumstances, an adolescent knows that he or she is unconditionally accepted and loved.

My observations confirmed this idea. The midadolescent students who struggled the most in nearly every category of adolescent development—for example, self-concept, sexual behavior, substance abuse, and trust in friends or authority figures—almost universally came from a family system in which the home was not a safe, supportive environment.[2] For example, midadolescents known as sexually "loose" often come from families in which the father is not present or there is a specific and usually observable disconnect between the child and the father. (This was true of both boys and girls, although it was more easily recognizable in the behavior and attitudes of girls.) Based on dozens of conversations and many observations of this aspect of midadolescent life, I found that those who had learned (or were learning) to use their bodies to find comfort and connection through sexual play were trying to prove to themselves and to the world that they were worthy of love. Upon directed reflection, most adolescents came to the conclusion that those who were the most desperate for affection were not receiving it at home. Even midadolescents themselves could see how family life and

I grew up in a home with a Christian mom and a non-Christian dad. My entire life I have struggled between growing in faith and trying to hide it from my dad. As I passed through the three years of middle school, I realized the problems this fractured identity had created within me. Battling with depression, I often felt worthless. I could not gain a social identity because not even I knew who I was.

high school student

parental relationships affected them. And the effects were not limited to external behaviors such as sexual experimentation, substance abuse, or partying. They also related to attitudes, confidence, and just about every other aspect of a person's life. The family is paramount in the developmental and psychosocial life of adolescents.

Yet according to a recent article published by the American Psychological Association, there is no longer a standard definition of *family*. It simply means what one wants it to mean: "Families today can take many forms—single parent, shared custody, adoptive, blended, foster, traditional dual parent, to name a few."[3] Yet in many cultures of the world, the central role of parents has been maintained as responsibility for the nurture of the young.[4] As mentioned in chapter 1, the family has been defined in the same way for centuries in American society: "two or more persons related by birth, marriage or adoption who reside in the same household."[5] Not only has that definition become simply one form among many and been assigned the label "traditional dual parent," but it is also mentioned last on the above APA list of the many forms of contemporary families.[6]

Not only is there no longer a standard definition of *family*, but it has become a word that allows for the justification, meaning, and structure of whatever situation adults find themselves in. During my time with midadolescents, I never encountered a dissenting voice that challenged how a household defined family. The rhetoric universally and unquestionably affirmed anyone and everyone's definition.

Here are some of the ways the word *family* was used among the students:

- Geri lived with her little sister and mother and her mother's latest boyfriend in his house with his three kids (when they were not at their mother's). Her family was her mother, sister, and the boyfriend (but not his kids).

- The man Kim calls Dad is actually her mother's former boyfriend. Kim never met her real dad, and she refers to the man she now lives with, her legal stepfather, by his first name. She told me she does not have a family.
- Kara lives with her mother, older sister (whose boyfriend occasionally lives with them), and the grandfather of one of her closest friends. The word *family* is used only to talk about her mother's family, meaning Kara's maternal grandparents, aunts, and uncles.
- Greg, the youngest child of a two-time divorcée, lives next door to his mother's boyfriend of ten or so years, and his mom forces him to call this man Dad. He blames his mother for forcing the father he seldom sees out of their lives. His mother refers to both households, his immediate family (his mother and himself) and the family next door, as "their family," but this usually happens only during holidays when some of them gather for "family holidays."
- Sam lives with his two moms and has never had a dad. His two moms are his family.

These are but a few samples of how varied and complex the notion of family is to many adolescents in American society. I had wrongly assumed that those in traditional dual-parent families would see these other expressions as somewhat less than ideal or at least contrary to the norm. Yet that was not the case. The concept of family is fluid for the developing midadolescent.

Because the family is the primary source of the relational and emotional stability necessary for healthy development, these changing definitions are noteworthy. The family system can shift and change at the whim of adults with little care given to the consequences of these changes on the developmental life and health of children and adolescents. Unfortunately, those who advocate the changing labels and fluid definitions of family do not consider these consequences. In this study, however, the erosion of the family as the central, stable institution designed for and dedicated to the protection and nurturance of the young revealed significant (if not devastating) consequences for the psyches, relationships, worldviews, and overall lives of midadolescents.

One particularly challenging—and rapidly growing—new form of the family unit involves cohabiting couples. Susan L. Brown contends that "the growth in heterosexual cohabitation exemplifies the informalization of the family and the increased emphasis on emotional (rather than legal) ties to others. Cohabitation is a distinct family form, neither singlehood nor marriage. We can no longer understand American families if we ignore it."[7] She goes on to report that children living in these situations "exhibit lower levels of well-being" and warns that "the private nature of cohabitation may be advantageous for adults but harmful to children . . . as dissolution can occur without court intervention that would determine custody and support."[8] As other studies have emphasized "the difficulty of any family structure change for adolescents,"[9] parents must begin to take seriously the selfishness of this kind of shift and consider carefully the damage it may be doing to their kids. Furthermore, what happens in the family of a midadolescent spills over and affects every person who comes in contact with that adolescent. The changing definition of family, therefore, does not simply affect a few unlucky adolescents. It affects the entire society.

Family/Parental Behaviors That Affect Adolescents

Determining the effects of family life on midadolescents was a more difficult undertaking than understanding other areas of their lives. For the most part, students were closemouthed when it came to details and feelings about their families. The conclusions discussed in this chapter, therefore, are based on random comments as well as observations.

The first and most striking observation is that parents seem to be fragmented. The time they need to keep their lives in order affects their ability to be there for their children.[10] I encountered many healthy and involved parents, but there were far more uninvolved, stressed-out, and stretched-thin parents. The most common reaction I saw in teens was a sense that their parents do not make much difference in their lives. The feelings of those whose parents were involved and active in their lives ranged from being fairly satisfied with their parents to being frustrated over their parents' need to control them. Those who saw their parents as being too preoccupied with their own lives and needs to be of any significant help to them reacted with a fatalistic and resigned view that they were doing fine on their own.

For most, however, the resignation was actually a thin veneer that covered everything from disappointment to a deep sense of hurt and betrayal. In many cases, parental patterns of neglect and/or inactivity had developed long ago, and many adolescents felt they had been on their own since late elementary school. I heard story after story of uninvolved, disengaged, and self-focused parents who, by neglect, busyness, or a false understanding of what it means to be a parent, had pushed their children into a world they were not prepared to handle. Through

What I have to say about being a high schooler may seem confusing or contradictory. But then again, what about high school isn't confusing and contradictory at times? First of all, I almost agree with parents when they say that their teen "knows everything." I often feel like I know more than my mom and her not letting me do something is ridiculous. Teens reach a point where they will disregard what their parents say and will do what they want to do. Parents try to protect us because they think we are too young to make big decisions on our own. I firmly believe that you have to make your own decisions about things and learn from your own experiences to ever truly learn and grow. There's no way that I would feel the way I do about smoking, drinking, dating, and other relationships if it hadn't been for my own experiences. Now, I know I just said how I believe I know a lot, but there is so much I don't know. Lately, I've realized how very much of a child I am. I have so much to learn, so much desire for consistency, and a great need for a happy, secure place I can call my home. I am not a child; I am much younger than that. So yes, this does contradict my frustration when I am spoken to as though I'm a child. This may not make much sense to you, but it doesn't even always make sense to me.

high school student

his in-depth research on middle class adolescents, criminologist Elliott Currie observed this same reality.

> The abdication of parental responsibility in the face of trouble or transgression, the assumption that children themselves bear the primary responsibility for their own well-being and for steering their own path in life, the readiness to sever ties with them when things get tough—recurred again and again in my conversations with troubled middle-class adolescents, and these themes reflect an underlying vision of the problems of families and children that is widely prevalent in America.[11]

Many midadolescents have been set adrift by parental and familial authorities, and they are operating as if they are on their own. This reality penetrates the behavior and worldview of all midadolescents, even those whose parents are actively involved and committed to providing a stable environment, because they learn from their peers (and the media) that there are many ways to parent. Many adolescents, even those from involved and nurturing homes, may take advantage of the freedoms and lack of rules characteristic of students who are on their own. This is noteworthy because it has been shown that the familial environment contributes to delinquency in all its forms.[12]

The second observation addresses the intensity and amount of conflict that occur during midadolescence between parents and their children. For the majority of the students, conflict with a parent was almost a daily concern. Such conflicts fell into one of two categories: the nagging skirmishes that seemed to take place on a daily basis (spontaneous conflict over day-to-day matters such as clothes, homework, use of the computer, the shape of one's room, and a basic lack of communication)[13] and arguments over more global or important issues (conflict based on parental concern regarding things that might affect the child's future, such as driving habits, substance abuse, grades, dating, and friendships).[14] There is disagreement over whether these typical, almost daily conflicts are negative or positive. As Jeffrey Arnett points out, "Some scholars have suggested that conflicts between adolescents and their parents are actually beneficial to adolescents' development, because it promotes the development of individuation and autonomy within the context of a warm relationship. This may be true, but high conflict may make adolescence a difficult time for adolescents and their parents even if the conflict ultimately has benefits."[15]

In many cases, I got the impression that the parent-child relationship had created a series of communication patterns and responses to daily life. From the adolescent's perspective, conflicts were almost always

My parents divorced when I was seven years old. I live in two houses, switching every two days. My parents get mad at me when I need to go to the other house because I forgot something. I get so angry because no one ever asked me if I wanted to live in two houses. No one ever asked me if it was okay with me having to keep track of which house my schoolbooks are at. No one ever asked me if I wanted to split my life in two!

high school student

about trust. The majority of the conflicts that occur between parents and children, then, seem to be about the dynamics of the relationship rather than a particular issue. Research has shown that parent-child conflict increases during adolescence, especially during midadolescence. These conflicts are often rooted in how a parent deals with a growing adolescent rather than in a specific issue.[16] For midadolescents, who are in the midst of daily internal conflicts, this hidden cauldron can have discouraging consequences, regardless of the nature or resolution of the verbalized issue.

What matters most in the lives of adolescents, then, is how parents deal with conflict. Most midadolescents rapidly get over the day-to-day conflicts they experience at home,[17] especially if they feel close to their parents. But parents are not as resilient. For many parents, even simple conflicts can push their buttons and drive a wedge in their relationships with their children. Over time, midadolescents pick up on this general sense of separation. This causes them to pull away from their parents. To complicate matters further, the rise of private cell phone use—particularly text messaging—among teens has enabled teens to "establish 'secret networks' off limits to parents" which, as might be expected, "may exacerbate whatever conflicts already exist within the family."[18] Thanks to technologies such as cell phones and the internet, shutting out parents has never been easier.

Parents have a tremendous responsibility not to be thrown off or emotionally entrapped by parent-adolescent conflict.[19] Adolescents know that their parents are supposed to be the adults, those who are to lead and guide them, without letting any conflict or emotion get out of hand. Far too often students described their parents as "out of control," "always mad," or "totally upset." They responded by backing down to avoid conflict and becoming relationally disengaged. When pressed, few midadolescents wanted a distant relationship with their parents, yet most feel they have no choice but to distance themselves from emotional entanglement with their families. To them, this conflictual situation is further confirmation of adult abandonment.[20]

Midadolescents and Time with Their Families

I asked the following question point-blank during the study: "Do you wish you had a closer relationship with your parents?" For the vast majority of students, this was not an easy question to answer, and so they tended to fudge. Grudgingly, most said something like, "Yes, I guess I would like to be closer, but . . ." The various qualifiers that followed would not come as a surprise to anyone: "they are always on my back," or "they don't know how to listen or how to be a friend." I found that unless they viewed the relationship as irreparably fractured, they answered affirmatively.

This confirms the research on parent-child relations, at least in terms of time together. As the American Psychological Association's Healthy Adolescents Project maintains, adolescents know they need more time with adults, and especially their parents: "In a report by the U.S. Council of Economic Advisors, based on the latest research and presented at the May 2000 White House Conference on Teenagers: Raising Responsible and Resourceful Youth, teens rated 'not having enough time together with their parents as one of their top problems.'"[21] In general, my impression is that this rings true.

Conclusion and Musings

Recent studies have demonstrated that during midadolescence, peers have more influence on adolescents than family and parents do.[22] I observed this during my study as well. I also observed, however, that during adolescence, teens have a desire to find safe and satisfying relationships at home. In fact, adolescents actually desire the approval of the family system for the way they live and the choices they make.

Parents must commit to two vital strategies in leading and loving their midadolescent children: first, to understanding them and their world, and second, to providing them with safe and secure boundaries while still allowing them the necessary room to grow.

The healthiest and most productive strategy is for parents to be so involved in the lives of their midadolescents that they can understand how complex, incongruent, and layered this phase of life is for their children. Parents who lovingly seek to understand that their son or daughter is in the midst of wildly changing psychosocial experiences and events will be well on the way to being the kind of anchor the child needs during this period. Parents need to realize that adolescence now lasts up to fifteen or more years. They need to see their parental role as a marathon, recognizing that building a relationship in which their child trusts them is even more important than whether they can trust their child regarding the immediate issues of the day.

Moreover, especially during midadolescence, teenagers need room and flexibility to develop into who they are going to be and to learn what it means to create an internal locus of control (what has been called identity and autonomy). Mary Eastham writes, "The role of parents is to support the emerging young adult in his/her quest for a unique identity, independent of them and yet related in terms of their overriding values. Parents are to listen to their children's dreams and goals, advise them, be there

Understanding the Selfishness

I'm such a terrible kid
I only think about myself
I can never make anyone happy
At least that's what they keep telling me
I can't understand it, I can't see
I'm always wrong
I can't do anything right
At least that's what they keep telling me
I'm ungrateful and high maintenance
I'm never satisfied, always asking
I'm not good enough for anyone
At least that's what they keep telling me
I'm so self-centered
Yet I give you all I have
I love you more than I should
I always try to make you happy
I try my best, hoping you'll be satisfied
But I'm your terrible kid, your sad mistake
One day maybe you'll understand the pain
The pain inflicted upon my unborn heart
Don't say you want me to be happy
When you're making me cry so hard, so often.

high school student

to support them, and yet allow them to make the important decisions in their lives."[23] This does not mean, however, that they need or even want to be separated from the one community that they believe will always be there for them. The peer cluster, as has been noted, is important and is even perceived to be their paramount support system. At the same time, most midadolescents recognize that this peer system is fraught with performance and conformity demands, making it a less than ideal place. Even the most independent, cluster-driven midadolescent needs (and at some level wants) to know that, regardless of behavior, problems, conflict, or looks, the family is a safe place.

This means that parents must provide a safe, warm environment for midadolescents while simultaneously maintaining a stable force of authority and control. Parents must seek to understand their children but must also provide flexible and reasonable boundaries that will allow them to change and grow, relate to others, and make choices that matter, all while under the clear, purposeful, and deliberate leadership of their parents.

Boundaries and understanding take a great amount of dedicated energy and resources. Parenting has, in many ways, never been more difficult. There are stock "principles" or absolutes. And parenting, especially with midadolescents, requires tedious negotiation and constantly shifting expectations. When parents recognize what their children need and then take the time to be that kind of parent, they discover that their children become stronger, healthier, interdependent adults. And the fruit of a carefully cultivated, lifelong friendship will be enjoyed for decades to come.

sports

The numbers—and what do sports train us to trust more than numbers?—
tell us that high school athletics have never been healthier. Roughly four
million boys and three million girls, more than ever before, participate in
one or more of some 50 athletic endeavors before kiting off to the rest of
their lives. . . . The win-at-all-costs coaches and preprofessional priorities
commonplace in college sports have seeped into grades 12, 11, 10 and
below. . . . As coaches demand year-round proof of dedication, kids spend
a greater and greater proportion of time practicing rather than playing, and
many state high school federations, which once enforced strict rules on
summer activities, throw up their hands, sometimes eliminating those
rules altogether.

Alexander Wolff, "Special Report"

Craig is a star water polo player, Carrie is a dancer on what is called
the varsity Song Squad, and Grant is a second-string football player.
Craig hangs out mostly with water polo players (there are only two
non–water polo players in his cluster). Carrie's cluster tends to ignore her
dancing. Grant has found security by being aligned with football players
(although half of his cluster stopped playing after their sophomore year).
Three students, three sports, three experiences. In their own ways, these
students allowed me to see how coaches and parents have added a layer
of performance anxiety to their love of sport. The stories are unique, as
are the circumstances, but what provides the backdrop for the struggles

these midadolescents face as they "play" comes from the same source: they are the casualties of systemic abandonment by those charged with their care. Sports (including dance) are no longer about fun, exercise, experience, and play. They are about competition, winning, and defeating an opponent. Sports are no longer child's play; they are a grown-up dog-eat-dog reality.

Surprised on a Saturday Afternoon

One Saturday I attended the peewee football game of a close friend's son. The players were seven to nine years old, and most of them could barely hold their heads up when they ran, most likely due to the weight of the helmets they wore. They looked like miniature football players, right down to the wrist bands, receiver gloves, neck rolls, and taped fingers. But most of them wandered, yelled, pouted, and ran like little children. The sidelines were packed with parents, either videotaping or chewing their nails. Most were yelling. Near the end of the game, if "our" team could somehow take the ball away from the other team, we would get one more chance to score. Then the man next to me, camera in hand, nearly lost his hat as he screamed at his son, "If you don't strip the ball, you're walking home!"

My wife, a relationally sensitive but nonetheless culturally savvy and experienced football mom, and I glanced at each other, not believing what we had just heard. Sure, we had been passionate sideline parents ourselves and had seen our share of over-the-top parental enthusiasm.

> The pressure from athletic coaches is really bad. The pressure to be the biggest and the best pushes kids to use steroids and other supplements, play hurt, and take one for the team. The coaches don't seem to care about your well-being. They just want the trophy and the recognition that come with a championship. A perfect example is my school. No team in its history has ever won three regional titles in a row. We've already won two, and the coaches are making practices longer and more strenuous to the point of dehydration and broken bones.
>
> high school student

How this man behaved, however, completely stunned us. His venom was so pointed, his threat so real, that we both actually feared for the boy were he to miss the play.

Sure enough, no one was able to strip the ball, and the team we were rooting for lost another game. The son cried as he approached his father. His father, with visible reluctance and more than a hint of sarcasm, told his son, "I guess you can't win 'em all. Let's get the hell out of here!"

The Pros and Cons of High School Athletics

The above true story hints at what every high school student has experienced on some level throughout his or her athletic career. The pressure is intense—to compete, to excel, to perform, and to remain in the game. By the time an athlete gets to high school, his or her chance of participation, much less success, in a sport has been all but settled. Certainly, an outsider could catch the eye of a coach and be catapulted above others to active participation. But in most high school sports, the main players are set even before the season begins. The ones who are safely nestled into the security of a starting spot are called jocks, and most of them wear the badge proudly.[1]

There are, of course, many positive aspects to high school sports, and they have been well documented for years. The recent report of the American Psychological Association's Healthy Adolescents Project offers this well-worn benefit of high school athletics: "Participation in sports, which has important direct health benefits, is one socially sanctioned arena in which adolescents' physical energies can be positively channeled. . . . These activities provide adolescents with opportunities for getting exercise, making friends, gaining competence and confidence, learning about teamwork, taking risks, and building character and self-discipline."[2]

Adolescent participation in sports has consistently been linked with higher levels of self-worth and self-esteem, higher likelihood to engage with both peers and adults, and positive short-term and long-term educational outcomes,[3] especially for boys.[4]

Yet in comparing this view to both the conversations I had with athletes and nonathletes and the observations I made during practices and at sporting events, I found that few students participate in activities because they get exercise, make friends, and so on. Certainly, some of these aspects become side benefits along the way, but for the most part, by the time athletes get to high school, the level of expectation and the pressure to perform make their participation an all-consuming commitment.[5] For many athletes, even the nice and concerned coaches can be hardheaded, demanding, and, while rhetorically committed to what is best for each student, ultimately more concerned with what is best for the team.

The report also describes the reasons many adolescents do not participate in sports: cost, lack of transportation, time commitment, and so on. What was not on the list is what I believe to be the most important reason of all: there are not enough sports or enough room in the ones that are available for "average" student-athletes to compete. Even if there were more opportunities for participation, I am convinced that few of these average players would enlist, mostly because they have been told since before junior high that they did not have what it takes to be an athlete. This attitude creates inside the developing identity of an early adolescent a defining stereotype that most have a hard time shaking. Trying to convince a late-blooming tenth grader to try out for basketball is asking him to risk a great deal, especially if he was derided as a child or early adolescent. One more rejection, especially for the fragile midadolescent, may be one too many to risk.

Actual research on the positive aspects of high school sports has produced mixed results at best. Certainly, in some ways, participation in sports is a good thing. There are, however, a few downsides to contemporary society's fascination with sports. Merrill Melnick, Kathleen Miller, and Donald Sabo report:

> Conventional wisdom has it that participation in high school athletic programs positively influences adolescent health-related behavior. Coaches, athletic administrators, the mass media, and the general public often assert that interscholastic athletic participation helps teenagers develop healthy habits while steering them away from tobacco, alcohol, drugs, dangerous dietary practices, physical inactivity, and other detrimental behaviors. . . .
>
> On the other hand, some sport critics focus on a variety of negative health-related behaviors they believe are associated with athletic participation such as binge drinking; drug use; on- and off-the-field aggression; the "female triad," namely eating disorders, amenorrhea, and osteoporosis; actions that result in unintentional injury and death, such as irresponsible automobile, motorcycle, and bicycle use; and unprotected sex.[6]

In my experience, adults' views on sports participation varied according to whether their children were "slow" or "gifted" athletically. Parents of nonathletes had to create an explanation for the crushing disappointment of exclusion and often saw sports in a negative light.

In terms of who is "good" and who is not, two thoughts struck me throughout the study: First, there are many more non-all-stars than there are all-stars. Second, by the time second-stringers enter high school, the die has been cast, and the athletic roles they will play throughout their high school years have already been settled.

In *The Hurried Child*, David Elkind quotes sportswriter John Underwood as he courageously takes on the "Little Leagues—the worst destroyers of the playfulness of sport."[7] The article, written more than twenty years ago for *Sports Illustrated*, is even more ominous today.

> The sine qua non of sport is enjoyment. When you take that away, it's no longer sport. Perhaps the worst creators of specialists are the Little Leagues in all sports. Although some observers believe there's much value in them, the Leagues have their own ethics. "Abolish the Little Leagues," says philosopher Robert Weiss. "Forbid 'em," says sociologist David Riesman.
>
> Sports psychologist Bruce Ogelvie laments the sickening arrogance of Little League coaches, too many of whom are unqualified. Some coaches, says another psychologist, Thomas Tatlio, even "think sports is war." They make eight year olds sit on the bench while others play, learning nothing beyond the elitism of win-at-all-costs sport. Token participation—an inning in right field, a couple of minutes in the fourth quarter—can be equally demoralizing.
>
> To visit on small heads the pressure to win, the pressure to be "just like mean Joe Green" is indecent. To dress children up like pros in costly out-fits is ridiculous. In so doing, we take away many of the qualities that competitive sports are designed to give to the growing process.[8]

The most alarming piece, though, may be the story of Carl Stotz, the founder of Little League Baseball himself, who, as author and journalist Mark Hyman explains, was stiffly dismissed in 1956 from the movement he started nearly twenty years earlier.[9] Stotz initially welcomed the national attention Little League received, and eagerly leveraged the publicity into more leagues to span the breadth of the teenage years. Despite the celebrity it afforded him, the expansion eventually began to reach levels that made him uncomfortable, but his advocacy for reform came too late: Little League had become big business, and it continues as such today. What began with neighborhood boys on makeshift ballfields enjoying America's pastime has now mushroomed into a worldwide brand and sophisticated financial enterprise, complete with equipment sponsors, advertising revenue, and an international World Series broadcast in High Definition on ESPN. We enjoy so much seeing an amazing catch or a clutch hit, we forget that those who make errors or strike out do so while bearing the name of their neighborhoods, or their states, or even their countries across their twelve-year-old chests.

What our hyperfocus on competition has inserted in the place of these qualities is a lucrative niche industry of club sports and private coaching. In days past, high school athletes looking to hone their skills might practice privately or attempt to put together a pickup game. Not so anymore. Today, students in all fifty states have the opportunity to

participate nearly year-round on a club team in any number of sports—
soccer, lacrosse, softball, volleyball, swimming, etc.—so long as their
skills are acceptable and their families' finances are in order. As Eric
Sondheimer of the *Los Angeles Times* reports, the last twenty years have
seen a meteoric rise in the club sports industry, "with private coaches
being paid thousands of dollars to develop elite athletes—and the parents
of those athletes paying up to $7,000 a year to participate."[10] Some clubs
have established official partnerships with professional teams both in
the United States and abroad, so that kids as young as seven compete
while wearing the exact garb of multimillionaire athletes on the other
side of the globe, right down to the corporate logos.[11] So consumed are
many clubs with winning—and thus maintaining their sponsorships
and brand recognition—that oftentimes the most gifted student-athletes
must choose between competing for the club and competing for their
high school.[12]

What often goes unmentioned is the physical toll that year-round competition exacts on young bodies. As Mark Hyman writes, "Lyle Micheli,
the youth sports medicine pioneer, estimates that of the seventy young
patients who file into his clinic each Thursday at Children's Hospital
Boston, 75 percent are victims of overuse injuries. . . . Back in the early
1990s, the figure was at about 20 percent. . . . Adults are the great en-
ablers of overuse injuries. . . . Children entertaining themselves at their
own pace, in their own way, simply did not play sports until it hurt."[13]

By the time many of the student-athletes fortunate enough to play
beyond high school enter the university setting, they have endured so
much extra competition that, while they have become highly skilled
players, they are also "orthopedic time bombs."[14] At the same time,
such may be the price for the opportunity to play at that university
level, or even the high school level; students who do not practice or
play year-round for upwards of fifteen or twenty hours per week simply cannot compete with those who do. Factor in the fringe benefits of
the club system—namely, social belonging and identity formation, for
both students and adults[15]—and it is clear that the system is not going
anywhere any time soon.

A Little Experiment

I performed an experiment in the middle of the study, attempting to get
a handle on how preadolescents and high school seniors felt about the
athletic "haves" and "have-nots." I included three groups: preadolescent
athletes, seniors in high school athletics, and nonathlete seniors.[16] The
questions I asked were intended not to elicit specific answers but to get

them talking about their impressions regarding the high performance and competitive aspects of youth and high school sports and how these aspects might affect different kinds of children and youth.

The first group contained three preadolescent boys who played organized baseball and three young girls who played competitive soccer. They were between eight and ten years of age. Most were from relatively affluent intact families in which there was a great deal of emotional support. They all considered themselves "good" to "pretty good."

They were at the highest level in their respective sports, and they did not feel it was wrong for them to get to go to special tournaments, get more playing time than other kids, and be separated from the "not-so-good athletes" in how they were treated by coaches, parents, and their teammates. Not only did they feel fine about this performance segregation, but they also felt it was "more fair" than letting those who were not good take playing time away from them. Every one of these children believed that the good should get to play, and those who were not of their caliber should have to wait until they (the better athletes) were tired. I asked at what age this should begin to happen, and they immediately agreed—as soon as they start sports! "If we're better than they are, then why should we suffer?" one child said.

Then I talked with six seniors, three male baseball players and three female soccer players, who had always been starters. While they acknowledged that children's feelings could possibly get hurt if they were not given much playing time or, somewhere around the fourth grade, no longer allowed to compete, they seemed to deflect any understanding of how it must feel for those kids. They all defended the process of highlighting the better athletes, even at ages as young as eight years old. As much as they tried to feign concern for those who were not born with athletic skill and talent, they had little compassion for the nonathletic students.

As much as the first group was marked by entitlement and the second by defensiveness, the third was marked by hurt and even resentment. These seniors, who for one reason or another had been told at a fairly young age that they did not have the ability to participate in sports, left me sad and a bit angry. The stories varied, from a boy who quit all sports because his soccer coach told him in third grade to quit because his play was costing the team games, to a girl who lost her best friends in fifth grade when she was cut from a competitive soccer team (the pain was as fresh as if it had happened the day before). Most of these students hated jocks and everything related to sports.

I walked away from these conversations contemplating how our culture had gotten to this point. In our competitive and performance-driven world, by the time a child is in the fourth or fifth grade, ten or eleven years old, he or she has it or does not. For a variety of reasons, this message

> I always played sports until I blew out my ankle and had recon-
> structive surgery. At that point I went from JV volleyball, varsity
> basketball, and varsity softball to the girl with the blown ankle. The
> remainder of my high school career I played only volleyball, when I
> could fit my foot in my shoe. So everything I once identified myself
> with was gone. I slipped into a depression. I started doing drugs
> and skipping school.
>
> former high school student

is not in and of itself enough to cause lasting damage to an adolescent. Some kids who are told they don't have it become firmly committed to showing a coach, friend, or parent how wrong they are. Yet we have a long way to go in understanding how our intensity concerning sports has impacted our young, especially those who have been excluded from participation and denied a sense of personal worth because they developed late, were not able to contribute, or simply got in the way of a coach's, a parent's, or even a teammate's drive to excel.

Every adult has been reared on the notion that youth sports build character. In light of what I have seen—the advancement of the best at the expense of the weak, the preference for the skilled even as the eyes of the awkward plead for a chance, the pressure of the parent who lives vicariously through his or her child's "play"—little character is being built. I have observed just the opposite in fact. True character is built when one is rewarded for hard work, when one is willing to sacrifice for a friend or teammate, when one experiences the instilled value that proclaims the love of sport and not the lust for competition. This is perhaps the most obvious arena in which abandonment has made its mark on the adolescent psyche. We still use the rhetoric that youth sports build character, yet in reality what we have taught our children builds nothing other than arrogance, self-centeredness, and a performance ethic that is destructive to healthy, communally connected development.

The Dethroning of the Esteemed Athlete

I discovered something else during this study. The jocks no longer occupy the highest rung on the status ladder. The historically definable and clearly observable social ladder is being dismantled in favor of a web of social influence. In the school where I conducted this study, athletics still mean a great deal, hundreds of people attend sporting events, and sports are still seen as somewhat cool. But even at this school, jocks' influence has waned. They are no more esteemed than any other group, including the band. Students no longer put up with the stereotype that athletes rule the school, and perhaps in a subconscious attempt to get back at the childhood athletic systems that hurt them, many nonathletes disdain jocks.

I came to this study being drawn to and even slightly defensive of those with whom I felt comfortable in high school. In my case, I was aligned with the athletes. In this chapter, it may appear that I am taking a hard line against successful athletes. My original bias notwithstanding, I am determined not to take a stand for or against any individual or group of adolescents. I am equally concerned about those who have been rejected by the competitive world of sports and those who by innate design, hard work, or both have achieved athletic prowess. The former's pain and disappointment are obvious and easily documented by anyone who would but look at life through their eyes. The latter's struggles lie far deeper, but I am convinced that even the top stars feel pangs of loneliness and insecurity as a result of being raised in a culture in which athletic excellence is measured only by the last pass, kick, or basket. All have suffered at the hands of a culture of abandonment when it comes to the decay of play and fun.

I opened this chapter with three students who take pride and find a sense of identity in their ability to perform well enough to be included on a team. Craig, the water polo player, is a naturally gifted player. He is also a leader in a sport that is considered second tier (especially when compared to football, basketball, or baseball), and he therefore feels the need to convince people that water polo players are "the best athletes in the school." This need to prove himself has become a major element of his personality and his relationships. He can no longer play for fun and sport. He must make sure that others know that he, as a water polo player, matters.

Carrie has always loved to dance. As a little girl, trying out new moves for her parents, putting on a fancy dress for the Christmas recital, and freely floating around a room with giggling friends made the pain of learning how to stand on her toes worthwhile. When she started fourth grade, dance was no longer a joyous adventure of free expression. It had shifted to a physically grueling gauntlet every weekday in preparation for the next competition. By fifteen, the pressure from the driven coach, the early morning practices, the continual (misguided and unnecessary) fight with her weight, and the daily pressure not to mess up and hurt the team had taken its toll. She quit the team after one year on varsity. She had lost her love of dance in order to become a dancer.

Grant was never quite good enough, or so the head varsity coach told him, to play "at this level." He had played football since he was ten, had even started for most of his sophomore season, but once he got to varsity, the head coach made it clear that he was barely welcome. He would be on the team, but he should not expect to play. As much as Grant saw himself as a football player, and his cluster and others on the team treated him as an equal, the coach never came around. Grant received an award at the banquet, but the head coach made it clear that he had not contributed. When I asked the other guys about Grant and the coach, the response was predictable: "The coach is a jerk. Grant should have started, at least a few games. He was a leader on the team." Grant's saving grace was his cluster. His friends showed compassion, loyalty, and concern. The coach was too concerned about being in charge, regardless of whom he hurt in the process.[17]

Conclusion and Musings

How do we fight our socially ingrained, competitive instincts to recommit ourselves to making sports fun? How do we remove our adult need to live our lives through our kids so that they can recapture the love of sports? How can we revamp our systems and structures so that even in high school sports are about play?

During this study, I became more convinced of how insidious and self-serving youth and high school competitive activities have become. These activities are no longer for or about the students; they are for and about the adults in charge. The deification of competitive prominence and the defeat of one's "enemies" have choked much of the life out of the human desire to play for play's sake and even to compete with class and honor.[18]

Of course, there are exceptions to this, as there are with every assertion I have made. I got to know many of the coaches at the school, and as individuals, they are a top-notch lot. The system they operate under, however, and the ethos of that system are focused on competitive excellence (defined simply by a season's record), and this is what is taking its toll on our young. A sensitive, savvy coach in an overly competitive system may be able to ensure that that sport or that season does as little developmental damage as possible, but the wave of winning and performing is a large force indeed.

As with every aspect of the consequences of abandonment, the most potent tool we have in helping adolescents overcome the damage caused by the negative aspects of sports and other competitive activities is to help them see that in the final analysis competition doesn't matter. We have been giving lip service to this message for decades ("It's all about trying your best, kids. It's not winning that counts; it's how you play the game."), but our rhetoric and our behavior have not lined up. When the father of the football team's kicker screamed at his son in front of hundreds of parents and students after he missed an extra point, he demonstrated that the message of "doing your best" was merely a convenient and hollow postgame speech coaches use to try to motivate athletes following a loss. Shame on that father! And shame on us for allowing a destructive system to continue in the name of sport.

It used to be fun to play sports, but for far too many of the students I talked to, their involvement ceased to be fun a long time ago. I cannot think of any other area of life in which we as a society have abandoned our young more thoroughly. From the time they hear "Play ball!" they know that they had better come through and perform, even if they are only playing for fun.

8

sex

While the study of adolescent sexuality is of unquestionable importance, I am now amazed and saddened that so many of us have studied sexuality removed from its context, which is often, but certainly not always, a romantic relationship. It is ironic that scientists have neglected the study of adolescent romance since it is a topic of such great importance to so many teenagers.

Terri D. Fisher, "Teen Romance under the Microscope"

We live in a sexually saturated culture. Adolescents grow up in a society that is regularly accused of being sexually outdated and puritanical and at the same time sexually preoccupied. Europe and much of South America see Americans as sexually repressive and arrogantly naïve. In much of Asia, the Middle East, and Africa, Americans are seen as decadents who are bent on destroying centuries-old cultural, religious, and familial traditions. The way we (and the West in general) portray sex and sensuality in television shows and films seems to reduce life to one juvenile, narcissistic, sexual escapade after another. Because adolescents are the products of this cultural reality, and the direct targets of society's fixation on a sexuality with no boundaries or rules, I wanted to discover what was happening in their world in terms of their sexual attitudes and experiences.

For decades, social scientists have investigated the sexual attitudes and behaviors of adolescents. These studies are vital in our attempts to lower teen pregnancy and sexually transmitted disease rates. But almost always these investigations focus on what can be directly measured and reduced to numbers. These numbers get reported not only in academic settings but also in *Time* or on *60 Minutes*. But these numbers, such as the percentage of fifteen-year-old recent immigrant females who say they have had intercourse, provide only a small slice of information for someone who wants to understand the complex issues related to adolescent sexuality. When I began this study, I had in my computer more than one hundred studies and articles that reported quantitative data related to adolescent sexual behavior and attitudes. I wanted to see if I could understand the experience behind the numbers, the reality beneath the conclusions. It is not that I do not trust the numbers when it comes to adolescent sexuality;[1] but I am aware of the severe limitations of the kind of research employed in this field of inquiry. When dealing with a private human arena such as sexuality, especially among midadolescent high school students, it is nearly impossible to collect conclusive data regarding their inner attitudes or actual behaviors. Short of hidden cameras and manipulative deception, the only way to understand is to watch and listen carefully to adolescents as they talk about the reality of sexuality in their world.

As a result of this study, I became aware that the adolescent world is not as saturated with sex as it is infused with palpable loneliness. I have since witnessed a subtle yet observable shift into an even more overtly sexualized environment. I originally expected that my adult perception of the barrage of sexual images, metaphors, allusions, and an anything-goes ethic would be duplicated among midadolescents. In other words, I thought that high school boys and girls would easily and constantly be swept up in a world of sexual lust and wild, irresponsible relational dalliances. I was surprised to realize that for most midadolescents the issue of sex has lost its mystique and has become almost commonplace. They have been conditioned to expect so much from sex and have been so tainted by overexposure and the emptiness of valueless sexual banter and play that they have become laissez-faire in their attitudes, even jaded. As one student told me, "Sex is a game and a toy, nothing more." As I was to find out, it is actually more than that—it is a temporary salve for the pain and loneliness resulting from abandonment.

A Word and an Event

One word and one event summarize the radical changes in sexual attitudes and behavior that seem to be taking place in the world of adolescents. Both of them are disturbing, to some perhaps extremely so.

Yet what was apparent from this study is that adolescents do not find what is reported in this chapter shocking, disturbing, or even morally or socially deviant. I offer these two scenarios as windows into a dark, new world where midadolescents live.

Near the end of the semester during my time at the high school, I overheard a group of boys talking, and a word popped up that I had not heard before. It was used in the context of evaluating a girl. Since I knew these boys fairly well, I asked what "MILF" meant. They laughed and said, "Dr. Clark, that one's for you to find out." Remember, this was in 2002. By the mid- to late-2000s the term had become so commonplace that this discussion would not have taken place at all. But at the time, I was completely thrown off guard by this discovery.

It took me less than a day to find out the definition of MILF: a "Mother I'd Like to F—." I also found out something else. Even in 2002, this word had been around for a while. The 1999 film *American Pie* popularized the term and for years it has been common across the United States, and even around the world in countries that have access to American media. When I first heard the word, I tried to stealthily find out how pervasive it was, especially in parts of the country where adults had been emphatic that it was limited to "LA and other big cities." So I tested this with adolescent boys and college men with whom I have a trusting relationship. No matter how close we were, there was almost always a pause when I asked, "Do you know what MILF means?" Sometimes they fudged or outright lied, but when it became obvious what I knew, the most common reply was, "How did you find out?" Not, "Sick, huh?" but, "You know something that is reserved for us!" Today, the concept, if not the term, has become so commonplace that by the mid-2000s Dr. Pepper used it in an advertisement, using the popular song "Stacy's Mom" by Fountains of Wayne.[2] So, for anyone reading this that does not yet know, we now live in a society where to banter about intercourse with a peer's mother is simply part of the everyday rhetorical landscape. Neither the concept nor the term MILF shocks anyone today.

The second scenario involves an event that happened with six seventh-grade girls at a sleepover. During the course of the evening, a seventh-grade boy came over to the house and, after some small talk with the mother hosting the event, was sent up to the host girl's bedroom. Apparently, there was little or no discussion of the appropriateness of this action. The parents were home, and they knew the boy, so they did not think twice about letting him visit the girls for a few minutes.

Of the six girls attending the party, five were from intact families with caring, upper-middle-class parents. The sixth girl lived with her mother and a supportive, involved stepfather. Four of the girls and their families were actively involved in faith communities (all self-described Christians). The mothers and the fathers were close to their daughters, and the parents affirmed that none of them had experienced serious behavior problems with their daughters that would have caused them to draw stricter boundaries. Each of the girls was popular among her peers. They were all involved in extracurricular activities, did well in school, and were well liked and respected by their teachers and other adults. They were the prototypical "good girls," but not in the sense of being socially inept. They were routinely described as "sharp" by those who knew them. In short, you could not comb a junior high in America and find a better sample of exemplary adolescents.

The boy lived with a supportive single mother and two younger siblings. He had no previous romantic experience, and his relationships with girls had always been as friends. He had come over simply because he lived nearby, was bored, and was friends with these girls. He apparently had no preconceived ulterior motives.

After this boy had been in the room for thirty minutes or so, the mother decided to check on the girls. She heard some giggling coming from the room and with slight nervousness but no hesitation opened the door to the bedroom unannounced. Even now she cannot fully describe the horror of the scene before her. The six girls were on their knees in a line with the boy standing in front of them with his pants down. It was obvious that he was near the end of a line of each performing oral sex on him. The mother gasped and quickly shooed out the boy, attempting to maintain some semblance of decorum in a situation she could not have even imagined.

The boy, obviously embarrassed but more scared that he had been busted, pulled up his pants and hurried out of the house. The girls were at first shocked but quickly turned to a mixture of embarrassment and worry over what the punishment would be. Apparently, they were more concerned about what was going to happen to them than about the event itself. To the adolescents involved, the only moral aspect of the event was that the mother had no right to enter the room without knocking.

When appropriate, I sometimes used this incident as the starting point for informal conversations and focus groups about midadolescent sexuality.[3] The responses from both males and females ranged from mild amazement to resigned acknowledgment that, while not exactly appropriate, the event was not surprising. What I was looking for, I suppose, was some level of moral outrage or at least an expression of incredulity, especially from teenage girls. I never saw that. Some young women expressed wonder as to how these girls could be so stupid. Occasionally, an adolescent boy would say something similar. For the most part, however, both boys and girls seemed to recognize that this is a normal experience in their world, the kind of thing that happens when adolescents follow through on their impulses.

"Was this wrong?" was my standard query.

"I don't know about wrong exactly, but it wasn't very smart," was the summation of the comments I received.

"Why was it not smart?"

"These kids were experimenting," was one reply from an eighteen-year-old senior girl. "They didn't really know what they were doing. They were just trying to have fun. They probably saw it in a movie and figured it was kind of cool. But they were idiots for not locking the door! Wow! They deserved to get busted."

As persistently as I tried in various settings, I had a hard time finding anyone in the high school world[4] who expressed outrage based solely on the act itself. Six girls performing oral sex on a male, I was told, was "maybe not very moral," but it "probably happens more than you think." I tend to doubt that assessment, at least regarding the population of the high school I studied, but I was astounded that the students themselves believed this was more or less an accepted reality and clearly fell in the range of normative sexual behavior. When I asked if it would have been more shocking if sixteen-year-olds had done this, I was told, "It would have happened only with girls who were so drunk that they didn't know or care or girls who were just stupid." Would a guy do it? "Absolutely! Any guy. Every guy!"

One time this discussion was followed by the comment, "I would not be at all surprised by a threesome." In mixed company, not one person feigned surprise at the remark. I, again, was incredulous. With over-the-air television programs, to say nothing of cable shows and specials, pushing the edges of societal norms for decades, from *Friends* and *Seinfeld* to *Two and a Half Men*, altering our cultural conversation while unblushingly referencing such formerly taboo sexual activities as ménage à trois (an arrangement in which three persons share sexual relations, now typically referred to as "a threesome"), it is little wonder that the concept of multiple sex partners at a single event would be considered mainstream by adolescents. Since the first edition of this book we have compiled scores of similar data that demonstrate that we have entered into a society with no sexual rules or boundaries. Today it is only the novel that surprises us, and only as long as it lasts as a YouTube featured video, like middle school girls wearing colorful "sex bracelets" that indicate what act they will perform for the guy who rips one off their wrist,[5] eight- and nine-year-old dancers erotically gyrating to the Beyoncé hit "Single Ladies (Put a Ring on It)," or the "self-proclaimed role model" Miley Cyrus giving "a lap dance to a 44-year-old film producer or pole-dancing on an ice cream cart at the Teen Choice Awards."[6]

It is clear that there are no longer any rules regarding sexuality in mainstream society, especially for adolescents. The fact that a group of eleven-year-olds can so easily participate in such sexual antics reveals that we are far removed from any modern version of a Victorian sense of sexual morality. By the time a typical child reaches ten or eleven years of age, he or she has heard about, and seen on television and in movies, not only sexual intercourse but also oral sex, multiple sexual partners, masturbation, anal sex, and any other form of sexual expression and experimentation a human can invent.[7] It has been decades since the "innocent" young were shielded from these behaviors.

On any given day, these behaviors (or at least their mention) are regular fare on afternoon television programming. Children and early adolescents are subjected to this daily barrage of sexual expression and innuendo without having the understanding of how relational and psychosocial dynamics intersect with sexual activity. I observed the results of this trend firsthand during this study. Sexual joking and sexual language were common and even intrusive. Not a week went by that I was not somehow shocked by the explicit nature of sexuality on the campus. For example, here is a sampling of what I encountered in just one week:

- A group of girls was judging a guy's backside. Pleased with the attention, he erotically posed for the judges.
- A student dropped a note that was filled with a sexually explicit description of the adventures she had planned with two male students.
- I walked in on a couple embracing and kissing. The boy's arm was through the girl's thong, which was exposed above her low-cut jeans.
- I overheard a group of students talking about things that would have been banned from all but the most severely rated movies twenty years ago.

What follows is a summary of the sexual behavior and sexual attitudes I observed during my experience in the adolescent landscape. I also briefly discuss some of the sexual forces that influence the daily lives of midadolescents and what the future holds for them in the realm of sex and sexuality.

Sexual Behavior and Attitudes

While there has been some recent scholarship addressing the sexual behaviors of adolescents,[8] to continue to work toward as comprehensive an awareness as possible of adolescent sexual behaviors and attitudes, we must begin with how sex is defined by teenagers. As Andrea Solarz writes, "Because teens may have different ideas about what constitutes 'having sex,' professionals must take care that both they and the adolescent understand exactly what behaviors they are talking about when discussing issues of sexuality. For example, although both will view vaginal sexual intercourse as having sex, they may differ in their perceptions about whether such activities as oral sex, mutual masturbation, or even kissing constitute having sex."[9]

This ambiguity was confirmed in my study, but more pointedly, I came away with a clear impression[10] that almost no midadolescent believes that sex is anything other than penile penetration into a vagina. Everything else, including oral sex, is generally not considered sex. This observation has not been softened from the first edition to this, but sexuality has become even more of an everyday reality, not just with adolescents, but with children as well. Sexuality is not simply about *sex* per se, but about using our bodies to promote sexual attraction, discussion, and activity. In wealthy schools and poor schools, in malls, in the parks, and even at camps and churches, there is an increasing loosening of sexual boundaries that is common in everyday conversation and behavior. Most adults are somewhat concerned by this trend, and perhaps have been for years, but we now cannot get away from daily reminders that life is about sex, and apparently *only* about sex. From the sports page ("Sex for life!" ads) to billboards (advertising television shows like *Cougar Town*) to commercials (the Carl's Jr. fast-food chain, for example), to say nothing of the cable shows and films, an insatiable appetite for sex seems to drive people of any age. It seems as if there is no place to hide from the pervasiveness of this message, even for very young children. As Peggy Orenstein asks in *The New York Times Magazine* in her article, "Playing at Sexy," "Is the neckline too low on the new Barbie Basics Model 10 doll—nicknamed, seemingly redundantly, Busty Barbie?" But there are those who are trying to address the downside of this onslaught. In her interview with Deborah Tolman, author of "Dilemmas of Desire: Teenage Girls Talk about Sexuality," Orenstein writes that sexuality has "become the latest performance, something that girls act out rather than experience. 'By the time they are teenagers, the girls I talk to respond to questions about how their bodies feel—questions about sexuality or desire—by talking about how their bodies look. They will say something like, "I felt like I looked good." Looking good is *not* a feeling.'"[11] Stephen Hinshaw, University of California psychologist, explains that "sexualizing little girls—whether through images, music, or play—actually undermines healthy sexuality rather than promoting it."[12]

Current Trends in Teenage Sexuality

Several indicators point to the fact that sexual intercourse is less prevalent among adolescents today than in the past several years, or perhaps
even decades.[13] Because of the limited scope of my study, I was not able
to discern whether this is true. One such indicator is the report that the
U.S. abortion rate in 2000 was at its lowest point since the year after the
Roe v. Wade Supreme Court decision legalized the procedure.[14] While
on many levels this is good news, the abortion rate is a rather meager
indicator of sexual activity in the lives of midadolescents.

Another common indicator is birth rate. Whatever the current statistics show, studies sometimes offer different pictures of birth rates,
especially when they are being used to infer rates of teenage sexual activity.[15] The statistics related to this can be deceiving because most reports
fail to take into account the distinction between married and unmarried women giving birth. For example, women ages fifteen to nineteen
had 45.9 births per one thousand females in 2001 compared to 68.3 in
1970. At first glance, it would appear that teenage girls were therefore
less sexually active in 2001 when compared with thirty years earlier. A
statistic that is often overlooked, however, is the marital status of the
women giving birth. In 2001, there were forty nonmarital births for every
one thousand women ages fifteen to nineteen compared to twenty-two
in 1970. Thus in 2001 there were almost twice as many nonmarital
births as there were thirty years ago. Yet in 2006, according to a report
by the National Center for Health Statistics (NCHS), a branch of the
U.S. Centers for Disease Control and Prevention, for the first time in
fifteen years the teen birth rate in America increased.[16] Even religiosity
is not always an accurate predictor of teen sexual activity as measured
by birth rate. As Joseph M. and Jillian C. Strayhorn note, the "teen birth
rate is very highly correlated with religiosity at the state level, with more
religious states having a higher rate of teen birth. . . . Thus, even after
taking into account the abortion rate and controlling for income, the
correlation between religiosity and teen pregnancy remained high and
significant. . . . Religious teens do not use birth control as frequently as
non-religious teens."[17]

It is also difficult to gauge sexual activity from reported episodes of
sexually transmitted diseases. We do know that chlamydia is greatly
increasing in the midadolescent population, while gonorrhea rates are
falling for midadolescents even though they are rising for those age
twenty to twenty-four.[18] The latest studies show an even more disturbing trend, one that is rarely discussed in the public arena. In 2008, the
Centers for Disease Control reported that "one in four (26%) female
adolescents in the United States has at least one of the most common

sexually transmitted infections (STIs)."[19] As bad as it is, this statistic is incomplete, for it is only a report of those who were tested by those who report such data, and that is not the entire population. If we were able to discern the rate for males, which is currently impossible because very few are tested for STDs, we would have a more comprehensive picture, and there is little evidence that the results would be more positive. In addition—though this statistic is frightening on its own—by the time they reach their twenties, virtually all adults in even quasi-romantic relationships engage in intimate sexual behavior, and since few get tested, the number is bound to leap exponentially.

Because we have solid, easily replicable findings that demonstrate so profoundly a societywide problem that will not go away on its own, I am at a complete loss with those scholars, bloggers, writers, and pundits who unflinchingly contend that contemporary adolescent life is fine and well. Those who criticize or dismiss as alarmists or ideologues the people who focus attention on the darker, more destructive, and painful aspects of growing up today rarely consider such data as they promulgate their positions. This statistic alone—the rate of STDs among teenage girls *who have been tested and reported only when they have gone to doctors*—should compel us all to come to the table and find out just what is going on with our young. When roughly half of teenaged girls in the United States report having had sexual intercourse, and we have more than one quarter having "at least" one STD, we are in the midst of a significant crisis that cannot be ignored. And yet it is. When this CDC study came out, I scoured the news sources to find anyone who would sound the alarm that we have allowed our society to inflict serious damage on our young, but the only outcry I encountered was a full page ad in *USA Today* that said, "American teens are in a health crisis, and nothing will change unless we all act. Become part of the solution: go to trojancondoms.com."[20]

Whatever the facts are concerning the actual number of adolescents who have engaged in sexual intercourse, there seems to be little debate that sexual activity has greatly increased and is now considered normal for even a casual dating relationship. The only possible ethical boundary that exists in the midadolescent world concerns actual intercourse. Oral sex has gone mainstream over the past two decades,[21] clearly contributing to the rise of STDs. Although the most recent research implies that the actual numbers of those teens who reported having had oral sex are not that much greater than for those who have had intercourse,[22] I suspect that the number is far higher than reported on surveys and interviews. Regardless, with all of the attention given to the "abstinence vs. protection" debate, one reality has emerged: our young are engaging in behaviors that have the power to change their

> I just finished my freshman year in high school. I'm fifteen, and my boyfriend is eighteen. We started dating in October when we were fourteen and seventeen. A little after Christmas things started to get crazy. We pretty much let go of moral values. While we haven't (and have promised each other we won't) had sex, we've done quite a lot. We've lied about it to our parents, friends, and anyone who cares to ask.

lives forever, and few institutions or organizations seem to much care. Oh, except one: Trojan Condoms.

There is, in addition to the physical dangers associated with unbounded sexual expression, another whole aspect to adolescent sexuality that almost never makes it into the academy: the emotional and relational outcomes of this hypersexualized world. During this study, I witnessed several episodes of anger related to sexual activity gone awry, from a teary cold shoulder after a one-night stand to a violent breakup after months (and in a few cases years) of intimate dating and sexual experimentation. I heard story after story of betrayal, misunderstanding, regret, and self-hatred. I watched countless midadolescent boys and girls develop apparent indifference and even callousness in response to the pain they experienced as a result of highly intimate yet uncommitted sexual relationships. In many cases, I found that behind the defensive joking and flippancy students were burdened by a heavy cloak of genuine sadness. In many students, I witnessed the heartache, emptiness, and loneliness that followed the loss of an implied promise of love and sexual activity. Even social science research is beginning to recognize that nonmarital sexual activity and intimacy can have measurable negative consequences.[23] In today's culture, sexually intimate behaviors tend to be a natural expression of connection when two young people, sometimes regardless of gender, become relationally intimate or consider each other a source of safety and comfort. Yet no one is helping our young to realize that it is impossible to separate the mind from the heart, or the body from either. Because each human is one matrixed whole, we cannot disengage one aspect of our humanity from any other. There are, simply stated, relational, emotional, psychological, and sociological consequences to the kind and scope of sexual perspectives and expressions we've handed our children. And as they grow up they do not have the experience, recourses, or capacity to cope with this wide range of complexities.

In the original study and since, I have found that the issues related to teenage sexuality and sexual expression are far beyond "salient": they are central, catastrophic, and yet, apart from debates about the hard numbers, virtually ignored by academics and even those who work directly with students. Considering the havoc that societal abandonment has wrought on today's adolescents, it is little wonder that they are ill equipped to deal with adult behavior or responsibility, especially in an area as accessible and emotionally charged as human sexuality. When considered in light of the emotional and developmental devastation it causes for midadolescents, the issue of adolescent sexuality should be a wake-up call to all who care about the young of our society.

In my observation of today's teenagers, the central reason for the decreasing age of intimate sexual activity is loneliness. Few argue that the age of menarche is getting younger around the world. This fact alone has been suggested as the primary reason why early adolescents are engaging in intimate sexual behaviors earlier than in the last several decades.[24] It is far from clear, however, whether physical development is influential in regard to sexual behavior. Such behavior has at least as much to do with psychosocial development as it does with biological preparedness. Sexuality has at least as much to do with psychosocial identity as with our bodies. Although our bodies are the physical tools for expressing our sexual longings, the decreasing age of menarche is but a minor issue in a complex psychosocial web affecting the sexual choices and behaviors of midadolescents.[25]

My conclusion after reflecting on the data from this study is that adolescent sexuality, and perhaps all human sexuality, has more to do with a desire for relational connection and a safe place than with a physical, albeit sometimes pleasurable, activity of the body. Many midadolescents are almost desperate in their loneliness, with few opportunities to share or even deal with the effects. Sexual activity and desire are obviously related to the natural drives and hormonal changes of this phase of life, but buried underneath any physical hormonal drive there is an even deeper, more profound need that uses sexuality and sensuality to heal. Today's midadolescents are desperate for the safety and protective embrace of a world that cares, and as products of lifelong systemic abandonment, they are crying out for attention and affection. Expressions of popular culture occasionally concede that this may be true for girls but rarely if ever cast boys in this light. I consistently observed, however, that midadolescent boys are just as vulnerable and desperate as girls but may not be as aware of their need for care and affection. Sexual behavior and sexual fantasy are immensely powerful in that for a very

> I've had to overcome many struggles with sex drive stuff and being lonely in a group of friends who are couples. It's a hard struggle. Feelings of loneliness are overwhelming.
>
> high school student

brief time they can ease the pain of disconnection and loneliness as they mimic authentic love. This is why unbounded, indiscriminate sexual activity for adolescents is even more dangerous and potent than most adults recognize. Adults limit the power of "sexual urges" to changing hormones, but in reality far deeper forces are at work that, due to the sexual training and exposure young people have grown up with, entice and woo the midadolescent toward a wide array of sexual expression. Boys are interested in sex not only because it is "natural" or "normal" but because they—like girls, though in somewhat different ways—are desperate for meaningful human connection. The primary motive for the sexual decisions of both boys and girls, at the core of who they are as people, is to be valued and cherished.

In addition to this driving desire to find attention and affection, most who are not sexually active (meaning not having sexual intercourse) are nonetheless sexually intimate. Although academic literature has not been able to discover the extent to which nonintercourse sexual activities are occurring among midadolescents, ample evidence supports my impression that the occurrence of such activities has dramatically increased over the past several years.[26] The most common explanation given for this increase is the movement referred to as "technical virginity," a term that describes a female who has experienced every form of sexual intimacy but not vaginal intercourse. "Reliable data on other kinds of sexual experiences, such as oral sex or anal sex, are not currently available for adolescents. There is some anecdotal evidence, however, that adolescents sometimes engage in these 'outercourse' activities as an alternative to vaginal intercourse in order to protect against pregnancy or maintain virginity."[27] In a few settings, students attempted to defend nonintercourse intimate sexual behaviors as nothing more than "messing around," using apologetic phrases such as "What's the big deal?" and "Everybody does it." The justification was that because it is not intercourse, it is not "technically" sex. I met dozens of self-proclaimed virgins who regularly practiced many forms of sexual intimacy with multiple partners and who (apparently) felt no sense of guilt or moral or even logical incongruity (many were committed to "staying pure" until marriage "because that's what God calls me to do"). This behavior reaffirms that the very definition of sex has indeed changed. And as the occurrence of nonintercourse sexual activity rapidly increases, dialogue about and anticipation of the activity have slipped into the midelementary years. As William Damon of Stanford University recently said, "By the time a child is eight years old, they know all about oral sex."[28]

Generally, the vast majority of midadolescents prefer relational sexual expression, but again, for many, it is not absolutely necessary, depending on a variety of circumstances. Although ample research claims that adolescents are becoming more concerned about sexual activity being connected to romance or at least affection,[29] I observed this issue as a mixed bag. Due in part to the media, adolescents experience acculturation and a barrage of messages that propagate the view that sex is enjoyable and appropriate regardless of the intimacy or longevity of a given relationship. There is a genuine belief in the midadolescent world that sex with a relative stranger can be the route to happiness and fulfillment.

In an editorial, David Brooks recounts his experience with college students, especially as he was attempting to describe the difference between the "hook up" (casual sex with a relative stranger) and the "hang out" (spending a brief time together before engaging in sexual activity, usually intercourse). He writes, "This is the point at which us fogies are supposed to lament the decline in courtship. Indeed, I was out drinking late one night with a group of [college] students, and a woman to my left mentioned that she would never have a serious relationship with someone she wouldn't consider marrying. 'That sounds traditional,' I said to her. She responded, 'I didn't say I wouldn't f— anyone I wouldn't consider marrying.'"[30]

Sex and sexual play hold the promise of easing unresolved and intense loneliness, satisfying an unquenched longing for adventure,[31] or providing a new and exciting experience. Yet it is clear that few teenagers are even remotely aware of the emotional and relational downsides of sexual intimacy. By the time they are in college, the expectation that there may be a viable connection between love and sex has all but been extinguished. In high school, however, the notion of romantic love that can be discovered through sexual experimentation, or even moving toward such an ideal, is still seen as a potentially obtainable goal. Many students I encountered held loosely to the philosophy that sexual activity is generally better reserved for someone you love or at least are interested in, but that sentiment is not so strong that it precludes a random sexual encounter with a stranger given the opportunity. Who knows? Perhaps that stranger will turn out to be that one who will take away the loneliness so many young people feel everyday.

Conclusion and Musings

Since conducting this study, I have had a difficult time watching television, going to movies, and driving by billboards on the freeway. I was aware of the sexual nature of our culture, but I now see it in a new light, specifically in regard to the developmental needs and lives of our children and adolescents. I cannot help but lament the fact that we have lost any hope of maintaining sexual innocence and sanctity for the current generation.

Massive shifts in thinking about sexuality have occurred in our culture over the past several decades. The definition of sex is now limited to the technicality of intercourse. Holding an appreciation for sex as the wonder and mystery of the intersection of bodies, minds, and hearts is but a distant and rapidly fading memory. Will this generation be able to comprehend the power of love that gives sacredness to a physical act? As I listened to teenagers talk about how they felt about love and romance and how these related to sexuality, I had difficulty finding any who could make the connection, though many wanted to (especially girls).

While writing some of these thoughts, I ran across an article in our local newspaper that seemed to summarize how far we as a culture have come regarding our attitude toward ourselves as sexual beings. The school these students attended is similar to the one where I did my study.

In an upscale area of Orange County, California, three adolescent boys were ordered to stand trial on "two dozen felony charges related to the videotaped alleged sexual assault of a 16-year-old girl." The boys and the girl had apparently been getting together for "sex parties" a few days before the event in question, and the boys had allegedly decided to videotape this one evening "for fun." When a judge saw the 20-minute videotape, he told the court, "It's pretty clear to me she's just being used like a piece of meat." The defense argued that "the victim had sexual intercourse with all three boys in the days leading up to the videotaped incident. [He] also said the girl consented to have sex the night of the alleged attack."[32]

This event demonstrates how far we have fallen in our societal understanding of and communication about sex to our children and adolescents. For eons across cultures, with few exceptions, humanity has believed that there are essential qualities that make us human, and bring out the best in life, like love, faithfulness, trust, and authentic intimate relationships. Expressed throughout time, the human spirit affirms the subservient and secondary role of human sexuality when compared to committed and sacrificial love relationships. The hope I carry is that the pendulum has swung as far as it can go in thinking about sex as a toy and that it will be brought back to the center by generations who have seen how devastatingly empty such a world can be. For now, all we can do is remind the young of our culture that love matters, that people are not objects or playthings, and that our bodies and our hearts cannot be separated. For this message to gain any traction, adults need to get involved in the battle for healthy balance. There are some promising signs showing that teens who have significant social capital in their lives, especially those who report that they "get along with their parents," are less likely to engage in early intimate sexual activity.[33] When it comes to sexual longing and opportunities, we are all constantly bombarded by conflicting and disconcerting messages, but as adults we need to do whatever we can to help adolescents recognize that there is a difference between unbounded and relationally disconnected sexuality and the kind of healthy love we all crave, where sex is an expression of authentic and lasting intimacy with someone we can trust.

busyness and stress

Today's child has become the unwilling, unintended victim of overwhelming stress—the stress borne of rapid, bewildering social change and constantly rising expectations.

David Elkind, *The Hurried Child*

In a meeting with a small group of government employees whose job was to focus on the unique needs of youth, the subject of stress came up. Because I was in the midst of this study at the time, my data-gathering antennae went up. I was not surprised by what I heard, but I was nonetheless a bit taken aback.

I had come to see that today's midadolescents are about as busy as humanly possible. They average five to six hours of sleep a night (when some experts insist they should get eight to nine, especially during adolescence).[1] The ever-mounting demands on their time and energies; the heightening expectations from coaches, bosses, and activity leaders; the proliferation of homework; and the accessibility of many communication options make the typical day in the life of a midadolescent a balancing act. Nearly every student I encountered during this study described life as busy to very busy.

I had also noticed that they were observably tired, some to the point of near exhaustion. Instead of being a general laziness or a semibored listlessness (both of which have long been associated with this age group), the tiredness I observed was like what I feel after staying up most of the night due to a delayed flight. Many students experience this zombielike feeling on a daily basis. When I asked why they were so tired, the answers had to do with everything from homework to work to a late practice.

The fact that adolescents are both busy and tired had emerged early on in my study. Until the meeting mentioned above, however, I was not planning on making the topic a major aspect of this book. Following the morning with this eclectic group of experienced, committed, well-trained, self-described youth workers, I was compelled to reexamine much of the data I had compiled.

"I have been working with kids for forty years, and today's kids are the most stressed out I have ever seen," said one gentleman.[2]

"They are on the edge, that's for sure," said a thirtysomething social worker who spent a great deal of time in the district where I was serving. "And the worst part is, they don't even know how stressed they are!"

The supervisor, a fifteen-year veteran of city government who was involved in numerous youth organizations throughout the community, jumped in. "They have no other framework, so they don't even know what stress is or looks like. I was talking to a kid last week, a sharp junior—student government, involved as a leader in the YMCA Youth In Government program, a star volleyball player, who looked like he was a great student—who told me he won't be able to get into a four-year college because of his grades. He saw my expression and said, 'Man, I don't have time to do homework, and I'm just too tired to stay awake in class. After volleyball, the Y, and Young Life, I have to gel and catch up with my friends. Just getting up in the morning is a miracle!' I tried to get him to step back and to see what's important, to get him to consider his future and make some priorities in his life. He just looked at me like I was his mom telling him to clean his room. All he said as he turned away was, 'You just don't get it, do you?'"

The rest of the conversation was more of the same. Then a kind of cloud of disappointment, discouragement, and even helplessness settled over the meeting. The agenda had to do with creating a strategy to help individuals and agencies serve those not yet at risk but on the edge. After this initial ice-breaking conversation, however, our efforts seemed feeble, and no one had the energy to try to strategize any solutions. We made it through the meeting, but the air had definitely been let out of the tires.

I drove away aware that what I had noticed but dismissed as a relatively minor issue was actually a core aspect of midadolescent life. I was discouraged by the apparent no-win convergence of multiple expectations, a lack of ability to see above the fray of their immediate contextual experience, and an unwillingness to trust adults who might be able to help. Midadolescents today seem to want to be incredibly busy. They do not know any different. And they are turned off by anyone's attempt to put limits on them or to suggest priorities and boundaries. Midadolescents live in the midst of the only reality they know. They are exhausted in the present but afraid of the unknown. The result of this commitment to busyness? Stress.

The stress is real and powerful, and yet few midadolescents see it as stress or even as a negative aspect of their lives. "It is what it is," one student told me when I asked why he was so tired. "I have to work, I have to be with my friends, I have to be up for practice, and I have to live my life. I'm doing okay, so don't hassle me . . . unless I snore in class."

The Reality of Their Lives

During the research I conducted across the country with both adolescents and adults, whatever the town, whatever the segment of society, the view was consistent: the busyness, fragmentation, and stress level adolescents experience are relatively new, and they are increasing. Whether midadolescents have greater resources today than in the past to cope with the stress and multiple expectations they face is, in reality, beside the point. The issue is what they face and how it affects them.

In an article on the state of college students at prestigious universities, one editor remarked, "Their main lack is time. Students boast to each other about how little sleep they've gotten, and how long it's been since they had a chance to get back to their dorm room."[3] In high school as well as in college, the lack of enough time to get done all they need to do is a consistently mentioned plague. For some, this is surrounded by a desire to have a full résumé. Most midadolescents who have proven they

You have no one to ask you what's wrong. You can't take it anymore. There's too much pressure. So what do you do? Do you find someone to talk to? The pressure is too high, choking you like a noose. So you think, What's the point of fighting it? You try to think of the old days when you were little, when life was about having fun. All you need is someone to talk to, but it can't be your parents. They're always fighting.

high school student

have the ability to compete academically for coveted admittance into a good school are well aware that the game is less about brainpower and more about tenacity and sheer determination. They know, as this same editorial observes, that "the system does encourage students to exert themselves. Actually, it demands it. As one student at the Yale Political Union astutely noted, the system doesn't necessarily reward brains; it rewards energy. The ones who thrive are the ones who can keep going from one activity to another, from music, to science, to sports, to community service, to the library, and so on without rest. To get into a competitive school, you need a hyperactive thyroid as much as high intelligence."[4] But pursuing this kind of success comes at a price. Researchers Suniya Luthar and Shawn J. Latendresse found that "individuals who place high value on occupational success and prestige relative to gratifying personal lives have been found to be at escalated risk for emotional distress."[5] Indeed, after reassessing the adolescents in their study near the end of their high school careers, they found that "on anxiety, incidence of clinically significant symptoms among girls increased over time, from one in five to almost one in three by the end of high school."[6]

As Madeleine Levine puts it: "We need to investigate the possibility that some aspects of this culture: materialism, individualism, perfectionism, and competition may actually contribute to psychological problems."[7]

By the time many students reach the middle of their junior year of high school, they want (most of them say "need") more money, and almost always that means finding a job. Research has shown that getting even a part-time job exponentially adds to the level of stress and busyness in the life of a midadolescent. The developmental cost of having a job seems to be much greater than the relational and material cost of not having a job. As the American Psychological Association reports, "Adolescents who work 20 or more hours per week during the school year experience consistently negative outcomes. Findings from the National Longitudinal Study on Adolescent Health suggest that these young people are more emotionally distressed, have poorer grades, are more likely to smoke cigarettes, and are more likely to become involved in other high-risk behaviors such as alcohol and drug use."[8]

The Sources of Stress

Before determining the sources of stress, we need to define stress. David Elkind writes that "stress is any unusual demand for adaptation that forces us to call on our energy reserves over and above that which we ordinarily expend and replenish in the course of a twenty-four-hour period. Although stress, or extraordinary demands for adaptation, can be of all kinds—accidents, breakdowns, being late, major decisions, major failures, successes, and so on—the response to stress is fairly specific and well documented. In other words, our bodies have a very specific way of calling upon and utilizing our energy reserves. . . . [This is called] the 'stress response.'"[9]

There are several specific and unique stressors in the lives of midadolescents. In his book *The Hurried Child*, Elkind offers a stress test for children. A point system charts a child's stress level based on changes in his or her life. If, according to this instrument, a child's score in any given year is beyond 150 points, he or she has a "better than average chance of showing some symptoms of stress. If your child's score was above 300, there is a strong likelihood he or she will experience a serious change in health and/or behavior."[10]

Here are some of the stressors he lists and their point values:

Parent dies	100
Parents divorce	73
Parents separate	65
Parent travels as part of job	63
Parent remarries	50
Parents reconcile	45
Mother goes to work	45
School difficulties	39
Threat of violence at school	31

This is but a sampling of the kinds of things that induce stress and anxiety in the life of a child. A popular assumption is that adolescents, being older and more streetwise than children, are less vulnerable to these and other stressors. Because of the added burdens of abandonment, social fragmentation, and being forced to live in multiple selves, however, midadolescents are even more prone to stress, with fewer points needed to push them over the edge.

In my observation of midadolescent busyness, stress, and pressure, I noticed three areas of stress that took their toll on most students: the pressure to succeed, the pressure to maintain stability at home while remaining loyal and connected to the peer group, and the general pressure associated with relationships. In fact, a 2009 study of significant stressors for students in high school general education programs revealed just these sorts of issues: "parent-child relations, academic struggles, conflict within family, and peer relations, as well as role transitions and societal problems."[11] These pressure points, while perhaps not overwhelming

It's hard to have so much on your shoulders or things on your to-do list when you're so busy.

high school student

for all students, at different times and in different ways seem to have a significant impact on the emotional equilibrium of most students.

The pressure to succeed, whether in the classroom, on the athletic field, or in another endeavor that creates a sense of worth and accomplishment, produces an elusive, never-quite-good-enough feeling that students wear like a cloud. When students do something well, they believe it is only a step in the direction of adequate performance. I encountered few students who allowed themselves to do their best in a given arena and then let the chips fall where they may. For most, the pressure to continue to reach loftier heights was the defining sentiment. When someone did well on a test or had a great tennis match, the time for celebration was short-lived. As one student remarked, acting as a spokesperson for several others in a small-group setting, "We feel an incredible pressure to succeed in every area, or it will all fall apart." When I asked what specifically would fall apart, the group could not put a finger on it, but they were convinced that the statement was nonetheless accurate.

What they are striving for is not the thing itself but rather what the accomplishment will bring with it. Performance, then, is not about the touchdown, the A, or a role in the school play. It is about how others will perceive them. In other words, adolescents have learned that what matters is not who they are but what they do—or more pointedly, what they can point to and say, "Look at me! I am worthy of attention and affection." For most students, the accolades that seemed to penetrate were those that went beyond a deed and focused on their intrinsic worth. This also seemed to diffuse some of the need to perform and the stress that came along with it.

Students regularly feel that their greatest struggle is when there is stress in their relationship with their parents. A fight with a mom, dad, or stepparent just as they are walking out the door to school can produce a brooding mood that lasts much of the day. They do not like to talk about it much, but they are easily discouraged when there is unresolved conflict at home.[12]

Midadolescents desperately want what they know they cannot have: parents who affirm everything they do and care enough about them to be their biggest fans, and yet who know when to keep their distance.

Even midadolescent logic can, when summoned to do so, see that these desires cannot coexist when it comes to parents. There is no way a parent can be a caring, involved parent who draws boundaries and makes certain a child is appropriately guided and nurtured and at the same time is such a great pal and fan that they never interfere in their child's life.[13] This paradox is nonetheless what a midadolescent believes is not only possible but also preferable.

The greatest rub occurs when parents attempt to step into the protective strategy of the midadolescent: the cluster. Parents are under considerable strain as they seek to exert influence over their child and to know when to back off. This is not easy for a parent or a child, and it can cause stress for both.

The most delicate and yet easily disguised source of stress for midadolescents is keeping people happy. Midadolescents may not seem to care about how others react to them, but that is an act. They actually care deeply about what others think. Much of the time their self-focus and self-centeredness keep them from reading the cues available to them. They also may wear dismissal by an adult or a student they do not like as a badge of assertive honor. But inside, they know they are taking a risk and desperately want everyone to respect, affirm, and hopefully like them.

A student handed me a note after class one day that read, "The thing we worry about the most is not disappointing others." The cynic in me immediately recalled the exceptionally rowdy and flippant class, and I was tempted to dismiss the note as a sarcastic attempt to manipulate my research. Yet the next day I felt different about the tone of our conversation. It seemed to me that what I had read as callous indifference and even arrogant disregard was actually a test. Did I really care about what they thought or, more importantly, about them? Was I interested in each one as a unique and valuable person, or was I one more adult who was willing to use and exploit them for my career? When I recognized what was at the core of their response to me, I saw twenty-eight fragile midadolescents who wanted to know that they mattered to me. What a gift that note was!

Developmental Issues Related to Busyness and Stress

In a report published by the American Psychological Association, the section titled "Adolescent Emotional Development" begins with the following sentence: "Emotional development during adolescence involves establishing a realistic and coherent sense of identity in the context of relating to others and learning to cope with stress and manage emotions—processes that are life-long issues for most people."[14]

As I watched the frazzled busyness, the burden of multiple layers of expectations, the overlapping and competing commitments to activities, and the desire to access and utilize the latest technologies, I could not help but feel that midadolescents have been backed into a difficult corner. On the one hand, a major aspect of their developmental responsibility is to learn how to cope with stress and manage their emotions. On the other hand, adults have continued to pile increased burdens and complex demands on them. What occurs when these two competing forces clash? Midadolescents feel the need to flee from both the pressures and their responsibility to cope. This becomes one more factor—sometimes the deciding factor—in the creation and sustenance of the world beneath.

Mary Pipher, in *Reviving Ophelia*, says that adolescent girls "need good habits for coping with stress" (though I assume she would include boys as well).[15] In context, she means that adults must teach and train the young how to handle the stress of everyday life. Perhaps there is some truth in the concept that development ultimately comes down to the individual journey of an adolescent, but the search for a satisfying and unique identity that includes the abilities to cope with and manage stress and emotions also has a great deal to do with one's environment. As Patricia Hersch notes:

> What kids need from adults is not just rides, pizza, chaperones, and discipline. They need the telling of stories, the close, ongoing contact, so that they can learn to be accepted. If nobody is there to talk to, it is difficult to get the lessons of your own life so that you are adequately prepared to do the next thing. Without a link across generations, kids will only hear from their peers. The Carnegie Council on Adolescent Development report A Matter of Time: "Young adolescents do not want to be left to their own devices." In national surveys and focus groups, America's youth have given voice to serious longing. They want more regular contact with adults who care about and respect them.[16]

Albert Bandura suggests that an intricate relationship exists among social environment, self-efficacy beliefs, and development for adolescents.[17] According to Bandura, "Individuals play a proactive role in their adaptation rather than simply undergoing happenings in [the environment]. . . . The success with which the risks and challenges of adolescence are managed depends, in no small measure, on the strength of personal efficacy."[18] Self-efficacy beliefs "moderate the relation between what the environment affords by way of incentives and demands and the level of success attained."[19] Bandura offers substantial evidence that stress affects adolescents differently (and significantly so) depending on the strength of their efficacy beliefs. His point is that those possessing belief in themselves have a far better ability to cope with the stress of everyday

Funny, isn't it, how one little incident could send me straight into tears and running away like I am nine. I feel ridiculous. I am seventeen and almost an adult. Why can't I handle it?

high school student

life, and they are thus less dependent on or subject to the environment when it comes to handling stress.

Midadolescence, however, is a period when even those who believe in themselves have difficulty with the expectations placed on them. Today's strongest midadolescents face challenges that their parents (and even their older brothers and sisters) did not. Those who possess the strongest self-efficacy beliefs, and who therefore have a greater ability to handle whatever the environment throws at them, still face periods of struggle, insecurity, and stress.

The Impact of Stress

The ordinary effects of stress in everyday life—such as recurring headaches, insomnia, or lack of ability to concentrate—are difficult enough for adolescents to bear. Unfortunately, however, efforts to cope with stress may lead to even more serious problems such as eating disorders, substance abuse, self-injury, and suicide.[20] One of the most unsettling trends among adolescents is the rise of what experts call nonsuicidal self-injury (NSSI), where individuals deliberately inflict some form of harm (cutting, burning, hitting) on themselves without suicidal intent. In their helpful review of recent research on this issue, E. David Klonsky and Jennifer J. Muehlenkamp report that self-injury of this sort typically begins occurring around age thirteen or fourteen and is by far most prevalent among adolescents and young adults. Studies have demonstrated that at least 14 to 15 percent of adolescents in North America have engaged in some form of self-injury. Common reasons given for this behavior include "to release emotional pressure that builds up inside of me," "to stop bad feelings," or "to manage stress."[21] One study of over three thousand university students conducted by Cornell and Princeton University researchers revealed that an alarming "17 percent of college students—20 percent of women and 14 percent of men—report that they have cut, burned, carved or harmed themselves in other ways."[22]

According to these researchers, this trend has led many professionals to conclude that "young people today possess fewer coping mechanisms and face more stressful situations than in the past."[23]

But self-injury is just one of a number of growing destructive trends among stressed adolescents. Similarly upsetting is the link between stress and eating disorders, particularly, though not exclusively, in female adolescents.[24] And while suicide may seem to be the extreme case, recent reports have demonstrated that it is an option that presents itself to significant percentages of young people. A recent study of stress levels among college students revealed that over the past year, 16 percent of the students had friends talk about wanting to end their lives, 11 percent of the students had friends attempt suicide, and 9 percent of the students had thought seriously about ending their own life.[25] It is nothing less than tragic that adolescents feel driven to these and other destructive coping strategies in order to deal with stress. The adults in their lives must take notice and begin to ask what may be done to help alter this course.

Conclusion and Musings

The most significant impression I had following my experience with midadolescents was this: just below the surface, today's midadolescents feel a sense of loneliness and isolation that betrays the confidence with which they present themselves, even to one another. The busyness they embrace keeps them from having to reflect on their dreams, their relationships, and their lives. The resultant stress only serves to compound the desperation they feel that somehow, in some way, they might be able to work hard enough or play hard enough to free themselves from the burden of loneliness and fear.

Certainly they are tired, and many are angry. Both of these, however, are but symptoms of a deeper threat to their well-being and ultimately to their ability to progress through midadolescence. At the core, they long for the safety and freedom of childhood and have no clear vision concerning what adulthood will be like. As a result of the abandonment they have faced throughout their lives, most midadolescents carry inside them a powerful defense mechanism that keeps them running as fast and as hard as they can. They know no other way to cope with life. The quicker they move, the less vulnerable they are to ridicule, critique, or even examination. Midadolescents know they must put on a mask of confidence, even arrogance, or they will be chewed up by those who would find them out. May we, the adults who love and care for them, not be fooled. They are busy, yes, and stressed, but they want someone to demonstrate in word and action, "You matter to me."

ethics and morality

The evidence is that a willingness to cheat has become the norm and that parents, teachers, coaches and even religious educators have not been able to stem the tide. The scary thing is that so many kids are entering the workforce to become corporate executives, politicians, airplane mechanics and nuclear inspectors with the dispositions and skills of cheaters and thieves.

Michael Josephson, quoted in Josephson Institute,
"The Ethics of American Youth: 2002"

Sociologist Mike Males used an interesting phrase in his article for the *Los Angeles Times* when he referred to adult concerns and fears about the state of the young as "bogus moral panics."[1] I have already discussed his attempt to discredit those who believe that adolescence is changing and presenting serious challenges for us as a culture (see chapter 2), but I have not yet considered his use of the term *moral panics*. Males and others may disagree with me, but if there is one arena in which adolescence is rapidly changing it is the realm of ethics and morality. To say that asking questions concerning the changing ethical standards, rules, and norms of adolescents is a "moral panic" is reductionism at its worst.

Ethics: Discarded or Redefined?

When plague afflicted the Greeks in the fifth century BC, an overwhelming sense of hopelessness impacted the entire society. Thucydides describes how this feeling affected people's ethical commitments:

Men now coolly ventured on what they had formerly done in a corner, and not just as they pleased, seeing the rapid transitions produced by persons in prosperity suddenly dying and those who before had nothing succeeding to their property. So they resolved to spend quickly and enjoy themselves, regarding their lives and riches as like things of a day. Perseverance in what men called honor was popular with none, it was so uncertain whether they would be spared to attain the object; but it was settled that present enjoyment, and all that contributed to it, was both honorable and useful. Fear of gods or law of man there was none to restrain them. As for the first, they judged it to be just the same whether they worshipped them or not, as they saw all alike perishing; and for the last, no one expected to live to be brought to trial for his offences, but each felt that a far severer sentence had been already passed upon them all and hung ever over their heads, and before this fell it was only reasonable to enjoy life a little.[2]

For much the same reason, contemporary midadolescents filter much of their thought processes through the lens of self-interest and self-protection. They see themselves as having been abandoned and left on their own to navigate the complexities of life. Living in the world beneath has left a mark on their ethical norms. Adolescents are not looking for the pleasure of the moment because they believe ethics are irrelevant in light of certain, unavoidable death. They are, instead, developmentally and practically preoccupied with the pleasure of the immediate because they have a driving commitment to create for themselves a world that makes life easier, safer, and more satisfying. But does that mean they have become lawless and have discarded any commitment to ethical rules and standards?

Systemic abandonment and midadolescents' subsequent burrowing into their own world have created a new standard and setting for ethics, one in which ethical norms are still important, for what society or even

> When I got to high school, I was ready to experience things. I tried weed and got pretty into it. It felt like a getaway. I began to drink and smoke as well. I lied to my parents almost every time I left the house. When I went to see my family, I would put on a big front. I felt so bad about it but would always try to give myself a reason why it was okay.
>
> high school student

subculture can possibly survive without an ethical system for defining and ordering life's choices and relationships? Yet the ethical system in operation in the world beneath is a pragmatically revised version of a culture's values. Many of the same ethical issues that are present in the larger culture are present in the midadolescent world, but the way these issues get resolved flows out of the reasons for the world beneath in the first place. The ethical system of the world beneath is limited to those primary ethical issues that affect midadolescents' abilities to feel safe, protected, and fulfilled. Loyalty (primarily defined as loyalty to friends but occasionally involving loyalty to one teacher over another, their school, or their community), staying within the preordained boundaries of social life (such as where to sit, whom to date, what activities to participate in), and other straightforward and easily negotiated ethical parameters of adolescent life make up the ethical scaffolding of midadolescence today.

What this means, then, is that many of the ethical standards of adult society have a secondary relevance for midadolescents. It is not that they do not care about some of the more "traditional" ethical issues—such as lying, stealing, and cheating—but these issues can be rather easily discarded if they violate the more pressing ethical standards of the adolescent world. Adults, on the other hand, at least nod toward an acceptance of ethical standards as an important guide for life. Adults may in actuality be no more moral in their behaviors and attitudes than adolescents, but they will typically have a harder time admitting their deviance from the acknowledged norm. In the General Social Survey study, for example, Gerald Celente of Trends Research states, "We are seeing precisely what this report is saying. They [adolescents] have been hardened by today's realities. They have seen an acceptance of disposing of ethics and morals if it serves a need. They see it is OK to do what you want to do as long as you meet your personal requirements."[3] This modeling by adults has served to further erode a commitment by midadolescents to live up to the lofty standards of ethical rhetoric. They have grown up in a world in which adults say one thing and do another. We even have a saying for this: "Do as I say, not as I do!" The young, therefore, have learned from the example of adults how little ethical standards mean.[4]

Adults see a wide discrepancy between what adolescents say and what they do. Young people seem to behave with inconsistency and defensive relativism. As one editorial that attempted to understand apparently conflicting data put it, "On some political issues involving religion, America's youth seem to be more conservative than their elders, but cheating, stealing and lying by high school students has increased with alarming vigor."[5] For adults to understand the world of midadolescents, they must understand where the ethical lines are drawn and what constitutes an ethical or moral issue.

This chapter identifies and describes two issues as examples of how adolescents view their standards of ethics differently than adults (or at least adult rhetoric): lying and cheating. These are not the only ethical issues in which adolescents function differently, but they do represent a sustained, regular, and even daily rejection of the ethical definitions of the adults who raised and trained them. When it comes to adolescent ethics, issues such as sexuality, alcohol, drugs, justice, racism, and a myriad of other topics are viewed through a similar lens.

Moral Categories

In any discussion of adolescent morality, the default academic position begins with theories put forward by people such as Jean Piaget (child and adolescent development) and Lawrence Kohlberg (moral development). Simply put, Piaget taught that developmental growth is a process of the increasing ability of internal reasoning.[6] Kohlberg went further by arguing that there are six stages of moral development, culminating in an internalized locus of moral commitment.[7] The process for both of these perspectives is linear according to stages (i.e., the older one gets, the more one grows toward a moral commitment). As theorists have worked to revise, reshape, and strengthen these perspectives, the generally accepted understanding of moral development has stayed relatively constant. It "refers to the development of a sense of values and ethical behavior. Adolescents' cognitive development, in part, lays the groundwork for moral reasoning, honesty, and prosocial behaviors such as helping, volunteerism, or caring for others."[8]

Cathy Stonehouse reworked Kohlberg's theory using three basic levels.[9] In terms of what she calls "the source of authority" for each level, level 1 is primarily concerned with the needs of the self, level 2's driving motivation is "how others might respond to one's moral choices," and level 3 is the pinnacle of moral development as one becomes more concerned with "internal principles" than with personal needs or even the perceptions of others.[10] Stonehouse's understanding of justice, related to moral choices and commitments, is also arranged from concern with personal fulfillment and satisfaction (level 1) to conventional standards of a culture (level 2) to the notion of blind and equal justice for all individuals (level 3). The implication is that as people grow up, they generally follow this path, unless they experience a block or trauma along the way that thwarts the process.

In my study of midadolescents, the stage theory, at least as set forth by Stonehouse, did not apply to the overwhelming majority of students. Kohlberg's classification and his six stages of moral development did not hold in terms of the ages most commonly associated with moral growth. In fact, there seemed to be a regression in moral development from middle school to high school (early to midadolescence).[11] Students seemed to bounce back and forth between levels of moral development. The most common stage of Kohlberg's moral reasoning I observed was the pre-conventional level, stage 2, in which a child is concerned primarily with satisfying his or her own wants and needs. The conventional level, stage 3, in which a child seeks approval from others, was in view when adolescents were operating within adult-controlled layers (e.g., school, sports teams, church, or work).

In the world beneath, Kohlberg's stage theory (and variations of it) was not able to address moral reasoning because midadolescents believe they must be in a constant mode of self-protection. A strong survivalist mentality exists just under the surface for many students, affecting their ability to move toward more advanced stages of development, especially moral development.

Lying

"Everybody lies, and everybody knows that everybody lies."

"Is it wrong to lie?" I asked.

"It depends," this junior girl from rural North Carolina went on. "If it doesn't really hurt anybody, and it is necessary for any reason, a 'white lie' is not really a lie, and then it's not wrong."

Some people call this relativism, others pragmatism. I suppose it depends on the perspective of the one doing the lying.

"Does everybody really lie? Even to their parents or ministers?"

"Especially to our parents and pastors! They can't be trusted with anything!"

I heard variations on this theme throughout my study. Researchers have come late to the game and often ask questions that are seen as almost silly by the respondents. "Everybody lies, and everybody knows that everybody lies." In typical academic understatement, one study reported that in an overview of literature dealing with deceptive behaviors of children and adolescents, previous studies had determined that the ability to deceive had been significantly underestimated.[12] When I shared with the students involved in my study that more research was going to focus on the extent of adolescent lying behaviors, they looked at me as if I had said that researchers were going to study whether adolescents breathe. Lying, especially as defined by adults, has become one more natural reflex of daily living, and besides, it is not even really lying!

Abraham Lincoln said, "When I do good, I feel good; when I do bad, I feel bad." In response to this quotation, a female student said, "It is like this: good and bad are relative. Sometimes I think something is bad when it is really not that bad. And sometimes when I try to do something good, it ends up messing me up. I don't think that quote applies to us. I do the best I can to live my life, and what is good or bad is not something I even think about."

I am not saying that every midadolescent moves through this process in the same way or even with the same effect. Some students do not seem to care what an adult thinks, and therefore their propensity to lie may be triggered less frequently than that of students who are trying to play the social game with excellence. All students, however, when they find themselves in a position in which a lie would be the easiest route to self-protection, will lie just as easily as the next kid. Pervasive and unchecked lying has become a central reality to almost every midadolescent in our culture.

There is no question that adolescents, especially midadolescents, lie. In studies on the adolescent tendency to deceive parents, for example, only 5 percent of adolescents said they never lied about where they were. This survey measured what adolescents said, meaning that it is possible that even fewer adolescents did not lie in such cases. The survey also revealed that girls lie more to parents about sex and more often to their dads than do boys; boys lie more often than girls to their moms. They are both highly successful in their lying; only 5 percent say they were often caught.[13]

I observed that the most regular defense offered for lying, especially to authority figures (parents, teachers, coaches), was a perceived need to protect oneself or one's friends. In incident after incident, the most often reported reason for lying was to avoid being punished for doing something that in general they did not believe was wrong. One student put it this way: "Most things are kept from my parents because of the repercussions." As research has shown, when students feel that an issue is none of their parents' business, or that full disclosure would lead to excessive restrictions on their autonomy, lying is not just an option, but a virtual certainty.[14]

I rarely encountered a midadolescent who believed that lying was unethical. Midadolescents reshape the idea of lying to the point where a justified deception, including an outright, bald-faced lie, is not actually lying. Nearly every student admitted to lying regularly, without remorse. Yet these same students actually believed that they were highly moral, ethical, and honest people! This is consistently confirmed by research. One study found that 85 percent of adolescents surveyed said yes to the question, "Are you basically an honest person?"[15] Here is a typical string of logic that I heard over and over again: "I lie, sure. So does everybody else. I'm an honest person, though, and that's what really counts."

Early on in my study, I became increasingly aware that terms and concepts that carry definitive meaning for adults are continually up for grabs according to the ethical mind-set of midadolescents. One day I was told by an athlete that when a coach looked him in the eye and asked why he was late for practice, he made up a semiplausible but fabricated story. As he told me what he had done, he made no attempt to conceal or even justify it to me. In fact, he shared it with me as if it were the most natural and normal thing in the world. When I pressed him, asking him how he could defend his deception, he looked at me with near amazement and said, "He would have made a big deal out of it, and it wasn't a big deal. He didn't deserve to know the truth."

"But you lied to him," I said. "Isn't that wrong?"

"I didn't lie, exactly. I just didn't think it was his business to know my business."

"What happens," I went on, "if that same coach told you that you were going to start next week, and then he turned around and had someone else start in your place? Let's say he was trying to motivate you, and it worked, and you figured out later that he never really intended to have you start. Is that wrong? Is that a lie?"

"Obviously. No coach can lie like that, and to a kid? That's wrong."

The more I tried to tie these two events together, the less this young man seemed interested in or capable of connecting the dots. To him, a lie was not a lie and was not wrong unless it was done to him. When I shared this story with adolescents around the country, it was clear that to some his statement reflected an ethical infraction, but to many others it did not. Even those who saw the inconsistency, however, still believed the guy was right.

During the summer following the year of this study, I spoke at three high school conferences. I told the students that I was finishing this research project and needed their help to correct any points or conclusions I had made. Among nearly three thousand students, there was not one dissenting voice regarding the major elements of the research findings. On the topic of lying, not one student disagreed with my near exaggeration of the phenomenon. After one conference, I received a letter from a young man. His three-page note was filled with personal struggles, despair over his sense of abandonment, and his being "fake more often than he was real." One line particularly struck me, as he was considered by his adult leaders, his school, and his community a moral leader among his peers: "I lie because I have never truly found a person to be honest with. Most likely I lie because I find it likely that any feelings I may convey to that person would eventually come back to haunt me, whether my parents, or even my friends, school, or church. I just can't trust anybody, so I need to protect myself. If I have to lie now and then to do that, so be it."

Despite the behavior, flippancy, and defensive rationalizing of mid-adolescents, lying does represent an important ethical issue for them, and when pressed, most of them do "get it." The issue for them is that the morality regarding truth telling is a second-tier ethic, meaning that while it is an important and necessary ethic on which any society is built—trust being central to social cohesion—these long-term and global realities may be placed on "developmental hold" when young people face a more immediate need to protect oneself (or one's friends).[16] It remains unknown whether the perceived need to lie is based on a fear of shame within the peer group, as some have argued,[17] or is simply an example of the limitations of the cognitive abilities and developmental reality of midadolescents. My hunch is that as midadolescents attempt to create a sense of continuity, congruence, and order while living in multiple layers, a concern for something as lofty as what lying does to the fabric of society does not register on their cognitive radar screens.

Cheating

As mentioned in chapter 5, some believe that cheating has become an epidemic, and research shows that it is widespread and growing among high school and college students.[18] Some of these studies, however, were flawed in that the authors often influenced their subjects by the framing of their questions.[19] That said, studies on cheating have provided insight into the prevalence of and attitudes concerning cheating: it increases during middle and late adolescence, students have a number of rationalities and reasons for cheating,[20] and midadolescents tend to blame their cheating on others (teachers, parents, the school itself, or even society at large).[21]

In one study, researchers found that high school students were far more carefree and casual about cheating than were college students.[22] This supports the notion that midadolescents, by developmental defi-nition, do not seem to give much energy to ethical issues that do not provide immediate self-promotion or protection. Even the definition of cheating varied from context to context[23] and, in my study, from situa-tion to situation. If, for example, a teacher was well liked and was seen as honest, respectful, and fair, then most students would self-police their own against too much cheating in that class. But if that same teacher "unfairly" gave a pop quiz, then whoever felt the need to cheat was only giving the teacher what he or she deserved.[24] These findings are consistent with a recent study showing that students readily justify cheating when they perceive a teacher to be incompetent and/or disrespectful.[25] This particular study took as its point of departure prior research that positively associated permissive attitudes about cheating with the perception that a classroom is driven more by performance than enrichment.[26] In another situation during my observation, when a student who was relatively respected felt that he or she had the right to cheat for one reason or another, it was up to the class to protect and defend that student's choice. But if another student who, for whatever reason, was not seen as a peer ally chose to cheat, that student would be turned in (this was actually quite rare, but it happened now and then).

Donald McCabe, in a study on academic dishonesty among high school students, offers some of the comments he recorded in a midadolescent focus group:

> "I think times have changed. Cheating is kind of considered, I don't know, just a kind of daily thing that's out there, almost kind of acceptable. Teachers know it and students know it. . . . Maybe when our parents were growing up or their parents were growing up, it was a lot tighter and stricter on people cheating. Today it's just not happening. I think grown-ups have gotten a little bit more with-it in terms of knowing that you're just going to kind of cheat. . . . It's almost a big deal if you don't cheat. . . ." It appears that cheating does not weigh heavily on the conscience of high school students. . . . "People cheat. It doesn't make you less of a person or worse of a person. There are times when you just are in need of a little help. . . . I think people are going to cheat so it will help them to get into an Ivy League school. . . . You can't change that; you can't change people wanting to get the A or whatever. . . . If cheating is going to get you the grade, then that's the way to do it."[27]

These comments could have been verbatim records of the conversations I had with students during my study. Others who spent time with midadolescents discovered the same themes. Cheating is rarely seen by midadolescents as a violation of some moral code, but instead is viewed as a pragmatic though potentially risky decision that serves larger, more important goals.[28] Gerald L. Zelizer, in an editorial in *USA Today*, reported that in a discussion with a handful of high school students he was chastened by a seventeen-year-old: "Don't you know, rabbi, cheating is pretty much the norm in high school? Besides, most of the teachers don't really care."[29] So how bad is it?

In a nationally publicized study conducted by the Josephson Institute of Ethics in the fall of 2002, researchers found that "stealing and lying by high school students have continued their alarming, decade-long upward spiral. A survey of 12,000 high school students showed that students admitting they cheated on an exam at least once in the past year jumped from 61% in 1992 to 74% in 2002. . . . The percentage who say they lied to their teachers and parents also increased substantially."[30] The methodology the Josephson Institute used consisted of self-report surveys. All this tells us is that 74 percent of those asked admitted to the behavior, and therefore, the number could be even higher. In addition, the way the question was framed implied that cheating is limited to personally and proactively cheating. Cheating has traditionally been defined as allowing someone to cheat from your work as well as allowing the behavior to happen in front of you. If this definition were applied, the number would probably be 90 to nearly 100 percent.

An example of adolescents' inconsistent understanding of the ethics related to cheating is found in a student's letter to the editor of the *Los Angeles Times* in response to the Josephson Institute report:

> I am an A student. I budget my time, even though I have basketball practice and don't arrive home from my bus ride until 6 p.m. But I have had friends tell me that they didn't study or they didn't know how to do the work or didn't try. They anticipate that the kid next to them studied, and they look at that student's paper. I have on occasion knowingly let someone copy from my paper. It was a smart kid who went blank on a question. I know he studied, so I put my paper to the edge so that he could get a look. Some say that it is not cheating if you don't get caught. But to me, cheating is cheating, for you are cheating yourself of an opportunity to learn.[31]

I know students cheat, or most of them, but I don't think I can do much about it. If I started pushing too hard, I would get in real hot water with parents. Parents are so clueless. They think, "My Johnny would never cheat. It had to be some other kid who set him up." I am sick of the whole thing, and I have learned that the best way to handle most of the small stuff is just to look the other way.

high school teacher

In the rest of the letter, the student remained critical of those who cheat who are not smart or do not really care. At the same time, she defended students who are smart by stating that "all types of kids cheat. Some are really smart, but they forget to study." I shared this letter with several students at the school where I did my study, and in the discussion not one picked up on her inconsistency until I pointed it out. At that point, they admitted that her behavior proved she was, like everyone she disdained, just one more cheater.

Another form of cheating that has been around for a long time but is now presenting a serious threat to the ethical standards of high schools, colleges, and even graduate schools is plagiarism, and it is not even seen by most kids as cheating.[32] Donald McCabe, a professor of management at Rutgers University and founder of the Center for Academic Integrity at Duke University, notes that the internet has provided an unprecedented opportunity for plagiarism: "Copying a few lines from an obscure website into one's own term paper is not defined by many students as plagiarism," and more than 70 percent of college students do not consider such an act "serious cheating."[33] An almost perfect storm of unethical scholastic behavior occurs when three factors converge: ours is a world in which adults and even the media portray relativism as the ethic of the day; ethics are related to self-interest, self-protection, and relational loyalty instead of to rhetorically affirmed moral standards; and the internet offers not merely a wealth of information and resources, but also an abundance of sites that offer essays, term papers, and the like for an affordable fee.

Like lying, cheating is clearly widespread and shows no sign of abating. Unfortunately, most adults agree that we as a culture have reached a point at which it is only an offense when one gets caught. Students in my study admitted that that is how ethics are defined in their world. If someone gets hurt or if one gets caught cheating, then that person is wrong. In the interim, however, the chorus keeps singing, "What is the big deal? So I cheat, so what?"

A final word that must be addressed is how midadolescents perceive and deal with cheating or lying when it involves one another. The assumption in articles, studies, books, and even this chapter is that the object of the deception is almost always an adult or adult institution. The adolescent world, though, is filled with its own deceptive and unethical practices. In my study, however, students were reluctant to talk about how such a breach of trust is handled within the midadolescent community. As I unintentionally bumped into scenarios, I was allowed a glimpse of how this behavior is handled. In general, when there is a violation of trust within a cluster or between friends, a flurry of accusation and counteraccusation takes place, followed by intense neutral party negotiations intended to heal the rift as quickly and as painlessly as possible. In the cases I observed, the conflict subsided as quickly as it erupted, with as little public fanfare as possible. A close group of friends is so committed to maintaining the status quo of stable familylike relationships that the system will not allow an ethical conflict to fester.

I did witness an exception to this when a guy felt he was being pulled to choose between his girlfriend and his cluster. The crowning blow occurred when the cluster perceived that he had lied to them to spend time with his girlfriend. This incident was quickly handled and seemed to blow over, but the sin was not wholly forgiven. Some of the guys in his cluster felt he had violated a sacred ethic—the sanctity of the cluster. Responses ranged from cold shoulders to outright ostracism. In this particular case, the cluster ultimately found a way for him to have a girlfriend and to stay friends.

Conclusion and Musings

In the film *The Emperor's Club*, Kevin Kline portrays a private school teacher who fudges the grade of a student to do the boy a favor. Although the teacher was attempting to motivate this wayward student, the boy later cheats during a public competitive exam. The boy grows into a man who functions as a world-class cheater, who views the world as a place in which to take any shortcut to get by. When the teacher realizes that his own cheating had hurt another student by denying that student's right to participate in the finals of the competition, he apologizes to the spurned student. The irony of the film is that the cheating of the teacher empowered the cheating of the first student. This was not resolved in the film, for the teacher remained the protagonist and the student the villain.

The Emperor's Club is a poignant reminder of how society has arrived at its current ethical position. To point fingers at the young for their relativism and deception is to display a naïveté of the worst kind. Our efforts at stopping the ethical slide of the young have not worked, although the popular media enjoys stories that seem to suggest that programs are paying off in moral dividends.[34] We may try slogans to reinforce ethical values, such as the "ref in your head" advertising campaign designed "to discourage academic cheating among middle-school youth, ages 10–14 years old."[35] But until we are willing to present the young with societal ethics, values, and moral choices that are tied to the actual behavior of those who are supposed to lead the young into maturity, we will not be able to affect their ethical processes.

William Damon and others, however, are doing some new and promising research on how moral character grows in the inner life and ultimately in the behavior of a child and adolescent—what is now called *moral identity*. His program promotes the "community charter," an effort to surround children and adolescents with caring adults who are committed to their development. The key is the coherency of the messages adults bring to the young. As Damon says,

> [Of paramount importance is] the extent to which all of those influences are coherent—the way they present to the child a message or a set of standards that the young person can make sense out of in shaping a moral self, a moral identity. An example of coherence is when parents are imparting the same messages that [other] parents, school, police, peers, media are imparting. Then moral identity can be developed. If all these things are happening, then the kid will be able to ask what kind of person the kid wants to be. If these things are not happening together (community cohesiveness), then there will not be the opportunity to develop moral identity.[36]

A system of ethics is operating in the world of midadolescents. Unfortunately, it is filled with inconsistency, self-centered justice, and relativistic ethical opportunism. Adults who care for the young, however, can make a long-term difference in the lives of students when we allow ourselves to be involved, to engage their ethical and moral belief systems and behaviors. If adults commit to train the young to care for others instead of just themselves and reinforce this view with commitment to integrity and honesty, then we have the best chance of influencing their moral development in a positive way.[37]

11

partying, gaming, and social networking

No matter how many stupid things you do while drinking (except driving, etc.), it's all worthwhile. Knockin' back beers with your best buds is the way to go.

high school chatroom, www.futazi.com

Everybody I know drinks and drinks a lot."
This statement from a male student was not surprising. After all, I was aware that my source was well known as a partyer. But when I heard it from a sophomore girl who described herself as a religious girl, a freshman girl in the school chorale, and a quiet junior boy who seemed to be limited in his ability to cross social boundaries, I began to wonder if this was a more widespread trend than I had assumed.

Precise data on private behaviors such as frequency of alcohol consumption, use of drugs, and sexual behaviors are difficult to come by.[1] I did not attend high school parties or invade private or semiprivate settings where an adult would clearly not be welcome. I wanted to understand the world of middle adolescents, but I also did not want to go where I was not invited. Thus, the information in this chapter is based on student reports of normative behavior among the campus community.

In our society, alcohol consumption and the recreational use of marijuana have always been viewed as dangerous and destructive behaviors for adolescents. Adults have attempted to educate, inform, and threaten adolescents to keep them from drinking and smoking marijuana. This issue is complicated, however, by a double standard: adults consume a great deal of alcohol, and many smoke marijuana. Apparently, however, this dichotomy has always been the case in nearly every society. As Tao Ruspoli notes, "The use of drugs has undeniably played an important role throughout human history. Each culture, with the exception of the Eskimos before the West introduced them to alcohol, has accepted at least one mind-altering drug as part of its tradition and practices. Drug use has also always been controversial. Each culture has had strong negative opinions of certain drugs while accepting and even encouraging the use of others."[2]

It was with that sober reality in mind that I sought to gain an understanding of the midadolescent use of alcohol and recreational drugs (primarily tobacco and marijuana). I chose to deal with marijuana and alcohol under the same general category. I recognize that some adolescents smoke marijuana but do not drink, while others drink but do not use marijuana. I concluded, however, that the behaviors and rationale associated with one are nearly identical to the behaviors and rationale associated with the other. This section most often discusses alcohol, with occasional reference to marijuana, but the information applies to adolescent use of both alcohol and marijuana.

"Everybody I Know Drinks"—or Do They?

Depending on the cluster being discussed, the quote that opened this chapter—"Everybody I know drinks and drinks a lot"—may be an overstatement, but not by as much as most adults believe. When it comes to substance use and abuse, midadolescents fall into one of two categories. The vast majority is comprised of students who drink and smoke almost exclusively in the context of a communal event, either a small group of friends or a party. The other category is made up of adolescents who use alcohol and/or drugs while alone or perhaps with one other person. This group is smaller, and those who fall into this category are often outcasts. This section, then, is devoted to the social partyer.

If one member of a cluster drinks, there are three possible scenarios for the rest of that cluster: all the members drink, that person is aberrant and the rest of the cluster refrains from alcohol use, or most members of the cluster drink but one or even a few do not.

All Members of the Cluster Drink
(and/or Smoke Marijuana)

One significant marker of a cluster is the rules and norms that hold that cluster together. The most common situation when one member of a cluster drinks alcohol is that the rest of the cluster also drinks at roughly the same rate.[3] This is true even if one or more members of the cluster did not drink when the cluster was being formed. The cluster made the decision, however (probably without much or any discussion), that being a partyer was a basic marker of the cluster. Because this value is an implied but nonetheless real commitment, the cluster follows this decree.[4]

Most Members Do Not Drink (and/or Smoke Marijuana), but Some Do

A cluster may be basically committed to refraining from alcohol, but it may have a lower commitment to that value than to the inclusion of the member who chooses to drink. When a member of a cluster seems to deviate from the rules or norms of the cluster, the cluster must decide what to do. It appears that most of the time this deviation was present when the cluster was formed, and therefore, members implicitly acknowledged that this behavior would not be seen as deviant. In this case, the cluster may seem to be committed to a corporate ethic that excludes drinking, but in reality, the decision whether to drink is left up to each member.

Most Members Drink (and/or Smoke Marijuana), but Some Do Not

When members of a cluster are actively involved in alcohol consumption, it is understandable to assume that the cluster has an ethic that supports it. Anyone who chooses to deviate from this expectation, as

> Everyone wants to fit in, so they do what everyone else does, such as drugs and drinking. People have to be extremely strong not to give in to these actions. I think a person's family influences actions in saying no. But drugs, they are extremely popular. They are everywhere. Drinking is also popular.
>
> high school student

the logic goes, would suffer from peer pressure to conform. But this is not necessarily the case.

As with the second scenario, the decision about whether to align with a person who does not hold to the norms of a developing cluster is made at that time. Things get tricky when a member, for whatever reason, decides to break from the established norms of the cluster. Over the course of the three to four years that midadolescents intimately confide in and rely on their friendship clusters, each member will face experiences that cause him or her to rethink a previously held value, to shift ethical commitments, or even to develop intimate friendships with people outside the cluster. At such times, the cluster and the member have to make a decision: do we allow the person to discard a previously agreed upon value and find a way to accommodate this change, or do we go through the pain and struggle of banishing the offender from the cluster?

I found that while some incoming freshmen tend to hold fast to the safe relationships they formed during early adolescence, most tend to branch out—subtly at first but often more boldly as the year goes on. As adolescents shift from a relatively nonreflective social reality in early adolescence to a more sophisticated social awareness in midadolescence, they make choices that create the safest and most satisfying arrangement for themselves, which causes them in some cases to distance themselves from even their closest long-term friends.

If a cluster is confronted with the need to renegotiate the rules and norms of the cluster, a significant dilemma can result not only for the cluster but for the individual members as well. The very notion of the cluster is that it is the safest possible community in the life of a midadolescent. This implies that, at least on the surface, the cluster is expected to flex with the changes of individual members. Cluster groups hold cohesion and unity as higher values—especially during the first year or two of forming—than the specific behavior of individual members. Exceptions to this would be those behaviors that are destructive to the cluster itself (such as a new relationship that violates many of the cluster values) or are a vast departure from the norms of the cluster (such as moving from drinking to hard drug use). It is rare, however, for a cluster to choose dismissal when confronted with a relatively minor shift.

My overall impression is that the rules concerning substance use (other than hard drugs) are not hard and fast and rarely jeopardize the integrity of the group. Almost across the board, clusters typically fall into an "It's okay if you use alcohol or marijuana and okay if you don't" arrangement. Accommodation is a small price to pay in comparison to throwing up for grabs the negotiated rules, ethics, and norms of a cluster.

The Partying Community

High school parties have been the stuff of legends for decades. They have been depicted in film, television, advertisements, and music ever since an adolescent subculture became part of the social landscape. I believe that the high school party is in many ways a uniquely North American phenomenon. Nearly all midadolescents want to party and are going to party, regardless of what parents say. It has been ingrained in the narrative of the population, and therefore it goes with the territory of being a midadolescent in this culture.

Unfortunately, the party scene is not really about parties at all. It is about drinking and, to a certain degree, drug use, sexual play and experimentation, and other risk behaviors (defined as behaviors that may cause harm to oneself or someone else).[5] Far too many students believe that it is simply impossible to have a good time at a party without alcohol, even if they do not drink themselves. Parents, schools, and communities have been trying for decades to reverse this perception but with few results. Perhaps adults have misunderstood the reason parties are so important to midadolescents and the factors that drive their desire to party.

During this study, it was tough to get students to move beyond sarcasm, humor, and even defensiveness whenever I would venture into these waters. I had a concern for the students and was (and am) a parent, so by and large I was not trusted by many students regarding this topic. But I was able to piece together a few preliminary thoughts.

First, as I sought to understand the desire to party, I realized that I needed to shift my focus from the alcohol (and the marijuana) to the communal experience itself. In listening to the stories surrounding the party world, I noticed that the stories had a common element: the experiences and antics of the players made the parties memorable, not the alcohol itself. Stories create a collective narrative of past experience that points to both a shared memory (which creates unity and binds people together in a common history) and the promise of a bright future, based on the narrative of the past. Parties are social gatherings that allow adolescents to participate in one of the most central and basic human experiences—community celebrations that remind people of their common past and guide them into the future. Parties are not about the party but about the longing for community.

Second, alcohol and marijuana are much like the symbols and sensory aids used for celebration and ritual in gatherings in other cultures (from candles and incense to peyote and reserve vintage wine). To put it another way, a party offers adolescent partygoers the deeply human elements of communal celebration and ritual as they attempt to discover what people they belong to—for everyone needs to connect to a story larger than his

Before this summer I was what people would call a party animal. I was the kind of girl who would go to parties and get smashed and look for guys to hook up with. My excuse was, "Oh, I was drunk. I didn't mean to do it, and I didn't know what I was doing." But truth be told, when you're drunk you have a sense of what you're doing, but you think stuff you normally wouldn't do is okay. When I started high school, I was thrown into the party crowd. This happened because my brother was a senior. I was immediately made out to be the cool new freshman who must party like her brother. Sad to say, I played that role for a long time, until God called my heart to be in a different place.

high school student

or her own. Regrettably, in our culture, the use (and almost always the abuse) of alcohol and marijuana as a central feature of parties creates an artificial celebration. Many times I heard the old saying, "The party begins when the beer shows up!" This statement refers to the beer not only as a sensory aid to combat inhibitions but also as a symbol of the ritual of adolescent celebration. As Beccaria and Sande have observed, "This ritual of drinking or getting drunk creates an experience of life, comradeship and equality amongst youth. Therefore, it resembles an act of initiation revealing the secrets of the adults' experience with drunkenness."[6] In other words, the party starts when the beer shows up, for those who drink and for those who do not. Certainly, alcohol (and to a certain extent marijuana) helps to enhance the collective stories of the adolescent community, and there seems to be an almost ingrained need for substances to create the desired experience.

This dynamic appears most obviously in the themed parties found on many college campuses, associated most often with fraternities and sororities but also a feature of many student clubs, associations, sports teams, and the like. High school students occasionally host themed parties, but it is the university setting that affords the most conducive conditions for unfettered behavior. These parties are painstakingly organized so that the décor, dress code, music, and beverage choices harmonize thematically, not simply for the purpose of uniformity, but because doing so turns a generic party into a unique environment that can be anticipated, experienced, and—most importantly—remembered collectively. It is no surprise that many of the organizations and clubs that offer multiple themed parties each school year utilize their social schedule as a recruiting tool. These annual social rituals, among other things, show what it looks like to be "part of us." A common phrase not particular to any university is especially telling: "Nights we won't remember, friends we won't forget." The power of shared party experiences to provide a sense of community overshadows any ethical taboo. As Jodi Dworkin writes, the "carefree attitude of experiencing college" means "you can get up at 8 in the morning and drink for a football game; you're not an alcoholic, you're a party animal. But if you do that in the real world, then you'll go to treatment."[7] Put succinctly, adolescent partying is rarely an end unto itself; far more often it is a means by which our abandoned young people attempt to satisfy their deep need for community, especially since the social lubricant of alcohol and marijuana, coupled with the prospect of sexual opportunity, provides at least a temporary salve to their loneliness.

Social Networking and Technology: The New Teen Hangout

Since precise firsthand data on partying is difficult to come by (as mentioned earlier), perhaps it would be helpful to supplement our discussion with research from an area much more easily quantified: teenagers' use of technology. First, we turn to text messaging. Unheard of until the last decade, the sending and receiving of text messages on mobile phones—some as long as 160 characters—has become the communication method *par excellence* for many adolescents. For instance, a 2009 *New York Times* article reported statistics from the Nielsen Company that revealed the average American teenage texter receives well over two thousand messages per month, with many sending hundreds (or even thousands) of messages every day.[8] Nationally, roughly one-quarter of all ninth graders send text messages on a daily basis; by the time they reach graduation age, the number has doubled.[9] It is not unheard of for an individual adolescent's monthly text quota to soar above ten thousand. It is not the thrill of typing with one's thumbs that keeps teenagers texting, but rather the chance to remain connected to one's peers at literally every waking hour—and sometimes in the middle of the night.[10]

Social networking websites are another vantage point from which to observe the adolescent drive for community. To the casual observer, the driving force behind adolescents' creation and maintenance of their webpage(s) might appear to adults to be an expression of adolescent narcissism, but as Sonia Livingstone explains, this is hardly the case.[11] The construction of a personalized online "identity" and the accumulation of "friends" within one's network are one and the same task. The disclosure, then, of personal information in cyberspace, while a significant risk, is the currency of intimacy among the adolescent, his or her cluster, and the greater adolescent world. For teenagers left starving for belonging by a fragmented adult culture that has abandoned them, the potential dangers of the internet are negligible compared to the perceived benefits.

A third significant area where teenagers utilize technology to meet their relational needs is the world of video games, or "gaming." In the first decade or so of video games, from "Pong" to the early Nintendo games, the activity was more than mere novelty; it was a way for those young people (and adults) who had been robbed of the opportunity to participate in communal sport or even casual play to experience the thrill of competition, even if the entity they "beat" didn't exist. When the internet began to add to that personal satisfaction by enabling collaboration with other players who were similarly entranced with the notion of nonactive competitive "sport," video games became a kind of social capital, giving players a system of shared information and experiences by which to define themselves both as individuals and as members of a larger community. The ever-increasing speed and accessibility of bandwidth, coupled with its ever-decreasing financial cost, has enabled people to network their gaming experiences with like-minded others in their towns, countries, and even across the world. The only things today's teenagers need to begin interfacing with others through their gaming system are a headset with a microphone and a networking cable.

Today the allure of gaming has shifted from providing a surrogate competitive sports opportunity to offering a more profound and contagious lure of intimate community and corporate purpose. Game-based communities did not form as a result of networking technology; rather, the technology merely provided a new, powerful avenue for gamers to expand their game-based social connections. For regular gamers, it is not about winning the game; it is about having a place in their gaming community. A 2009 study on networked games affirmed that gaming "is not an activity motivated by a wish to be alone, secluded in front of a computer screen," but rather by a desire for social belonging.[12] A common phenomenon in such games is the formation of permanent groups that schedule regular times for communal playing and, more importantly, positive social interaction. Another 2009 study confirmed that those who played a certain networked game derived significant social support from their community—support which increased over time—and therefore stood to improve in physical health and reduce negative psychological symptoms (e.g., depression, anxiety).[13] The following quote from a 2007 study sums it up well: "The virtual world that these games offer allows players to express themselves in ways they may not feel comfortable doing in real life because of their appearance, gender, sexuality, age, or other factors. They also offer a place where teamwork, encouragement, and fun can be experienced."[14]

In short, video games are, for many adolescents, a chance to experience a "win," both personally through their gaming efforts and interpersonally through their interactions with the gaming community. For the teenagers struggling under the weight of abandonment by the systems and communities meant to nurture them, the chance for a "win" is not merely a relief—it is a dream come true.

Conclusion and Musings

Adolescents are hungry for a transcendent experience that provides meaning, hope, adventure, and carefree celebration—whether they seek it through partying, social networking, or video games. We as adults, in our collective abandonment of this generation, have taught them all too well that there is no celebration unless we can falsely create one by altering the state of our lives and even our relationships. We as adults do not know how to celebrate life and relationships. We have created a vacuum in the psyches of our young that they must find a way to fill.

This chapter may sound disturbing to some, especially to those who have a bias against the idea of the teenage party. Once we realize that parties are one of the few avenues adolescents have to find a sense of community, ritual, and celebration, however, we may have a greater understanding and compassion for this potentially negative event. Parents and other adults who desire to protect and nurture midadolescents would do well to approach the issue of parties with respect for the communal experience. The best way to cause a midadolescent to dive underground is to uncaringly disparage what is in many cases an important community ritual.

I spent a great deal of energy attempting to understand teenage alcohol use. The party ethic of the high school world, coupled with the centrality of alcohol as a staple of the experience, is commonplace, and yet that has (apparently) been true for several decades. Is partying really any different today from what it was in the 1960s or the early 1980s? Why has *Animal House* retained its popularity with the adolescent community after all these years? Why do kids want so desperately to party, and what drives them to see alcohol as the core of the experience?

I am not satisfied with what I discovered. I was simply not invited into this arena of their lives. Few midadolescents are extremely reflective, especially if it may lead to self-discovery or to questions that may make them uncomfortable. Students simply do not want to consider the underlying forces that make partying attractive, powerful, and therefore normative.

So the only conclusion I came to is that for the vast majority of adolescents, drinking is not about drinking; it is about community. What I observed was that almost every midadolescent either loves to party or affirms the ritual of the party and therefore wants to be involved, even if he or she does not drink.

One of the major aspects of adolescent development is the longing for a place to belong. There is ample evidence across centuries and cultures that children become adults via a system of rituals that celebrates the society they are entering. Because we have abandoned our young, we have effectively taken from them a formalized expression of communal celebration and left them to their own devices to celebrate the life they have. Why is alcohol involved? All one has to do is glance at popular media, marketing strategies, and even adult behaviors to see why adolescents believe alcohol is necessary to experience community. We have taught our young that they need a mind-numbing substance to find the courage to relate to one another, and we have created a structure in which we advertise their need for it and provide access to it.

The popular sitcoms *Cheers* and *Friends* tapped into our longing for community. Even the *Cheers* theme song highlighted the loss of community: "You want to go where everybody knows your name." Midadolescents cannot yet explain their passion for parties or their love for alcohol, but their behavior, humor, and even social structure scream loudly that they cannot survive without a safe, welcoming place and a ritual. Unfortunately, that ritual requires alcohol.

12

kids at the margins

Shawn shouted across the room just as I was leaving for the lunch area, "Will you eat with me? No one eats with me!"

Since I had been his substitute teacher three times, I knew Shawn fairly well. He was a small guy, even for a freshman, and he could barely walk. It was true that Shawn rarely ate with anyone, and it appeared that he didn't have any, or at least very many, friends. He was part of a "special ed" class, and I didn't know quite where to discuss him in this book. While this encounter with Shawn haunted me for some time, in the first edition of *Hurt* I didn't mention it because I could not find a way to make it fit the macro design of the book. So I left out the story of this tender, lonely, wandering kid. In life, and in the book, he didn't fit. Shawn could be described as a kid at the margins.

During the follow-up study to the first edition of this book, I met Terry, a thin, darting young man whose only words to me were, "I hate school!" Terry clearly loved to laugh, mostly at others, and yet he could turn a smile into a mask of disdain on a dime. After a very brief introduction and conversation, it was clear that Terry didn't want to talk to me. I was at his school with one of my graduate students who spent most of his time in and around this particular neighborhood. Terry's school is among the poorest in one of the most impoverished parts of Los Angeles, and I had come to gather at least a bit of insight into the unique issues the kids of this neighborhood deal with, in contrast to the issues of the kids I included as part of the "macro" majority of American teenagers. My

> I am learning in English about this guy named Thoreau who said
> to march to my own drummer. Man, I really think that is right. Who
> cares what anybody else thinks! I'm gonna march to my own drum-
> mer regardless of what anyone else thinks!
>
> note from a freshman

grad student and I moved on from group to group, occasionally finding someone who would agree to chat, even briefly, but mostly just being visible and present. But the one person I remember most from that day is Terry. Something about his eyes told me how far apart we were. If I had met Terry before I had first written *Hurt*, he, like Shawn, probably wouldn't have made the final edit. He was too far out at the margins.

Sara was as close to the perfect teenager as any I had met. She was attractive in a cute, wholesome way, and she had the grace and demeanor of a dancer, the movements of a gymnast, and the poise of a choirgirl. Sara was committed—a committed student, a committed athlete, a committed child, and a committed churchgoer. But as we interacted when we first met, and as I observed her in a focus group I later facilitated at an elite private school, I began to notice that there was a difference between Sara and other teens I had encountered throughout the study. On the one hand, she seemed to be more genuine than most young people I had encountered. Yet at the same time she seemed younger than her age and her classmates, perhaps by as much as a year. I can only describe her as naively optimistic and developmentally sheltered. The more our team observed Sara and her peers, the more we noticed that they all seemed significantly younger and less emotionally aware than their peers from public schools. As of the first edition of *Hurt*, I hadn't yet encountered this disparity between the more mainstream teenagers and those, like Sara, who had extremely invested parents and tightly controlled school and social environments. Even if I had, I am not sure what I would have said about Sara and her friends. From the outside they appeared to be the elite among their age-group—and they clearly knew how to play the part well—but they belonged in a different category.

Sara, Terry, and Shawn: three teenagers who in many ways are equally part of the adolescent community that has been affected by systemic abandonment, and who are living, like their peers across the board, out of a sense of isolation and the need to perform. Yet they are all what I now call "kids at the margins," a designation that describes those young people who, though still in the same macro world as their peers, in some ways fall well outside of the sociological mainstream. This book attempts to provide a comprehensive description of a diverse population of midadolescents, but there is no question that many young people exhibit behaviors, values, and attitudes that do not cleanly fit such broad characterizations. Yet to get a sense of where teenagers are today, to really get inside their world, we must examine those at both ends of the sociological and developmental spectrum—what I call "the margins"—using the results of my ethnographic study and research triangulation to better understand in what ways their experience may be more difficult than for the mainstream young teen.

At the outset, it is important to note that while much of contemporary scholarship views adolescents as basically healthy, there are emerging voices who believe that the teenage life is not quite the free adventure many adults assume. Among those who study adolescents there is an increasingly pervasive perspective that growing up today is harder and more treacherous than in generations past.[1] As Osgood, Foster, and Courtney put it, "Moving into adulthood involves a long and often difficult transition in the United States and other industrialized nations in the West."[2] In both editions of *Hurt* I have attempted to make the case that, at least at some level, all midadolescents experience life as painful and precarious; they grow up feeling more isolated than previous generations and are therefore more stressed and lonely than adolescent populations in the past. I have observed and studied kids at the margins—both those who have less opportunity and resources than the average young person and those who seem to have everything—and I have wrestled with the literature regarding both extremes, but it is not an easy task to describe how these teenagers experience life in comparison to their peers. To simply say that both groups of young people struggle as they grow up would be insulting to those who have had few resources in navigating the transition to adulthood; the issues they face, like racism, poverty, and the like, certainly disadvantage them in ways their more fortunate peers will never understand. Yet at the same time there is ample evidence that—as Madeline Levine puts it in the title of her outstanding book *The Price of Privilege*—there is a high cost to what she calls privilege, especially in contemporary society. So instead of attempting to offer comparisons of who has it worse, in this chapter I will focus on describing what I have observed in light of the latest research that illuminates how kids at the margins experience life in different ways from their more, for lack of a better term, mainstream peers.

For every teenager, regardless of life circumstance, the three basic issues of the adolescent journey are *identity*, *autonomy*, and *belonging*. Those who fall outside the mainstream of the social or developmental spectrum are just as concerned with and consumed by the need to discover who they are as those who might be considered more typical. This chapter seeks to challenge cultural myths and stereotypes that keep us from recognizing what is going on with those at the margins. Although it may not seem that privileged teens would wrestle with the issue of autonomy in the same way as their peers, research indicates, for example, that they actually have a more difficult time recognizing and living out of a strong sense of self with the internal belief that they matter as a unique person. Even kids of privilege carry within them a longing to love and be loved, to find themselves embedded in a community where who they are is celebrated, needed, and desired. Cultural perceptions about kids at both ends of the developmental and social spectrum abound, but like all adolescents they also must seek identity, autonomy, and belonging. Yet kids who are particularly advantaged or disadvantaged are uniquely shaped by the circumstances that have placed them on the fringes of the mainstream. Thus this chapter will look at the distinctives of both the vulnerable and the privileged as they attempt to navigate these three tasks of adolescence.

The Vulnerable and the Privileged

The midadolescent population "at the margins," as I conceptualize it, includes those on the one extreme who, relative to their peers, have *fewer* opportunities and resources (and generally more roadblocks) to achieve healthy individuation and those on the other extreme who have *more* opportunities and resources. The former, whom I refer to as *vulnerable*, include those who grow up under extreme systemic or societal oppression or who have been beaten down by the impersonal vagaries of life circumstance. This group includes young people who face severe poverty, are homeless, or are where they are due to class and/or racial oppression. According to scholarly studies on vulnerable adolescents, especially those who are from poor urban communities, the majority are of color,[3] are more likely to be male,[4] are more prone to mental illness and depression,[5] and are far more likely to be involved in substance abuse.[6] There are of course exceptions to these generalities, but these are the broad categorizations applied to more at-risk adolescents.

Difficult life circumstances can also nudge children and adolescents toward the vulnerable category. Regardless of the events leading to the circumstances, this marginalized group consists of the disabled, the socially illiterate,[7] those who self-describe as GLBT (gay, lesbian, bisexual, or transgender), and those who fall into a distinct separatist subculture, for whatever reason, like highly religious students. While many teenagers who might self-identify with one (or more) of these categorizations are not actually outside of their peer-group structures and therefore should not be viewed as "kids at the margins," in my observation these are the two broad categories that describe the vulnerable.

At the other end of the continuum are those who have been commonly referred to as *privileged*. This term describes those teens that have a great deal more social capital, environmental resources, and relational and vocational opportunities than the average population. While not all private school students should be considered privileged, many privileged youth do attend private schools, especially elite private schools, and they are typically wealthy, have parents who are accomplished and deeply invested, and have been raised under the banner of possessing, for a variety of reasons, "exceptional" potential. They can be described as "special," often due to their pedigree or their parents' achievements, social status, fame, or power.[8] Privileged kids are taught at a very young age that they innately possess a special status among the world in general and their peers in particular, and they are programmed to live accordingly.

Identity

While there is debate over the precise definition of and process related to the term *identity*, most people recognize it as the way we see and define ourselves as "me." Scholars generally agree that identity can be described as having a well-formed "sense of self." Madeline Levine explains the need for the development of the self as an adolescent grows up: "The reason that a well-developed sense of self is so critical is that, in the desirable and inevitable absence of external support, a sense of self provides both a comfortable home base and an internal compass for navigating through life. Lives are never perfect—not our own, not our children's—but a healthy sense of self helps insure that life will be interesting, satisfying, and manageable."[9]

It is difficult to engage in adult society without at least a relatively grounded sense of the self as distinct from others. The development of identity is a much-debated topic in developmental literature, but there is little doubt it involves an internal quest to embrace one's unique sense of self while interfacing with a socially mediated and communally affirmed portrayal of who one is. As David Moshman put it, "Our efforts to construct an identity are constrained not only by external social factors but by a need to be true to ourselves . . . the actual construction of identity may sometimes partake more of creation, and sometimes more of discovery, but in general, it involves elements of both."[10] For an adolescent moving toward healthy interdependent adulthood it is vitally important to have help navigating this treacherous developmental terrain of discovery and integration. The question before us, then, is how do kids at the margins discover and create a unique sense of self that they can carry into the rest of their lives?

Identity Discovery for Vulnerable Kids

Every culture desires its children to grow up into healthy, productive, and contributing adults. In order for a child to become such an adult, however, it is essential that adults are present, available, and committed to providing the environment where each child can discover and live out of his or her unique sense of self. To take this obvious assertion one step further, every child deserves the opportunity to have the chance to grow up in such a way as to realize his or her distinctiveness as a member of society. This is a much more difficult task for vulnerable kids than for those growing up in the mainstream.

Part of the community's role in identity formation and self-discovery is to name, or label, what that community—whether parents, neighbors, coaches, teachers, or other adults—sees as the emerging self of the child. This naming has great power—power that can be either productive in affirming a child's growing sense of self or destructive in negatively determining his or her identity. Depending on the source and relationship of the messenger, negative labeling has great power to become a curse that a child must overcome in order to move into healthy adulthood. When a vulnerable child, for example, is labeled a failure (by being either explicitly told or implicitly treated as such), that child will learn to live into the label that the community confers. When such labels are harmful, damaging, or demeaning, because they come from those with the power of authority and the weight of the community, children often embrace this tag as the definition of who they are. As Vasudevan and Campano note, "The proliferation of labeling in American schools has garnered ample critique (e.g., Hudak and Kihn, 2001), particularly in light of increased high-stakes testing and an era of accountability as measurement (Darling-Hammond, 2006). Labels and classifications, by themselves, may not be harmful. . . . However, when labels create an exclusive norm for human behavior and reinforce an ideology of (in) ability, there invariably will be hierarchy."[11]

Take the impact of violence on identity, for example, which is a present reality for many vulnerable kids. Children who grow up in homes or communities that normalize violence have a greater chance of seeing themselves as violent, and thereby not only will be prone to perpetuate a lifestyle of violence, but also will view themselves as violent persons, a defining label.[12] It has been shown that for certain vulnerable children, high-risk behaviors provide a sense of security and stability as they attempt to find their own sense of self within a high-risk population. In one study, adolescents reported that they were able to achieve a "mature status in the eyes of their caregivers through antisocial behaviors such as criminal activity, sexual promiscuity, drug use and other forms of delinquency and risk-taking behaviors."[13] For homeless teenagers, a population about whom we know very little but that is estimated to number at least 1.7 million, the most common trigger leading to homelessness is household violence.[14] For most of the teens in the vulnerable category, the violence they see and experience creates an environment that stifles, if not directly shapes, their identity. Thus not only do they not have the same opportunities to discover their own unique sense of self or to explore the various options of their mainstream peers; it is also likely that vulnerable youth will be dragged down into perpetuating a lifestyle of violence.

The issues related to vulnerable youth have been well documented in academic literature, and occasionally have made their way into our national discourse, mostly through political posturing. But the actual plight and environment of vulnerable kids is rarely engaged by the general populace, especially with any credible data driving the discussion. When an acquaintance found out I had spent time with some members of the Los Angeles gang reduction staff and visited some of their sites, he flippantly remarked, "They just need to get with the program, and improve their lives. Nobody ever helped me out when I was growing up." This type of attitude is common today, especially among those who have never had to endure the realities that vulnerable kids face every day—from violence and drugs to systemic economic and racial oppression. What I observed at an urban public school versus at an elite religious private school, for example, made it impossible not to notice the differences in how our society cares about our young—discrediting the myth that in the United States we all have the same opportunity.

As we grow up our identity is shaped by the interaction between those voices and messages we receive and our internal conception of ourselves. Vulnerable kids often receive negative or destructive messages, which sets the course for their identity development. A resounding default perspective toward vulnerable young people is that it is their fault that they have a hard time finding their way out of economic, educational, and societal circumstances that hold them back. So we as a culture often ignore the needs of our most vulnerable and implicitly join in the chorus of those negative influencers. It is no wonder we are a divided nation; we simply do not offer everyone a level playing field, and then we try to rationalize the inequities in order to make ourselves feel less

I Wish . . .

I wish I could tell secrets
To someone who would listen,
To someone who wouldn't tell.

I wish I could meet that special someone,
Someone who loves me,
Someone who cares for me.

I wish I could talk to someone,
Someone who would understand,
Someone who wouldn't laugh.

I wish I had a best friend,
Someone I can trust,
Someone I can tell secrets to.

Someone who understands me,
Someone who will grow with me,
Someone I can talk to.

high school student

responsible. Vulnerable kids are told that they will never amount to anything, that they are not as smart, or as talented, or as gifted as those of privilege, and the cycle rolls on. Our children are the losers, and therefore so are we all.

Identity Discovery for Privileged Kids

While identity discovery is not an easy task for most adolescents—especially given the profusion of disparate messages bombarding them throughout their young lives—most kids have the opportunity to explore the interaction of external messages and internal sense of self. For privileged kids, however, this dance becomes even more complicated as their environment becomes more controlled and manipulated. They know that they are constantly being watched, evaluated, and judged. They learn from a very young age that their life is and will always be measured by externals, especially how they look, adapt, and perform.

Just as labeling can reinforce a negative perception of one's sense of self, it can also undercut the healthy development of the self. There is no doubt that on average privileged kids are able to perform at a higher level than their peers. In discussing the impact of labeling on vulnerable kids, Vasudevan and Campano assert that labeling at either extreme invariably results in a hierarchy for all young people.[15] The privileged, then, grow up believing that they are better than, smarter than, and more capable across the board than their peers. The educational culture we have allowed to control the defining of our young has used labels to separate them by employing phrases like "gifted and talented." As a result, privileged kids are conditioned to believe that they have an external standard and expectation they are destined to attain, while vulnerable teens are conditioned to expect that they have no chance in life because they are not gifted and talented, according to the prescribed definition.[16]

For the purposes of this discussion the concern is not whether some young people are more academically and environmentally "wired" for a rigorous degree of educational opportunity. The issue for privileged teens is the worldview that defines individuals according to their "potential," which goes well beyond academics and spills into sports, music, dance, commerce, and just about any other human activity. For privileged kids, there is simply the expectation that they are somehow a cut above others. This creates, then, an implicit—and at times explicit—label that they must carry and address as they seek to discover who they are.

As discussed in chapter 9, today's kids are under more stress than any previous generation. Privileged young people, however, because they are trained to see themselves as the elite, are under far greater pressure to live up to external expectations and agendas than the rest of the adolescent population. While most adults tend to view adolescents as spoiled or at least unfiltered and unfettered consumers who do not seem to have a care in the world other than themselves, another reality is buried beneath the surface of today's teenagers. They are attempting to discover who they are in a world that defines them by externals. In our research with privileged kids our team observed in every focus group and saw affirmed across a wide range of academic literature that growing up today with the requirement to represent oneself with strength and prowess adds yet another layer to what adolescents must bear. With privileged adolescents, this additional coating of entitlement and power adds a complex dimension to an already difficult life. Because privileged youth are trained to see themselves as superior to others, they carry the added burden of having to avoid showing any weakness or even struggle, sometimes even hiding the truth of human vulnerability from themselves.

For privileged young people, especially for those who are temperamentally or environmentally well suited for maintaining an air of causal power and capability, the effort it takes to perpetuate the myth of superiority overshadows and can even stifle the natural developmental process of identity formation and discovery. It is as if the "me" they need to become is pushed aside for the "me" they need to externally produce and display. Thus, as Madeline Levine notes, "When we coerce, intrude on, or take over for our children unnecessarily we may be 'spoiling' them, but the far more significant consequence is that we are interfering with their ability to construct a sense of self."[17] The effect of how children of privilege are raised and led by adult systems, and especially by their parents, is that their chief developmental task during adolescence is often ignored and even diverted while they are reminded that the greatest goal in life is the development of the externals that define them.

Again, Levine asks, "Why are children of privilege, in record numbers, having an extraordinarily difficult time completing the most fundamental task of adolescence—the development of autonomy and a healthy sense of self?"[18] Drawing on a wide array of studies and research perspectives, Levine analyzes and critiques pressure and performance, isolation (in this case directly related to individualism) to materialism, "the emphasis on things over people and character."[19] Performance is the rubric by which worth is measured and identity defined. Isolation, as a consequence of the ethic of "rugged individualism" (a hallmark characteristic of privilege), is clearly a universal plague among all mid-adolescents, and with privileged teenagers it is a carefully guarded but nonetheless visible companion. Materialism is a product of the pressure to perform, and is therefore "both a cause and a symptom of impaired self-development."[20]

The notion of materialism, which is clearly not limited to the privileged, is nonetheless one of the major influences that Levine and others identify that hinder healthy identity development. Curtis Miller, in summarizing literature on the effects of materialism among privileged teens, defines it in this way: "Materialism means the emphasis on things over people and character, and is rampant in affluent communities. Materialism directly attacks a child's ability to develop a secure sense of self because it means defining oneself *entirely* through outside markers of status. In other words, you are not defined by your character but by the things you have and by other people's perception of you. There is no internal self-development since all energy is being used to cultivate external perceptions."[21]

Thus many privileged adolescents have a much more difficult time doing the hard work required to achieve a healthy sense of self. As we have noted throughout this book, it is not easy for anyone. But for those who live under the labeling, expectations, and agendas of others (especially adults who define adolescents by pedigree, extraordinary talent, or circumstance), it can be even more difficult. For young people who are taught that isolation is the acceptable cost of the privilege and power, and who have been handed a world where materialism teaches that control, power, and desire are more valuable than people and relationships, the cost becomes growing up without a core sense of self.

Autonomy

The second primary task of adolescence, autonomy, has been largely understood in terms of its external expressions, like responsibility and making wise choices. Yet the development of an inner capacity for making the kinds of choices, and thereby assuming the level of responsibility, that is expected of an adult is much more an internal process of growth, awareness, and "owning" one's choices. In other words, what most adults—parents, teachers, coaches, counselors—are most concerned with is not that young people are developing the internal capability to wrestle through various competing issues and expectations in order to learn how to choose the right course of action for their life, but rather that they would make the kinds of choices and assume the level of responsibility that would serve the interests of the adult. Therefore we readily judge our young not by the trajectory of learning and growing they are on, but rather by how they are fitting inside the predetermined box we have expected them to live in. This trained compliance, however, is not the developmental task of healthy autonomy; it is learning how to adapt to the agendas of others. And these are very different things.

Autonomy can best be described as the ability to make a difference, to choose a life path, and to operate as an agent in the service of society. The key word, then, at the heart of autonomy is *power*. As Scot D. Evans notes, "power comes from developing capacity, experiencing voice and resonance, and having opportunities to play meaningful roles in the context of caring adult support and challenge."[22] For many adults the word *power* itself, when it comes to working with and guiding adolescents, conjures up a wide variety of potentially negative outcomes, even when it is couched in terms of developing "capacity" and "voice." For when a developing young person explores her own sense of self, and agency and voice, by that very act she becomes a threat to someone else's agenda, unless of course that agenda is to best serve the needs of the emerging adult. This is perhaps the most prominent and defining issue for adults as we seek to raise, lead, and guide young people: above all, each adolescent needs the chance to discover who he or she is as a person who matters and who has a significant role to play in society. As they explore and express their power, however, adolescents will inevitably bump into the power sphere of the adults in charge. Thus when an adult is in a relationship with a young person for any reason other than for their developmental health and well-being, the adolescent will eventually find himself in a situation where he hits the wall of adult control. This is the gauntlet that is thrown down any time an adolescent pushes against an authority or power agenda while under the domain of the adult in charge. Even if the adult believes that he or she is exerting authority and control in the best interests of the adolescent, it can actually end up being received as one more expression of abandonment. The mere presence of an adult with an agenda keeps kids from growing up believing that their voice and agency matters. An adolescent cannot become an adult without the opportunity to find her unique power and place, but adults are rarely willing to sacrifice their own power and place in order to allow that to happen.

The development of autonomy, then, is a necessary step in growing up, and for every adolescent it is a precarious journey. For kids at the margins, this is an even more difficult and elusive process. As a result of my work with young people from both extremes, I believe Evans has it right when he says that "research also suggests that adults need to find a way to help teenagers find their voice and influence in community settings. There is much recent evidence to suggest that this is happening in community organizations, and some school and city contexts. Unfortunately, many of these examples fall short of providing youth genuine influence and power. Many of these opportunities are simply token gestures that give teenagers the perception of influence without really sharing any power at all."[23]

All adults, not just parents, bear the responsibility to ensure that children are given the chance to explore who they are and what gifts they bring to society. Very few kids at the margins have relationships with adults who understand this as their role, much less with adults who are willing to adjust their own expectations and put their own needs aside to make it happen. Certainly parents hold the greatest influence and have the greatest opportunity of anyone to help their children discover their voice and power. Another influential group of adults, one that has almost as much potential to make an impact on adolescents as parents, is comprised of those who are committed to deeply investing in helping a child or teenager discover what power they have. In addition to parents, those adults who are closest to children and adolescents, like mentors, coaches, teachers, youth leaders, and so on, can provide a supportive environment in which an adolescent can recognize that her voice and her gifts matter, and that she is a powerful agent in the world. Adults can help youth to build a sense of power and autonomy in various ways, from boosting measurable aspects of autonomy, like confidence, to inspiring the kind of future adolescents will explore as they get older.[24]

In the following discussion of autonomy for kids at the margins I have chosen to spend a great deal more time and space describing this issue for privileged kids than for vulnerable kids. Adolescents on both extremes face adversity in finding their own voice and living out of that unique calling, but the issues for these two groups are very different. I have done my best to highlight some of the salient issues facing vulnerable youth as they attempt to find their own sense of power and autonomy, and I firmly agree with those who advocate that a hard, honest look needs to be taken at vulnerable kids and communities, but for the most part I will offer my own perspective and leave deeper discussion of these issues to other scholars and forums. What hinders privileged kids' ability to discover and explore their growing sense of power and voice is less clear, and in fact is something disputed by many adults (especially those who are charged with direct responsibility for nurturing them). Because the plight of privileged kids as they seek autonomy has not found its way into the cultural conversation, I have therefore given a bit more focus to this side of the spectrum.[25]

Autonomy Opportunities for Vulnerable Kids

There are multiple factors at work in denying vulnerable kids the opportunity to grow into healthy, productive adulthood. This is true as they seek to discover and live out of a sense of self (identity), and it is even more true as they strive to explore their own power and voice (autonomy). To many vulnerable kids, the greatest obstacles they face result from the overwhelming systemic forces that deny power not only to them but to their entire community. The oft-repeated cultural mantras that anyone can make it and that one only needs to work hard and good things will happen mean something very different to the vulnerable than they do to other teens. In a provocative and powerful article studying the perspectives of "female inner city youth," Ruta Valaitis reported how adolescent girls felt about their community's lack of commitment to the development of their autonomy: "In summary, youth's abstract ideals of community and their experiences with community were incongruent. These negative experiences coloured their perceptions about their position and power to influence their community. . . . Under the major theme of 'threats to empowerment,' there are three subthemes: 'grown-ups run everything,' 'we're just kids,' and 'they don't trust us.' . . . Youth's feelings of being 'put down' by adults help to further explain their perception of having low control."[26]

These perceptions mirror what mainstream adolescents report, especially in relationship to their sense of powerlessness and the lack of adult support they receive as they attempt to develop their own voice.

Yet vulnerable kids, especially in depressed urban contexts where even the adults in the community feel disempowered and pushed aside, face even greater developmental challenges. In communities where oppression and depression have been a constant reality for decades, there is little capacity available for helping children and adolescents believe that they can rise above the only life they have known. When the adults in a child's life model a general malaise of hopelessness and resignation, the child grows up believing that is his lot as well. Without meaning to discourage or hinder the future for their kids, such communities nonetheless reinforce and even participate in a repeating cycle of systemic disempowerment. This makes the development of autonomy, power, and voice an elusive if not unreachable dream, in spite of the fact that it is a core task in human development.

For vulnerable kids who may have access to relatively supportive adult relationships but still find themselves at the margins—like those with even slight disabilities or those who may have relatively low emotional or social intelligence—it can be equally difficult to develop a healthy sense of internal autonomy. Because society at large and their peer community consistently perpetuate the message that these young people are "less than" others and therefore do not possess the power or ability to function as viable agents,[27] these marginalized teens also find it extremely difficult to develop a healthy sense of internal autonomy. Even when there is an occasional encouraging voice, an assigned "mentor," or some other random source of support, the forces arrayed against them are potent. There is simply no doubt that vulnerable kids of all circumstances face a much harder road toward healthy autonomy than their mainstream peers.[28]

Autonomy Opportunities for Privileged Kids

Few adults would suspect that privileged kids have any struggle at all with the development of autonomy, especially when terms like *power* are used to define the task. Most are convinced that the more resources one has, the more able one is to handle anything that comes along. There is actually a growing body of evidence with an accompanying groundswell of support that would seem to indicate exactly this: kids with the most support, belief in themselves, and even academic achievement have a much greater ability not only to survive difficulties and obstacles, but even to thrive. In surveying this literature, youth service worker Maria Drews summarizes:

> A few essential elements are necessary to develop and protect that natural resilience we all possess. Studies show that good intellectual functioning

(including IQ, problem solving, and information-processing), competent and effective parenting (including monitoring, boundaries, and support), and the ability to regulate emotion and behavior are all essential parts of developing natural resiliency. If these systems are compromised, a kid's natural resilience will be hindered, and the chance of poor outcomes in the face of adversity will be much higher. On the other hand, if a kid has adults who care for them, normal cognitive development, and the ability to manage their attention, emotions, and behavior, they are more likely to develop a strong natural resilience to adversity.[29]

When examining the existing literature through the lens of thriving, sometimes also called "positive psychology,"[30] it is evident that there are distinctives that enable some to flourish and leave others to flounder, especially in the face of difficulty. Adolescents who, as Drew asserts, have "adults who care for them, normal cognitive development, and the ability to manage their attention, emotions, and behavior," or, perhaps better to say, who *know* and *believe* they have such a rich environmental pool to draw upon, there is a greater likelihood that their transition into adulthood will be smoother and healthier than it would be for someone who does not. Instead of finding what is wrong with youth, then, "positive youth development" as a theory prefers to focus on what is going right. According to the U.S. Department of Health and Human Services, "the Positive Youth Development approach understands that all young people need support, guidance, and opportunities during adolescence. It also looks toward creating supportive communities for all young people and at the same time, engaging youth to contribute to the well-being of the larger community."[31] According to advocates of this theoretical framework, positive youth development also emphasizes that youth are producers of their own growth, counting heavily on the idea that there is an innate and accessible "human capacity for motivation that drives development."[32]

That said, throughout this book we have demonstrated that, at least for a brief season during midadolescence, roughly fourteen to twenty years of age, very few report *feeling* like they have such a robust support system, either externally or internally. This is true across the board for this age group. In our studies with a wide variety of kids, the "human capacity for motivation" during midadolescence was in practice latent at best. For some kids (and in my observation this was a very small percentage of the midadolescent population) their developmental progress included an occasional and context-specific rhetorical nod to a forward-thinking motivation. Yet even for most such kids, and certainly for everyone else, an internal drive toward growing up was hardly on the observable radar. More pressing was surviving the myriad agendas and expectations their world was throwing at them while trying to make sense of the competing interests, needs, and longings that they were seeking to fulfill. For vulnerable kids this may be obvious, but this is also an expressed reality for privileged adolescents.

It clearly is important to focus on the positive where it is appropriate and to do all we can to help our children "thrive" by providing for them what they need to become successful, productive, even resilient, adults. But, and this is true even for the privileged, before we jump too quickly into what is good out there and identify whom we may perceive as thriving, it may be important to first look carefully at what is really going on with today's teenagers—all of today's teenagers. We need to investigate what lies beneath the surface and see how our adolescents are actually experiencing the environment they've been handed by us as a society. Acting and responding to circumstances with a positive outlook and commitment is important, yet before we respond we must have a clear picture of whom and what we are dealing with. In so doing, by recognizing and cataloging systemic abandonment and its effects, the eventual outcome for those who care about kids may be an even more robust theoretical understanding that could lead to a more effective strategic response so that more kids, families, and communities are well served.

Studies done by prominent psychologist Suniya S. Luthar, for example, reveal how far off from reality our perceptions of privileged kids are.[33] While most adults believe that kids who have greater resources and opportunities than their peers are generally happier and more satisfied with life, recent studies (and media headlines) overwhelmingly challenge that myth. Luthar and Latendresse found that teenagers in affluent communities have significantly higher rates of depression, eating disorders, substance abuse and addiction, anxiety disorders, cutting, and other self-destructive behaviors than all other groups of teenagers.[34] In addition, for several markers of mental health and development, affluent kids are worse off than even "high-risk" (or vulnerable) adolescents in urban centers. According to adolescent psychology expert Madeline Levine, the root of these problems is that affluent teens display a disturbing lack of independence and are therefore quite fragile in the face of relatively minor adversity. This lack of independence and fragility in the face of adversity can ultimately lead to the need for self-medicating and self-destructive behaviors.[35]

Research indicates that "competent and effective parenting" is an essential component of the landscape necessary for healthy development of autonomy and resilience, and yet for many privileged kids parents may end up providing exactly the opposite of what they need to thrive. There is current evidence that as privileged adolescents move into emerging adulthood their experience and perception of the kind of parenting they receive has a strong correlation with their ability to develop a healthy sense of internal power and autonomy, especially during times of crisis and stress. For parents who are able to convince their children over time to *perceive* that they are and have been "competent and effective" in their parenting skills ("monitoring, boundaries, and support," and the key word is *perceive*, because the predictors are tied to an adolescent's perception of the parental role, not his or her parents'), children will tend to ultimately create narratives of their histories and lives that demonstrate a growing sense of competency and resilience. Yet when children *perceive* their parents as controlling or as having an alternate agenda that is not for the ultimate good of the child, or when parents simply are not present, a child's historical narrative will tend to express dissatisfaction and struggle.[36] Parents know that to be perceived by their children as committed and supportive requires a finely tuned and mysterious dance, and that finding a healthy balance between "monitoring" and "support" is much easier said than done. As Michael Ungar found, "teens in this study demonstrate that they want a parent to remain involved in their lives, but not to dominate the child's own choices regarding how he or she nurtures health."[37]

Privileged kids, on average, have highly involved parents who generally take a proactive role in their children's lives. While most consider this to be their role as "good" parents, their involvement can easily become overly controlling. Having controlling parents, when coupled with the stressors of performance and maintaining a suitable image that privileged kids carry, provides a recipe for deep struggle and anxiety. The indicators of this struggle may not show up for years, because privileged kids are only given two choices when growing up under this level of scrutiny: comply and adapt, or rebel and face the consequences.

This has given rise to "helicopter parents," who hover over their children and control them almost to the point of living their lives for them. One example of this is the rise of parents writing college essays, a practice that parents usually defend by saying that their kids are "too busy" or "would do it well but can't focus right now." This line of logic and style of parenting is prominent in privileged households, and in our research this moral reasoning has been tilled into the soil of the children of these households. So not only are the children of helicopter parents ill prepared for living from the center as they enter the world post–high school; they are also taught that moral rules, like honesty and integrity, do not apply to them if it means getting something or somewhere they want.[38] Similarly, in the last few years we have also witnessed a new type of parenting style related to an adolescent's developmental journey: the "stealth bomber parent," who is committed to swooping in and "fixing" a problem or controlling an environment, yet does not have the nurturing commitment to remain and "hover" like the helicopter parent. This parenting style does damage to all parties, yet is becoming an increasing problem among privileged families and communities.[39]

There is ample evidence that privileged teens are far better at adapting to the expectations around them, as they have been trained and conditioned to do just that their entire lives. But the cost of such a commitment to adaptation—adaptation to the agendas, expectations, and sometimes even whims of those adults in control, including teachers and coaches as well as parents—actually stifles their ability to develop the internal sense of personal agency they will need as a healthy adult. For a privileged kid, to succeed is to capably adapt to the goals of the system handed to them, whether in sports, in a class, in playing an instrument, or in how one presents oneself on the outside. There is little room for adolescents to learn how to examine a situation or issue from a variety of angles and to experiment with choices and decisions, for the cost of failure in the system of the elite is often viewed as too steep for even the young to bear.

In my work with privileged kids, I found that they were unaware of their inability to think critically on their own and generally naïve regarding the need for critical thinking and decision making. If ever a population has been trained to live inside the box set before them, it is the subculture of privileged kids. Yet when they go to college, get jobs, get married, and attempt to move into adult life with a well-developed and healthy sense of how to navigate its complexities, they will likely be far behind their mainstream peers. Learning to adapt to the decisions of others more powerful than oneself is an important life skill. Yet learning to integrate conflicting viewpoints; to nuance personality differences; to navigate and interpret pain, failure, and brokenness; and to believe that we all need each other are skills that are even more vital. But the latter are not skills taught in the elite circles of our society, and our privileged kids are not led to develop their own voice while listening to the cherished and valuable voices of others.

Belonging

In a culture that elevates personal accomplishment and individual responsibility over mutual support and communal living, growing adolescents find themselves faced with an inescapable conundrum: is it more valuable to learn how to stand tall as a capable individual or to learn how to recognize my need for others and their need for me? In American culture, for some time we have been taught that we are ultimately on our own and that no one will ever care about us or our needs as much as we do. On the other hand, none of us can escape the fact that to live alone is to die, for we are social creatures who must have others to survive.

With adolescents, cultural mandates do not have the power to drown out the deafening voice of human history. Society is, after all, defined as our life together *as a group*. We need each other, and none of us can ever hope to live up to the rhetorical expectations of independence and solitude that we have been trained to pursue, even if we wanted to. We are simply not wired to live as autonomous creatures who do not need anyone other than those who can serve a utilitarian purpose. In defining the concept of need, Abraham Maslow called it a "deficiency disease," which he illustrated by reporting that "most neuroses involved, along with other complex determinants, ungratified wishes for safety, for belongingness and identification, for close love relationships and for respect and prestige."[40] These basic human "needs" are rooted in our innate need for interconnectedness and belonging.

This book has repeatedly demonstrated how adolescents experience an isolation and palpable sense of loneliness as a result of systemic abandonment. This chapter addresses how kids at the margins in particular deal with the need to connect and belong in a world that can often make them feel alone. Perhaps more than identity and autonomy, this third major task of adolescence is where there is the greatest difference between kids at the margins and their mainstream peers.

Belonging for Vulnerable Kids

The good news is that for those who are vulnerable due to systemic oppression or racial, socioeconomic, or other such factors, there is often a stronger sense of community than in mainstream American culture. The presence of this social network is sometimes, in certain communities, assumed to provide for an otherwise vulnerable adolescent a significant asset as they grow into adulthood. What is rarely acknowledged is that it takes more than the presence of a social network to create the kind of support a developing adolescent requires to meet her innate need for unconditional inclusion and authentic belonging to a group. Even for those vulnerable kids who have a close-knit extended family, for example, the lack of an integrated web of social support networks beyond their kin can create in them a sense that while their family accepts them, the rest of the world does not. This can cause them to have an antagonistic view of their family versus the greater society, which may in turn hinder their sense that they fit outside of their immediate, usually familial, community.

An example of this is the school system. The majority opinion today in the dominant culture is that our public educational system resolved the issues of racial separation long ago.[41] The facts are, however, astonishing. In December, *Time* magazine chose as its "most underreported story of

2009" a report that revealed that "African-American schoolchildren are more segregated than they have been since the time of Martin Luther King Jr.'s death in 1968. In the 2006–07 school year, nearly 40% attended schools—many of them subpar 'dropout factories'—where students of color made up 90% to 100% of the student body."[42] The UCLA study cited notes that "fifty-five years after the Brown decision, blacks and Latinos in American schools are more segregated than they have been in more than four decades."[43] While there are many problems and issues that accompany this reality, perhaps the most significant is that the vast differences in the educational opportunities for today's vulnerable kids compared to the privileged tangibly demonstrate one way that our society excludes the vulnerable from belonging.

The issue of separate educational opportunities often has the effect of excluding the vulnerable from feeling they are a part of "us"; however, those from the populations where most vulnerable kids live universally believe that this is but a symptom of a much greater truth: the mainstream and elite are committed to maintaining the walls of exclusion while perpetuating the image that we are one. (Even writing this sentence, sitting in the company of a planeload of the mainstream and elite, I can just imagine how my flightmates would react to such an assertion.) While this book is not about American society on the whole, our divisions directly affect the developmental health of the children and adolescents we are seeking to understand. One African-American teen, for instance, who could only be considered vulnerable due to his ethnicity, asked me point-blank, "Dr. Clark, have you ever been followed by a police car because you were driving in a neighborhood where you didn't belong? You ever been pulled over by a cop who kept you from leaving for a half hour because he said he didn't believe you, and you know full well that's because you're black? Well, until that happens to you, don't say you understand me, because you can't." This young man was absolutely correct, and an even greater injustice occurs when I have the audacity to pretend that I do understand. Perhaps that is among our greatest failings as a society: those of us who are by race members of the dominant culture are trained to believe that, regardless of ethnicity or class, we are all the same, with the same opportunities and privileges. This is simply not true, and until we are willing to be honest about this disparity and systematic racism and classism, we will continue to perpetuate this cultural divide.

Belonging for Privileged Kids

When adolescents grow up being conditioned to believe that personal achievement and individual prowess are what ultimately matter most in life, the developmental task of belonging comes to be seen as an optional luxury worth pursuing only if it is not too costly to the quest for status and power. Most privileged adolescents have been trained— even programmed—to believe and live as if they reside at the center of social groups and networks. The way privileged kids are conditioned to view life as one competition after another, coupled with the high value on individualism they have been steeped in (which Levine asserts is ultimately equated with isolation), produces in many privileged adolescents a deep sense of loneliness. Madeline Levine details this clearly and profoundly, summarizing that "the link between materialism and competition is particularly strong."[44] This third developmental task of adolescence, belonging, is the greatest deficit privileged kids experience as they grow up. When you are raised to see others, and sometimes even friends, as means to an end, the internal drive to belong to others both in peer relationships and as a society is simply pushed aside. The outcome, however, is to grow up wondering, does anyone actually care for me, or do others see and treat me as I have been taught to see and treat them?

Both privileged and vulnerable kids have no greater and no less of a driving need to belong in a meaningful, affirming, and genuine community—to know they are loved and appreciated not for what they can contribute but for who they are. And for kids from both margins the need to belong is not limited to their family or even to their closest group of friends, but is instead a need to belong to the society at large, and to those whom they must somehow relate to for the rest of their lives. The film *Crash*, which won the Academy Award for best picture in 2006, did a masterful job of reminding us that whether we grow up in a poor barrio in East Los Angeles, are second generation Asian, or have parents who went to Harvard Law and UCSD Medical School, we are all the same and we all need each other. But when you've been raised at the margins of mainstream society, this is a difficult if not insurmountable discovery to make. Adolescents at the margins are too often programmed to believe that, in the final analysis, they simply do not, and never will, belong to everybody else.

Conclusion and Musings

Doing the research, spending the time with these kids, and then finally writing this chapter has been a difficult, even painful, journey for me. After skimming the first edition of *Hurt*, one sociologist remarked to me that it wasn't a helpful sociological take on the midadolescent population because I was "an advocate." Since then I have discovered that many sociologists, among them many of the most renowned in the history of their field, find themselves advocating for those they study, especially when over the course of their work they uncover injustice, oppression, or perhaps even relatively fixable issues that cause damage and pain to a group of people. If social science research must be a disconnected analytic quest for "data," but does not bring action and change that improves the lives of real people, then the academy has written itself out of relevancy.

This chapter caused my heart to break for kids on both ends of the margins. From Shawn, the disabled boy who had few friends, to Terry, my hard-eyed urban adversary, to Sara, the sweet and smart wealthy girl, I have come to see that marginalized young people need what every other adolescent needs: adults who care for them without any self-serving agenda. All kids, regardless of their background, family, ethnicity, gifts, or power, are desperate for a society that will help them discover who they are, what gifts and voice they have, and how they belong in a multigenerational community that values all. Because of the work I have had the honor to do with these kids the last few years, I am now more committed than ever not only to writing as an advocate, but also to advocating with my time, my money, my career, my calling, and my life. I invite all of you who are reading to join me. Our kids, *all* our kids, deserve no less.

part 3

where do we go from here?

> I'll tell you why I don't trust anybody at this school or my parents. Everybody is out for themselves. Teachers, coaches, parents, even my church group leaders—they are all out for themselves. *Nobody* gives a (expletive) about me! *Nobody!*
>
> a sixteen-year-old girl following a presentation on trust

This statement is representative of hundreds of comments I heard from a wide variety of midadolescents. The issue of trust for this population is not whether they can be trusted[1] but whether they feel safe enough to trust an adult. Many midadolescents feel that adults are more concerned with their own agendas than with the needs of adolescents, and therefore, they cannot be trusted.

Part 3 is relatively straightforward. It deals with what midadolescents need and five strategies to turn the tide of systemic abandonment. These ideas are the outflow of hundreds of hours of research, analysis, and evaluation. The lists are neither definitive nor complete. Perhaps they can serve as a springboard to additional ideas.

When I completed the formal aspect of this study, I made the commitment to make a change in how I lived my life. I knew I had no business telling others to get personally involved with kids unless I was willing to do so. So that is exactly what I did. In September 2002, I began spending a few hours a week as a volunteer in a youth club known as Young Life. I soon connected with three junior football players and started having dinner with them every Monday night. It has been taxing, tiring, and downright hard at times, but I have fallen in love with three guys—Daniel, Nigel, and John. They have changed me, and my dream is that showing unconditional tenderness toward them has made a dent in their belief that they have been abandoned.

Beware as you read, then. You may find yourself being drawn into a deeper, more committed calling to care for the young of your community.

13

what do midadolescents need?

Sometimes, I'm not who I seem to be
Sometimes, I keep it all inside of me
I know I could use a friend
But how can I tell you what's in my head?

That's when I cry
I let the tears run down my face
In the darkness
Where you can't see me
And you can't ask me why.

But when you're there
I keep my head held high
With a smile upon my face
So you don't know my pain or what I'm going through.

It's too late, you can't help me now
It's too late, you can't help me now.

Don, a high school student

Throughout this book, I have struggled with the constantly nagging question, so what do we do about abandonment and the world beneath? Almost everyone who read the initial chapters came away with the same question. My friends and associates wanted answers to "fix" this situation, not just more observations and questions. Unfortunately, the issues raised in this book are so subtle, evolutionary, and complex that solutions too quickly offered could trivialize the midadolescent plight and do more harm than good. We live in a culture that tells us we have the ability, with enough focused resources and energy, to conquer any problem, no matter how large. The sweeping changes society has gone through over the past few decades, however, make the multifaceted nature of the issues facing adolescents all the harder to diagnose, much less address. As one teacher lamented near the end of my study,

> It is as if the problem of caring for kids is just too overwhelming. As a teacher, I have so many things to think about and deal with—keeping up with grading, staying on schedule, maintaining order and discipline in the classroom. All this and still having to get my kids to perform for the standardized tests that we all feel so much pressure from.
>
> But when I think about it, I know I could listen a little harder, stay a little later, and show a bit more personal interest in the lives of my students. And I sometimes do. But then there are those days when I snap at the least little thing, when I am tough and hard when somebody gets under my skin. I guess more days are like that than not, but to be honest, the demands of the job allow me little time even to think about it.

What Does It Take to Make a Difference?

In *X-Men 2*, Jean Grey saves the day for her friends by using her mutant powers to hold up a crumbling dam, only to sacrifice herself in the process. In the film *Precious*, an unflappable and overly committed teacher breaks with convention and sincerely cares for a young woman who has been beaten down by life's circumstances, taking her in and nurturing her back to health and confidence. In both of these films, I could not help but think that this is what those of us who care about the state of contemporary adolescents are up against. A lone figure with hands

> Power, no matter how well intentioned, tends to cause suffering.
> Love, being vulnerable, absorbs it.
>
> Philip Yancey, *What's So Amazing about Grace?*

upraised cannot alter the societal push of abandonment. That does not mean, however, that we cannot soften its impact or compensate for its cruelty. We are not powerless. When we are willing to walk beside even one young person, we can make a difference.

One of the hallmarks of abandonment is the cultural shift from a nurturing focus on individuals to a focus on the group, the crowd, the statistics, the record, the program, the institution. Granted, addressing the larger, more global issue of abandonment will take an intense, lengthy, proactive assault from every corner of society. But I have reached the conclusion that the most significant help we can offer our young is to address their needs from the bottom up, at the point of the individual adolescent. Adults must care for and reach the individuals who have suffered from abandonment throughout their lives.

This study, along with other current research dealing with intervention strategies that have affected the maximum number of young people,[1] reveals that our cultural ethos of bigger, faster, and splashier does not apply to the issues facing contemporary adolescents. They need adults who are aware of the power of small, deliberate, and consistently authentic applications of relational concern, care, and nurture. As men and women who care about what abandonment has done to our young, we have the opportunity to make a significant difference if we but realize that the biggest need every student has is satisfied in an adult who is there for him or her. Our response must begin with an individual student who needs the encouragement and leadership of an adult who genuinely cares.

One of the main reasons for the retreat of adolescents from the adult world into the world beneath is that many adults have let them down throughout their lives. Most midadolescents carry with them a list of adults who did not protect or look out for them, whether it was a Sunday school teacher who kicked them out of class, a peewee soccer coach who angrily took them out of a game for making a mistake, or a teacher who called on them when they weren't prepared. These experiences become the locus of a lack of trust in adults who say they care.

If adults are willing to wade through this lack of trust, and if they honestly desire to come alongside and nurture adolescents as they make their way into the community of adults, it will not take long for adolescents to recognize the sincerity and allow these adults into their lives. The only qualification an adult needs is the willingness and fortitude to authentically care. Once this foundation is laid, adults can focus on the three specific needs of midadolescents:

1. Youth need refocused, nurturing organizations and programs.
2. Youth need a stable and secure loving presence.

3. Youth need to experience authentic, intimate relationships with adults.

Youth Need Refocused, Nurturing Organizations and Programs

In the not-too-distant past, even in the United States, communities were just what the name implied—networks of friends and neighbors who knew one another and carved out a life together. The community existed for its members, and the young were no exception. Even as late as the early 1960s, community was a central aspect of life together. In larger cities, as community boundaries became less identifiable, this became more problematic. By and large, however, even in the most urban of centers, people attempted (until the last thirty or forty years) to maintain a sense of community.

Across our nation, in villages, towns, and even cities, adults and children celebrated life together. They ate together, danced together, and played together. Little children were scolded by merchants, who often played the role of a relative. A teenager considering college was the talk of the barber shop. An invitation to a state band concert, a bad case of the chicken pox, or a home run at a county softball tournament captivated the interests of the entire community. Everyone mattered, and that included teenagers, even though they were still a few years removed from full adult status.

The benefits of this tribal connection are obvious, especially in light of how far our culture has drifted from that. Not too long ago, even single parents were not alone in raising their kids, for someone was always looking out for them. Even as "rebellious" adolescents, young people knew they were valuable members of the community, were genuinely enjoyed and appreciated, and therefore were given boundaries and protected. Even when teenagers pushed against the adult rules and the seemingly unjust and unnecessary constrictions placed on them by both their parents and the community, it was simply a part of society continually redefining itself as it assimilated new blood and fresh ideas into the life of the village. Adults knew their responsibility to nurture and protect the young, and therefore they held fast, realizing that the young were their most precious resource. They even started activities and programs intended to organize communal nurture of the young.

Today, that kind of community, especially in terms of how adolescents are viewed, is all but lost. This study showed that what is true about midadolescents in Los Angeles County is also true in Washington, North Carolina, rural Minnesota, central Georgia, Upstate New York, suburban Chicago, and inner-city Seattle. The young of every village, town, and city in America are in need of the same thing: a community of people, organizations, and institutions that have their individual needs and interests in mind. Some examples of this may be

- parents banding together to encourage youth sports leagues to allow all children to play the same amount and to affirm them for their contribution
- getting a school system to study how other districts have reduced the homework load on students while increasing test scores and student enthusiasm for learning
- communities sponsoring regular meetings at which all those who work with adolescents—school officials, sports and recreation leaders, parents, church leaders, employers, police and social services—come together to help one another assess their unique and collective efforts to care for each child and adolescent in the community

These are three fairly straightforward and simple examples of what it means to connect adolescents to nurturing adults. The need is real to recover the original intent of nurturing opportunities and to reshape how we serve the young in every community.

Youth Need a Stable and Secure Loving Presence

Connie was confident, proud, smart, and witty. She stopped me after a talk I had delivered on the topic of this book and said, "I just don't get how you can put us all in a box!" Connie's initial point was that while she appreciated those adults who took an interest in her, she wanted me to know that she did not need their help. She felt she needed to figure out how to live life on her own. "I am sick of feeling like I can't do anything right and always having to defend myself." We sat down, and she told me her story.

Connie was the oldest of three children. Her parents fought all the time. They were still together, but her dad had left at least twice during the past few years, usually flying out the door in a huff. She had become, apparently with little thought by her parents, the stable one in the home. At seventeen, she did most of the laundry, drove the other two kids, and cooked more than half the meals. She was an athlete, involved in student government, had a boyfriend, went to her church youth group, and was a good student.

My talk that morning had focused on the longing for a safe place, personalizing and placing in context the notion of abandonment. Connie

> The courtyard is filled with teenagers,
> Fake smiles, fake friendships.
> They are everywhere.
> Freshmen, sophomores, juniors, seniors,
> Jocks, preps, freaks, geeks,
> There is no exception to the rule,
> All desperately wanting to feel wanted,
> To feel needed, included, loved.
> Do you not realize this is pointless?
> That all the empty phrases,
> All the fake hugs and hellos are worthless?
> That will never satisfy their longing.
>
> high school student

felt she didn't have a safe place, and there was nobody in her life who was truly concerned about her needs. She felt alone, stuck, ignored, and used. Yet she simply could not see a way to escape the unending pressure she felt from every area of her life. The only solution she had come up with, prior to hearing me that morning, was to step up and live her own life. She felt abandoned and desperately wanted a place where she could rest. Connie wept when we talked about her childhood memories of sitting in her father's lap watching television and going on walks in the park with her mom and little sister. Suddenly she sat up, wiped her eyes, and exclaimed, "Those days are long gone. You know it and I know it. I am on my own. I just can't let myself think this way. It's stupid to even think about. I can't take it. I've got to go." With that, she left.

Her story describes life for many midadolescents. The source of the pressure may be different and may come with unique intensity and challenges, but the feeling of lost childhood, the loss of a safe embrace,[2] and the seemingly unreachable hope of finding true security, safety, and rest are universal. Young people do not want to be smothered or too tightly bound. They need the opportunity to venture out into the world, all the while confident that they have a safe place to return to.

This is the cry of many midadolescents. As they become aware of the difficulty, pain, and complexity of the world, the hurts of the past are magnified. Worse, this causes midadolescents to dive underground and grab on to a few friends for emotional and sociological survival. Midadolescents seem impenetrable, callous, without a need for adults. This is not a smokescreen. It is an authentic depiction of how they have chosen to cope with the danger of abandonment by those they had trusted. Adults should not be fooled by the reactions or even the words of adolescents. They should trust that each one is desperate for a safe and secure loving presence, regardless of whether they know it or not.

Youth Need to Experience Authentic, Intimate Relationships with Adults

Building a bridge between adults and adult-run systems, structures, organizations, and institutions is not enough to bring vital healing to the wounded psyches of adolescents. Each individual, by the time he or she is a midadolescent, needs to know that at least one adult knows him or her well and will do whatever it takes to bring him or her into the community of healthy adulthood.

In popular rhetoric today, that is a job exclusively relegated to parents. One teacher, when he found out the nature of my research project, told me he had a student who showed up late for class almost every day. The teacher had tried everything he could think of to motivate the student to be responsible, and eventually he tried to work with the boy's parents. When he was finally able to talk to the mother (a single parent), she took no responsibility for the boy's behavior and truancy. "She said she couldn't control him. If only the parents would do their job, we wouldn't have to be burdened with doing their job for them!"

The frustration displayed by this teacher was understandable, and I could certainly empathize with him. But this typical scenario of a parent who is clearly at her wits' end and a teacher who has simply gotten mad is but one more example of how societal fragmentation has hurt the young. In a segmented, fragmented culture in which neighbors do not know one another's names and families are so busy that they don't have time for an evening meal together, even the best of parents cannot possibly hope to meet all the nurturing requirements of raising a postmodern adolescent. Teachers, even the best ones, get overwhelmed by the multifaceted demands of their jobs, and it is little wonder that they sometimes feel as if they are society's last hope of nurturing the young.

Yet the fact remains that every child needs authentic, intimate relationships with adults until he or she has completed much of the adolescent process. This responsibility cannot fall to parents alone or to teachers, who can influence individual students for a year at best. The only way we can stem the tide of the consequences of abandonment is to encourage a wide variety of adults to take part in the lives of the young. Nothing else will make a difference—not more baseball fields, more programs and events, or more job opportunities. Because the root of the issues related to contemporary adolescence has to do with leaving this age group to flounder on its own, the answer is relationships with adults who sincerely care. That is the most fundamental need of this abandoned generation.

five strategies to turn the tide
of systemic abandonment

F or more than a year I have been thinking about the things I heard and saw and learned from the midadolescents gracious enough to let me into their world. I have wept for some and laughed with others. I recall the myriad expressions and emotions I saw on the faces of these great kids—the smiles, the stares, the fear, the wonder, the sadness, and the ecstasy. I treasure the countless memories I shared while walking alongside each student I encountered. This experience was a gift to me, and I will always be grateful to everyone who made it possible.

Now, what do we do about it all?

As June 2002 came and went, I spent a great deal of time pondering that same question. I had reconnected with an age group that had, as Dave Barry once described his own son, grabbed me by the pinky and had not let go. I was simply hooked. I had grown to care about each one. I had come to see that every child when he or she reaches midadolescence is intensely engaged in a battle of emotional and social survival. Each one has a story, a unique history, that influences and shapes who he or she is becoming. I had heard many stories and knew I could not go back into my world pretending I had not been a part of theirs.

This last chapter, then, describes how we can begin to turn the tide of systemic abandonment and serve as advocates for this generation. What I offer here is not the final answer, but my hope is that these strategies will be a starting point for making a difference in the lives of midadolescents in our communities.

Those Who Work with Youth Should Be Trained in the Changing Youth Culture

Over the course of this study, I encountered people in a variety of settings and occupations who functioned as if adolescent life is the same as it was when they were that age. In two conversations in the same week, for example, a late-fifties city youth services worker and a twenty-eight-year-old YMCA recreation supervisor both prefaced their comments regarding my study by saying, "When *I* was in high school . . ." and then proceeded to describe their own personal experience as normative. The deeper I got into the changes that have occurred, the more I wondered whether most of these committed, caring people have seen adolescent life only through their own historical filters. I am now convinced that everyone who works directly with adolescents needs to be trained and made aware of how different things are today than even a few years ago.

As I came to know my cell group leader more and more, I realized, Hey, she's got a lot in common with me. Maybe I can trust her. She's not gonna hurt me. She became my safe place. At this point, school was draining the life out of me. Anything I wanted I could get, most of the time for free. And I would take anything I could get. During this time, I confided in Monica, my cell group leader. She knew I was crying out for help, and she gave it to me in every way possible. I don't know how many times she picked me up, how many times she flushed drugs, how many times she and her husband opened their home to me. I got to the point where I wanted to end it all. I was going to kill myself. But Monica stayed on me and kept caring. Finally, she took me to my mother's office and made me tell almost everything. I was so ticked at the time, but I am so thankful now. If it wasn't for her—Monica—I would definitely be dead.

high school student

Although many adults interact with adolescents, adults in the following six occupations/roles should especially be made aware of what they are dealing with when it comes to postmodern midadolescents:

- educators
- government service agents (including police)
- counselors, therapists, and social workers
- coaches
- social and religious youth workers
- employers of youth

The areas in which these adults serve represent the most common settings in which abandonment has taken its toll on our young. The strategy to inform and train adults in these areas can include formal preparatory and/or educational classes, seminars, and informal talks in which the issues related to systemic abandonment can be presented and discussed. Those who work with adolescents should be encouraged to consider and wrestle with how abandonment in their setting could be avoided and what steps need to be taken to care for the needs of every individual.

Those Who Serve Adolescents Must Work Together

Adults must realize that, regardless of their resources or expertise, they cannot turn the tide of abandonment on their own. In most communities, schools, youth centers, churches, youth sports leagues, and other youth-focused groups function independently of one another. For each adolescent in a given community to be cared for, regardless of talent, ability, or even attitude, programs with similar goals must work together.

Obstacles to networking range from a lack of time to a lack of awareness of what others are doing in a given community. Most people and organizations who serve the young frequently feel overwhelmed by a lack of resources and the demands they face. What few seem to recognize is that a network of like-minded people and organizations creates a flow of additional resources and strategic opportunities. A seminar for parents, for example, would be expensive if a local PTA sponsored it independently. If a local community network comprised of various agencies and organizations hosted it, a better (and cheaper) parent seminar could be made available to all. Imagine what could happen if Little League sponsors, local schools, the police, the YMCA, and churches met together two or three times a year with the sole intent of addressing issues of abandonment in a community.

Occasionally, the reason people and groups do not work together to address common issues related to abandonment is because of institutional or even personal mistrust. A lack of collaboration, however, brings with it a high cost. Out of a commitment to nurture children and adolescents, all groups should be compelled to work through their differences and establish parameters for working together for the good of the community.

Those Who Serve Adolescents Must Understand Youth and Provide Boundaries

The basic response demanded by the issues related to abandonment may feel overwhelming, but it is actually relatively straightforward: to nurture adolescents, we need to understand their changing world and provide boundaries so that their choices have as few serious consequences as possible.

Adults need to understand some of the struggles and issues facing adolescents as a result of systemic abandonment. They must understand what abandonment is, what it has done, and how kids have reacted to it. The greatest hurdle is convincing adults that abandonment has taken its toll on today's adolescents. When adults realize that abandonment has taken place, or at least that adults are often more concerned about themselves and their commitments and interests than about the interests of adolescents, they soften to the idea of severe cultural change.

Providing boundaries for the young, which is a vital component of nurturing children and adolescents, is the responsibility of every adult in a given community. Most people assume that parents alone are responsible for raising their children. This is often declared, however, in the context of an attempt to skirt responsibility for a system, decision, statement, or behavior that has the potential of adversely affecting kids. A recording artist who blames parents for buying his albums, a director who cavalierly directs responsibility for monitoring teen-marketed R-rated films to parents and theater owners, and a volunteer coach who dismisses a parent's concern over the intensity of the "recreational" experience by claiming that "these kids want to win, and if your kid plays we can't win" are all guilty of avoiding their adult responsibilities. Parents alone cannot hope to provide the boundaries their kids need to stay within the zone of personal safety.

What does it mean for adults to provide boundaries? It comes down to a commitment to a simple truth: the nurture and care of the young in society is the responsibility of every adult in society. Every adult who cares about the young must do whatever it takes to address and confront any other adult, organization, or policy that adds to the effects of abandonment. Small, relatively simple actions can make a huge difference over time. Consider:

- an assistant youth football coach who takes it upon himself to meet with the coaching staff and parents to discuss ways to encourage every player equally, regardless of experience, size, or talent (During childhood and early adolescence, athletic competence is at least as much about confidence and encouragement as it is about ability.)[1]
- a high school teacher who notices other teachers' disparaging comments toward students and makes sure the administration takes steps to address such a flagrant violation of that profession's lofty calling
- a few parents who find out that a local merchant is selling chewing tobacco to football players and arrange a meeting with that merchant (and others in town), the city council, the school administration, and law enforcement to ensure that unsafe and addictive substances are not readily available to adolescents

The issue comes down to whose responsibility adolescents are. Those who recognize that all adults must band together to ensure that each young person is given the best opportunity to be welcomed into the adult community must be advocates until the rest of their peers catch up. The above examples are but a few of the countless actions that a caring community of adults can take as it seeks to provide boundaries for the young in a given community.

Parents Need to Be Equipped and Encouraged to Parent the Changing Adolescent

I have spent a great deal of time with parents, speaking at seminars and discussing in small, intimate groups what is going on with their children. I have found few parents who, once their children enter midadolescence, are not on the edge of panic at some level. Parents are well aware that much of high school life has changed and that the culture is far different from when they were in high school. Yet most feel insecure and alone. They see the layering, the relational disconnectedness and callousness, and the way they are pushed aside in favor of friends. The vast majority knows what it is like to be lied to, deceived, and manipulated. Parents need to know that what is happening is not their fault and that with some work and understanding they can build good and productive relationships with their children even in the midst of cultural chaos.

Parents are obviously the most significant people in the life of any child. What, then, should parents be aware of in light of the cultural systemic abandonment of the young? The easy answer, of course, is everything! But specifically, parents should be aware of the following three changes in adolescent development: the reality of lengthened adolescence, the phenomenon of layered and underground living, and the perception of adolescents that they are on their own to figure out how to live. If parents (including stepparents and guardians) recognize and understand these aspects of adolescence, they will be well on their way to parenting with a certain level of confidence.

Communities Must Make Sure That Each Student Has a Few Adult Advocates Who Know and Care for Him or Her

A popular myth that many of us have grown up with is the idea of a single role model. This has been perpetuated by otherwise outstanding programs such as Big Brothers and Big Sisters and by the overall concept of finding struggling kids a mentor to help them whenever they are in need. Unfortunately, an individual does not have the ability to be present in the variety of ways an adolescent needs. In this culture, the diversity of demands is simply too great. Second, even the best mentors eventually leave,[2] which in some ways can be worse than if they were never there in the first place. To a needy child or adolescent, the failed promise of intimate companionship and nurture is devastating. Third, research has consistently demonstrated that several positive and supportive relationships that offer the same messages must be present to have an effect on the life of a child.[3] If a child has a mentor who is gentle, supportive, and affirming during a weekly encounter, yet the rest of the week he hears that he is lazy, stupid, and incompetent, the negative voices will win out. One fan, even a great one, is not enough.

Every adult must attempt to add to the cumulative message of protection, nurture, warmth, and affection. It takes several consistently supportive and encouraging messages to counteract the effects of systemic abandonment. By far the best way to help our young is by being a chorus of support and a choir of commitment.

method

As noted throughout this edition, the content of this book is driven by the data, results, conclusions, discussions, and limitations of the initial two-part study, sometimes referred to as the *Hurt Project*, that a research team and I conducted from 2001 to early 2004, as well as the added data from the third phase (2004 to 2010). The initial phase of the project has been driven by the data discovered in my role as a substitute teacher from late 2001 to June 2002 in the Glendale Unified School District at Crescenta Valley High School using an ethnographic methodology known as participant-observation. At the same time, a team conducted a thorough literature review of all relevant material, in both popular and academic sources, that served to inform, shape, and nuance these observations and emerging perspectives. The second phase of the project, from the summer of 2002 to spring 2004, consisted of seventeen open-ended conversations with high school juniors and seniors where I sought to gather a new batch of data giving texture and thickness to the observations and literature reviews previously utilized. This is what was reported in the first edition of *Hurt*. The continuing phase of the project is an ongoing synthesis of observation, interviews, open-ended conversations, and deliberate focus groups that provide additional data to the original results. This phase reveals conclusions that have changed over the past several years, and focuses more specifically on populations and environments that the original study understudied.

The method used for the original *Hurt Project* and reported in this edition is basically the same integration of participant-observation, literature review, intentional open-ended conversations, focus groups, and occasional interviews. What has changed from the first edition to the second is the level of depth we have explored in the literature review, the intentional investigation and analysis of what we are calling "kids at the margins" (those who either have overwhelming obstacles to healthy development or have been smothered by a tsunami of adult directives), and several more conversations and focus groups with midadolescents that have provided additional and significant insight into how the world is exponentially changing for today's teenagers.

As in the original edition of *Hurt*, we are convinced that our results and conclusions generally fall into the category of "grounded theory." Our hope, therefore, is that other scholars from a variety of disciplines will take what we have seen and go deeper by engaging in the work of understanding how cultural change affects adolescents without a disciplinary bias or a priori assumptions that could keep them from moving this research forward.

The Method

While participant-observation was the initial and motivating strategy used for the study, all of the supporting methodologies we used were integrated in such a way as to bring out the most complete and robust picture of teenagers' sense of their world and life. While there are a myriad of possible ways to investigate the general sense adolescents share regarding their perception of their reality, what is vital is that any methodology must be able to provide a relatively authentic and honest portrait of those being studied. As Paula Saukko notes, "The worth or validity of [a] project depends on how thoroughly and defensibly or correctly [it] has been done."[1] This concern has been at the very heart of every aspect of the research process for *Hurt* and now *Hurt 2.0*.

As has been stated, the data reported in this edition are the integration of a four-part research process: my role as participant-observer in a high school; a literature review team investigating the issues that emerged from my observation; a series of conversations and focus groups; and finally an ongoing synthesis of these observations, conversations, and focus groups, interaction with new scholarship, and a proactive commitment to dialogue with practitioners and scholars, even those who have publicly or even privately dismissed the findings from the first edition of *Hurt*. In other words, the *Hurt Project* is an ongoing dialogue with scholars, parents, youth advocates, educators, social scientists, and a wide array of others who are interested in understanding the world of today's adolescents.[2]

Participant-Observation/Ethnography

Perhaps the most fundamental question a social scientist can ask is "How do we really *know* about a given population?" As the lead researcher in the *Hurt Project*, for nearly a decade I have wrestled long and hard with this question. As the world changes and widespread cultural trends increasingly demonstrate how these changes affect us all, this question nudges scholars to move in a little closer to those who can teach the most about their world, the adolescents themselves. Today's teenagers have a great deal more to share than what we can see and know through the more typical research methods of focus groups, questionnaires, or even individual personal interviews. Participant-observation of a population is especially important when studying adolescents, whose answers to self-report queries may not be consistent and whose actual perspectives, attitudes, and behaviors do not readily correlate with what they might say to a researcher. In order to even begin to paint an accurate picture of the complex, multitiered world of today's teenager, it takes someone who is outside of the direct experience of the constantly changing nature of adolescence itself to carefully and deliberately listen, watch, ask, invite, and pursue.[3] It takes someone who is close enough to get a well-rounded picture of what is going on, and at the same time is safe enough to be invited into authentic and unfiltered behaviors and conversation. Patricia and Peter Adler, leading ethnographic scholars, consistently affirm that participant-observation is the most productive methodology in studying adolescent life and behavior, as they describe in the *Journal of Contemporary Ethnography*: "Given ethnography's strength of getting inside groups' inner workings, this methodology has been central to the exploration of how teenagers make sense of their social worlds."[4]

The specific strategy I employed was to find a way to honor the agreement with the school and district by serving in the role of a substitute teacher. While I maintained the integrity of the role by following the directions the teacher had left regarding the class, the coprincipals and I agreed that the method required the students (and faculty and administrators) to also be made aware of why I was there beyond substitute teaching. In every class I would begin by explaining that I was on a lengthy sabbatical leave in order to listen to and observe the world of high school students and that I was planning on writing a book about what I saw and heard. At the end of each day, I would record impressions—without using any names of students or even specific classes—of what I observed that day. At the end of each week I would synthesize my diary notes into a loose but comprehensive narrative, and then put the daily logs away. Within a few weeks, themes began to emerge, and I would allow myself to reflectively test out these emerging themes in my future daily observations at that time.

During the semester-plus I was on campus I received over one thousand unsolicited poems, notes, songs, and letters from students (and a few teachers). Our team later coded these texts and, changing the names of students, created a database of impressions of my observations, conversations, and preliminary conclusions. This type of coding data is what Charmaz suggests is an important aspect of the participant-observer's process in order to allow for various random materials to be integrated and synthesized. She writes, "Coding gives a researcher analytic scaffolding on which to build. Because researchers study their empirical materials closely, they can define both new leads from them and gaps in them. Each piece of data—whether an interview, a field note, a case study, a personal account, or a document—can inform earlier data."[5]

Although participant-observation is objectively recognized as one of the most robust of research methodologies, a relatively consistent critique of it is the possibility that researcher bias may influence the reported conclusions, sometimes to the point of invalidating the entire project. Since the first edition of *Hurt* I have occasionally heard this as a critique of our study. In an undergraduate class at a major U.S. university, for example, a student asked his prominent sociologist professor how my work and *Hurt* in particular spoke into the theory he was espousing. The professor is reported to have said, "That guy spent a few months on a high school campus and calls that research? He was just out to prove what he already believed." When this student emailed me this exchange, I was less concerned about the professor's comments than I was with the potential that there were others "out there" who had similar misgivings about the academic strength of this research.

It is impossible to deny that when a researcher engages with a given population and has any affinity for or even relationship with members of the subject group, the potential for bias, and perhaps significant bias, is a very real concern. Yet many scholars who use this method for their own research question the perception that the potential for researcher bias plays as significant a role in the value, veracity, and power of ethnographic observations and conclusions as some assert. Research scholars like Michael V. Angrosino, in his article "Recontextualizing Observation," for instance, make precisely the opposite case, arguing for the value of an invested researcher being sympathetic to and even connected with her subjects. Because the method requires a great deal of time, for researchers to be trusted they have no choice but to build some sort of rapport with their subjects. It is in the context of this relational ecology, Angrosino argues, that the researcher has the best opportunity to uncover, detail, and report the reality being studied.[6] While I am clearly an advocate for the young and want to raise awareness of how they have been systemically led and treated, I believe that the observed data, the impressions forming into conclusions, and the results written herein are ultimately faithful and honest objective reflections of what other researchers would discover if they were to replicate the study with openness.

Literature Review

While the *Hurt Project* initially relied on my work as an ethnographer on a high school campus, the method used in this study is not limited to that singular strategy; we have also taken great care to align, or at least measure, our conclusions with relevant literature. Our commitment to a thorough interdisciplinary literature review, then, provides as much a dynamic data set as any of the other forms of data collection we used. This edition is a point-by-point, paragraph-by-paragraph revision of the first edition of *Hurt*, written in order to maintain the deliberative connection between my continuing observations of adolescents in contemporary culture and the most recent and best scholarship and thinking. In participant-observation, the literature review offers a grounding and delimiting structure that enables both open-ended ethnographic inquiry and, at the same time, a sense of place for contextualized analysis. The literature review is vital because it forces an ethnographic researcher to either position observations and conclusions within a previously delineated conceptual framework or, if necessary, to push for a new way of thinking. This is what keeps ethnography in general and participant-observation in particular located as a bona fide and trustworthy social science methodology.[7]

In participant-observation, the conceptual boundaries that literature provides, however, must not be allowed to shape ideas and perspectives before the observations themselves have bubbled to the surface of the researcher's impressions. In other words, relevant literature should be used as a potential corrective to observations and conclusions that violate previous theoretical assumptions, not to shape the impressions a priori. Throughout the *Hurt* study—both the initial study and the ongoing work—that is how we have employed relevant literature and theory.

Informal Conversations and Focus Groups

Focus groups and their research cousins, informal group conversations, have provided ethnographers with a wealth of insight not easily captured using other methods. First, even the most astute participant-observer is only able to see snapshots of a given population, so a focus group will be able to fill in gaps.[8] In addition, focus groups can help to prevent researchers from forming premature conclusions without having enough firsthand information.[9] I found our procedure of adjusting conclusions according to the focus group comments to be vital to our overall understanding of this population. And lastly, the greatest value of the focus groups was the way they allowed teenagers to "reveal unarticulated norms and normative assumptions"[10] that perhaps in many cases I generally suspected but that were made all the more clear by the collective descriptive and corporate assent of the group participants. Thus throughout the entire project, and since, we have utilized some form of small group interaction as a third primary source of data.

As stated, for the initial study I conducted seventeen "official" informal conversations, all with written parental consent. After the conversations were complete I received word that a small handful of parents from five of the groups were uncomfortable with their children's involvement, so we did not include any of the comments or impressions from those five groups in any of the books, articles, or lectures related to the *Hurt Project*. Interestingly, the issue was the same for every concerned parent: the adolescents had discussed, *without my prompting*, oral sex. To my knowledge no other issue caused any parental angst with any part of the study.

The groups were comprised of between fifteen and twenty high school juniors and seniors who were chosen from at least three, and usually six to ten, population pools that were all geographically proximate.[11] The cities and communities were chosen to represent a wide spectrum of the U.S. population centers, as well as a wide demographic—ethnic, urban, rural, suburban, etc. (I also conducted two Canadian focus groups, one each on the east and west coast). Before arriving in a city or town, I would contact at least two local nongovernmental agencies (and usually more) to enlist their help in connecting with a group of youth and youth-serving organizations with access to teenagers who could serve as potential subjects and who were articulate and willing to discuss with peers, many of whom they would not know, their impressions of the world they lived in, for a research project seeking to understand how teenagers perceive their life and world. Each city ended up with its own unique process, but our team insisted on the following conditions: if at all possible, no more than three of the students would know each other well; no more than 50 percent could be actively involved in any single major category (sports team, church and/or religious youth organization, service clubs, etc.); they must be available for a one-time sitting (including pizza); and a parent had to sign a release form. In most cases we followed up with a letter to each parent asking to reaffirm their willingness for their child to participate. In the years since the first edition I have conducted between eight and fifteen similar conversations, depending on how formally I would define "conversation."

The format of the groups was straightforward. I wanted to allow for any kind of perception or perspective to emerge without being shaped by the presence of the researcher or by the way a question was asked. Therefore I came alone to almost every focus group and took notes sparingly, for only a few direct and especially pithy quotes, thus trying to stay true to the observation method by relying largely on my memory. In deciding how to facilitate the groups, we chose to err in the direction of simplicity and openness by simply asking group participants to, for example, "Tell me about school" or "Discuss friends" (or dating or family or pressure). Once the teens achieved a level of safety with each other, usually within the first thirty to forty-five minutes, the most important work I had to do was to avoid groupthink, where the information being offered appears to be swelling into too clean a uniformity. The research on a facilitator's avoidance of groupthink is well documented and entails a relatively easily accessed skill set, with the researcher employing strategies like inviting a quiet person to answer a relatively unrelated question, or reintroducing or redirecting words one subject has said that would contradict the direction the group was headed.[12] This proved not to be a problem with any of the groups.

The Ongoing Work of the *Hurt Project*

The work of the *Hurt Project*, as we've already noted, was not complete with the release of the book. As a graduate school professor, I have continued to enlist students and graduates to investigate a wide range of literature, to ask ethnographic questions while in the field, and to personally work with and consult organizations and communities that seek to improve their ability to understand and serve their teenagers. Our teams[13] have intentionally chosen to see this research as an ongoing inquiry and to report what is seen and heard in the natural course of networks and relationships, as opposed to formalizing the project by means of a committee, grant, or institutional project. For example, when a private school invites me (or a member of my team) to spend time on their campus observing and interviewing students and faculty to determine the level and places of systemic abandonment, we operate under the guidelines of the institution and the authority of their board of directors. When given the opportunity to conduct focus groups, we do insist, as we have from the beginning, that the institution or agency is responsible for obtaining parental consent, but for the most part we observe and operate under the auspices of the inviting party.

Finally, the reason we have continued this project, and will continue this project for years to come, is that what was discovered in writing the first edition of *Hurt* is not improving. The level of responsibility and competencies[14] required of children from very early ages has risen exponentially over the past decade, and yet the ongoing adult support and guidance offered them without a self-serving agenda has diminished at roughly the same rate. We are convinced that today's children and teenagers have never experienced less social capital than they do today, and that they experience more stress than any generation in history. We stand with people who are committed to raising the flag of awareness, conversation, and action so that our children, and their children, will grow up where they are known, loved, and cherished as vital and valuable members of our community, nation, and world.

notes

Preface to *Hurt 2.0*

1. "MILF (an acronym of 'Mother [or "Mom"] I'd Like/Love to F—')—a sexually desirable older woman, though not necessarily one who has children. It was the name given to the marijuana sold by Nancy Botwin on the Showtime series *Weeds*. By 2008, the term was familiar enough to be used on television series such as *30 Rock* (episode 'MILF Island'), *Scrubs* (episode 'My Last Words') and *Pushing Daisies* (episode 'The Norwegians') without necessitating its definition (which would have violated Federal Communications Commission rules). In 2007, *Spirit Airlines* ran a promotional campaign titled "M.I.L.F." described as meaning "Many Islands, Low Fares" but deliberately playing on the double entendre. (http://en.wikipedia.org/wiki/MILF [accessed November, 2010]).

2. Cougar—The term is commonly applied to women who are forty or older and pursue younger men. The origin of the word is debated; however, it is thought to have first appeared in print on the Canadian dating website Cougardate.com. Since then, the term has been used in TV series, advertising, film, and even books. (http://en.wikipedia.org/wiki/Cougar_%28slang%29#Slang_terms [accessed November 30, 2010]).

3. See the website of the National Study of Youth and Religion, www.youthandreligion.org.

4. This discussion took place at Fuller Theological Seminary on March 8, 2008. The quote here has been edited for grammatical purposes only. The entire panel discussion, including Dr. Kara Powell of the Fuller Youth Institute, can be found at http://fulleryouthinstitute.org/2008/03/soul-searching -panel/ (accessed November 30, 2010).

Preface to the First Edition

1. See Patricia Hersch, *A Tribe Apart: A Journey into the Heart of American Adolescence* (New York: Ballantine Books, 1998). Hersch is sometimes quoted in scholarly works, but this is actually rare. Most often authors use her as an anecdotal example of how some people think about adolescents rather than seriously engaging her conclusions. I believe her book is one of the most important books for anyone intent on understanding the young of the new millennium, whether that person is academically oriented or just wants to understand how different their world is.

2. See Paul Atkinson and Martyn Hammersley, "Ethnography and Participant Observation," in *Handbook of Qualitative Research*, ed. Norman K. Denzin and Yvonna S. Lincoln (Thousand Oaks, CA: Sage, 1994), 248–61. For a more detailed description of the method, see the appendix.

3. David Hamilton, "Traditions, Preferences, and Postures in Applied Qualitative Research," in Denzin and Lincoln, *Handbook of Qualitative Research*, 67.

4. See John Stanfield, "Ethnic Modeling in Qualitative Research," in Denzin and Lincoln, *Handbook of Qualitative Research*, 175–88.

5. See Valerie J. Janesick, "The Dance of Qualitative Research Design: Metaphor, Methodolatry, and Meaning," in Denzin and Lincoln, *Handbook of Qualitative Research*, 209–19; and Patricia A.

Adler and Peter Adler, "Observational Techniques," in Denzin and Lincoln, *Handbook of Qualitative Research*, 377–92.

6. Goths wear black, dye their hair black, and sometimes display multiple piercings and/or other highly visible physical or clothing flags that let the world know they are different. It took them a while to trust me, but once I was accepted as a relatively safe presence, I found the Goths to be some of the most articulate, intelligent, and forthright adolescents I encountered. Their common narrative as well as their individual stories did not seem to be all that different from those of other students. What was different was their in-your-face commitment to marking their separation from the adult-controlled and ordered world.

7. Similar to Goths, Punks rely on outside appearance to create their sense of identity. Chains, multiple tattoos, and ornate and inventive piercings are some of the flags of this group.

8. One of the more interesting aspects of this constant changing of identity is that it appears to be mediated by the friendship group, both as it is being formed and as it evolves over time. This is noted by P. J. Curran, E. Stice, and L. Chassin, who state, "Peer cluster theory postulates that friendship dyads or small groups (clusters) are the silent proximal link between more distal causal influences and adolescent substance use. Adolescent psychological characteristics, behaviors, attitudes, and socialization may all exert an influence on subsequent substance use, but these effects are thought to be primarily, if not solely, mediated through the peer cluster" ("The Relation between Adolescent Alcohol Use and Peer Alcohol Use: A Longitudinal Random Coefficient Model," *Journal of Consulting and Clinical Psychology* 65 [1997]: 131). Although the article focuses on substance abuse, the issue of peer clustering is explored in depth as a contributing factor, and the authors' summary is one of the most succinct in the adolescent literature.

9. The media regularly reports scandals where adults function like adolescents, regardless of who it brings down.

Part 1 The Changing Adolescent World

1. For example, see Mike Males, "The New Demons: Ordinary Teens," *Los Angeles Times*, April 21, 2002, home.earthlink.net/~mmales/epheb.htm (accessed March 13, 2003).

2. In my more popular-level books on this subject, I refer to the concept of "multiple selves" by the analogy of "candles." See Chap Clark and Steve Rabey, *When Kids Hurt: Help for Adults Navigating the Adolescent Maze* (Grand Rapids: Baker Books, 2009); and Chap Clark and Dee Clark, *Disconnected: Parenting Teens in a MySpace World* (Grand Rapids: Baker Books, 2007).

Chapter 1 The Changing Face of Adolescence

1. Although the term *kids* is consistently used in popular literature and other media as a moniker for describing adolescents, a few adults bristle at the term. I have tried to avoid the use of this term where possible. I do reserve the right, however, to retain its use where I believe it is necessary.

2. As found in August Kerber, *Quotable Quotes on Education* (Detroit: Wayne State University Press, 1968), 265.

3. Augustine, *Confessions*, trans. Rex Warner (New York: Signet Classics, 2001), 28.

4. Sonia Livingstone, "Taking Risky Opportunities in Youthful Content Creation: Teenagers' Use of Social Networking Sites for Intimacy, Privacy and Self-Expression," *New Media Society* 10 (2008): 400.

5. See Jeffery J. Arnett, *Adolescence and Emerging Adulthood: A Cultural Approach* (Upper Saddle River, NJ: Pearson Education, 2000); Jeffery J. Arnett, ed., *Readings on Adolescence and Emerging Adulthood* (Upper Saddle River, NJ: Prentice-Hall, 2002); and G. Stanley Hall, *Adolescence: Its Psychology and Its Relation to Physiology, Anthropology, Sociology, Sex, Crime, Religion, and Education*, 2 vols. (Englewood Cliffs, NJ: Prentice-Hall, 1904).

6. See http://www.qis.net/~jschmitz/afu/youth.htm, accessed November 15, 2010; the actual quote comes from Plato, *Platonis Opera*, ed. John Burnet (New York: Oxford University Press, 1903), 562c, 563a.

7. Arnold van Gennep, *The Rites of Passage*, trans. Monika B. Vizedom and Gabrielle L. Caffe (Chicago: University of Chicago Press, 1960). Nearly every culture across time believed in the necessity of rituals and rites of passage to create a well-defined, clearly ordered movement from childhood to adulthood. For examples, see Ray Raphael, *The Men from the Boys* (Lincoln: University of Nebraska Press, 1988).

8. See Chap Clark, "The Changing Face of Adolescence: A Theological View of Human Development," in *Starting Right: Thinking Theologically about Youth Ministry*, ed. Kenda C. Dean, Chap Clark, and Dave Rahn (Grand Rapids: Zondervan/Youth Specialties, 2000), 41–62; and Chap Clark,

"From Fragmentation to Integration: A Theology for Contemporary Youth Ministry," *American Baptist Quarterly* 19, no. 1 (2000): 45–55.

9. Arnett, *Readings on Adolescence*, 1–31.

10. See John W. Santrock, *Adolescence*, 8th ed. (New York: McGraw-Hill, 2001); and Andrea Solarz, *American Psychological Association Healthy Adolescents Project: Adolescent Development Project* (Washington, DC: American Psychological Association, 2002).

11. As stated, this chapter is not intended to debate traditional and/or classic developmental theories and concepts. It is intended, rather, to provide a balanced view of those developmental and relational issues that most directly relate to the youth ministry task. This chapter draws together those areas of research, study, and debate that someone who works with young people needs to recognize and understand.

12. Some contemporary developmental theorists have challenged many of the assumptions of developmental pioneers such as Jean Piaget and Erik Erikson. For an example of this, see Robert Kegan, *The Evolving Self* (Cambridge, MA: Harvard University Press, 1983) and *In Over Our Heads: The Mental Demands of Modern Life* (Cambridge, MA: Harvard University Press, 1994). See also Nancy Chodorow, *The Reproduction of Mothering: Psychoanalysis and the Sociology of Gender* (Berkeley: University of California Press, 1978), who questions, for example, potential male and European biases found in traditional developmental theory.

13. The word *adolescent* is derived from a relatively innocuous Latin term, *adolescere*, literally, "to grow up into" something. See Arnett, *Adolescence and Emerging Adulthood*; and Santrock, *Adolescence*.

14. A comment made by a teacher when asked during this study to define adolescence.

15. Frederick Buechner, *Whistling in the Dark* (San Francisco: Harper, 1993), 2.

16. Santrock, *Adolescence*, 28–29.

17. Ibid.

18. See Clark, "Changing Face of Adolescence"; S. A. Boles, "A Model of Parental Representations, Second Individuation, and Psychological Adjustment in Late Adolescents," *Journal of Clinical Psychology* 55, no. 4 (1999): 497–513; and J. Garbarino, J. P. Gaa, P. Swank, R. McPherson, and L. V. Gratch, "The Relation of Individuation and Psychosocial Development," *Journal of Family Psychology* 9 (1995): 311–18.

19. According to Andrea Solarz in a report sponsored by the American Psychological Association, "Establishing a sense of identity has traditionally been thought of as the central task of adolescence [Erik Erikson, *Identity: Youth and Crisis* (New York: Norton, 1968)], although it is now commonly accepted that identity formation neither begins nor ends during adolescence. Adolescence is the first time, however, when individuals have the cognitive capacity to consciously sort through who they are and what makes them unique. Identity refers to more than just how adolescents see themselves right now; it also includes what has been termed the 'possible self'—what individuals might become, and who they would like to become" (*American Psychological Association*, 34). While I agree with the thinking that identity formation continues throughout the life span and even begins prior to the specific psychosocial stage known as adolescence, for the purposes of this book, I maintain that this argument can easily become technical to the point of irrelevance. Certainly, there is growth in terms of identity across the life span, but the primary grounding or application of one's uniqueness is a major component of the process of adolescence. Therefore, I will use the term *identity formation* to describe a central role in adolescent development. I am aware of potential problems that may accompany the complexities of such a concise definition.

20. Richard Knox, "The Teen Brain: It's Just Not Grown Up Yet," National Public Radio, March 1, 2010, www.npr.org/templates/story/story.php?storyId=124119468 (accessed July 1, 2010).

21. Ibid.

22. Joseph Allen and Claudia Worrell Allen, *Escaping the Endless Adolescence: How We Can Help Our Teenagers Grow Up before They Grow Old* (New York: Ballantine Books, 2009), 34.

23. Ibid., 44.

24. Peter Blos, "The Second Individuation Process of Adolescence," in *The Adolescent Passage* (New York: International Universities Press, 1979), 141–70.

25. Boles, "Model of Parental Representations," 497–513.

26. See the websites of these organizations for more information: www.ama-assn.org and www.cdc.gov, respectively. Earlier puberty is reportedly due to "better nutrition and body fatness" available in Western cultures. See also V. Matkovic et al., "Leptin Is Inversely Related to Age at Menarche in Human Females," *Journal of Clinical Endocrinology and Metabolism* 82, no. 10 (October 1997): 3239–45.

27. As reported in Patricia Cohen, "Long Road to Adulthood Is Growing Even Longer," *New York Times*, June 11, 2010, http://www.nytimes.com/2010/06/13/us/13generations.html?_r=1 (accessed November 30, 2010).

28. Allen and Allen, *Escaping the Endless Adolescence*, 19.

29. Robert Epstein, *The Case against Adolescence: Rediscovering the Adult in Every Teen* (Sanger, CA: Quill Driver Books, 2007), 5.

30. For instance, in *The Case against Adolescence* Robert Epstein articulates a somewhat radical minority view, arguing that teens who are deemed "ready" should be free to become emancipated from their parents, marry, start businesses, etc., as this will aid in their maturation process.

31. David Elkind, *Ties That Stress: The New Family Imbalance* (Cambridge, MA: Harvard University Press, 1994).

32. See Robert D. Putnam, *Bowling Alone: The Collapse and Revival of American Community* (New York: Simon & Schuster, 2000).

33. Elkind, *Ties That Stress;* and *The Hurried Child: Growing Up Too Fast Too Soon*, 3rd ed. (Cambridge, MA: Perseus, 2001).

34. Mary D. S. Ainsworth and John Bowlby, "An Ethological Approach to Personality Development," *American Psychologist* 46, no. 4 (1991): 333–41; see also Mary D. S. Ainsworth, "Infant-Mother Attachment," *American Psychologist* 34 (1979): 932–37.

35. Margaret Mahler, "Symbiosis and Individuation: The Psychological Birth of the Human Infant," in *Separation-Individuation: Selected Papers of Margaret S. Mahler* (Northvale, NJ: Jason Aronson, 1974), 149–65.

36. Peter Blos, *The Adolescent Passage* (New York: International Universities Press, 1979). As one example of a review and critique of Blos's view, see J. Lock, "Acting Out and the Narrative Function: Reconsidering Peter Blos's Concept of the Second Individuation Process," *American Journal of Psychotherapy* 39 (1995): 548–57.

37. William Damon, *The Youth Charter* (New York: Free Press, 1997).

38. Elkind, *Ties That Stress.*

39. This definition, used by the U.S. Census Bureau in 1990, was selected by only 22 percent of a random sample of twelve hundred adults in a 1990 survey conducted by Massachusetts Mutual Insurance Company (found on the website, Kearl's *Guide to the Sociology of the Family,* www.trinity.edu /mkearl/family.html [accessed October 27, 2003]).

40. The source is the Tufts University Sociology website, course description for SOC0020: http:// ase.tufts.edu/lgbt/resources/academic/courses.asp (accessed November 30, 2010).

41. See www.cdc.gov/nchs/fastats/pdf/43-9s-t1.pdf (accessed March 13, 2003).

42. According to the Centers for Disease Control and Prevention (CDC), www.cdc.gov/nchs /releases/01news/firstmarr.htm (accessed May 24, 2001).

43. Federal Interagency Forum on Child and Family Statistics, "Family Structure and Children's Living Arrangements." *America's Children: Key National Indicators of Well-Being, 2009;* available from http://www.childstats.gov/americaschildren/famsoc1.asp (accessed November 22, 2009).

44. There is a journal devoted to this stage of the adolescent process: *Journal of Early Adolescence.*

45. See Arnett, *Adolescence and Emerging Adulthood.*

46. For examples, see Joseph P. Allen et al., "Attachment and Autonomy as Predictors of the Development of Social Skills and Delinquency during Midadolescence," *Journal of Consulting and Clinical Psychology* 70, no. 1 (2002): 56–66; and "Solution Focused Counseling in Middle and High Schools, Part 2: What the Research Says about What Works," *School Counseling and Psychology,* ACAeNews, American Counseling Association, 1, no. 2, January 29, 1998, www.counseling.org/enews /volume_1/0102b.htm (accessed February 26, 1998).

47. See www.counseling.org/enews/volume_1/0102b.htm, section on midadolescence (high school) (accessed February 26, 1998). The embedded quotation is from H. R. Wallbridge and T. A. G. Osachuk, "Therapy with Adolescents," in *Basics of Clinical Practice,* ed. D. G. Martin and A. D. Moore (Pacific Grove, CA: Brooks Cole), 208.

Chapter 2 Abandonment—The Defining Issue for Contemporary Adolescents

1. Lucinda Williams, http://top40-charts.com/news.php?nid=4878&string=Lucinda%20Williams (accessed November 30, 2010).

2. In addition to being a graduate school professor of youth, family, and culture, I have also been a staff member and volunteer of Young Life, a Christian youth outreach program. This has allowed me to be connected to and involved with students, faculty, administrators, and parents on several local high school campuses over the last three decades.

3. Ron Powers, *Tom and Huck Don't Live Here Anymore: Searching for the Lost American Childhood* (New York: St. Martin's Press, 2001).

4. Ron Powers, "The Apocalypse of Adolescence," *Atlantic*, March 2002, www.theatlantic.com /issues/2002/03/powers.htm (accessed May 3, 2003).

5. Males, "New Demons."

6. Ibid.

7. This is a phrase often used by those in academic and scholarly settings that qualifies information or an opinion as folklore. It is, in essence, the academic equivalent of an expletive.

8. See William Damon, Deanna Kuhn, and Robert S. Siegler, eds., *Handbook of Child Psychology*, vol. 2, *Cognition, Perception, and Language*, 5th ed. (New York: Wiley, 1998); and Rune J. Simeonsson, ed., *Risk, Resilience, and Prevention: Promoting the Well-Being of All Children* (Baltimore: Brookes, 1994).

9. Powers, *Tom and Huck*; and Powers, "Apocalypse of Adolescence."

10. Comment made on CNN about child prostitution in United States urban centers (March 21, 2002).

11. See Robert Epstein, *Teen 2.0: Saving Our Children and Families from the Torment of Adolescence* (Fresno, CA: Linden, 2010).

12. David Elkind, *A Sympathetic Understanding of the Child: Birth to Sixteen* (Needham Heights, MA: Allyn & Bacon, 1994), 197. See also Elkind, *Hurried Child*, 3rd ed.

13. Hersch, *Tribe Apart*, viii.

14. Ibid., ix. Triangulation in participant-observation methodology refers to bringing together data from multiple sources to get at the greatest understanding of the people being studied. It usually refers to the addition of outside literature, both popular and academic, to the researcher's own experience and the observations emerging from the study itself. In this study, I also employed focus group responses and feedback from presentations given to large groups of teenagers.

15. This is an important element of the ethnographic research process in which observations are compared and contrasted with literature and often feedback interviews. See the appendix for a more detailed explanation of the methodology used in this study.

16. David Elkind, *The Hurried Child: Growing Up Too Fast Too Soon*, 2nd ed. (Reading, MA: Addison-Wesley, 1988), xv.

17. Elkind, *Hurried Child*, xv. This and all subsequent references are to the third edition.

18. Elkind, *Ties That Stress*, 10–11.

19. William Mahedy and Janet Bernardi, *A Generation Alone: Xers Making a Place in the World* (Downers Grove, IL: InterVarsity, 1994), 24.

20. Hersch, *Tribe Apart*, 19.

21. Good Schools Pennsylvania, "Education History: A Timeline of Public Education in America," www.goodschoolspa.org/students/index.cfm?fuseaction=history (accessed August 13, 2003).

22. I deal with this in chapter 6.

23. Madeline Levine, *The Price of Privilege: How Parental Pressure and Material Advantage Are Creating a Generation of Disconnected and Unhappy Kids* (New York: HarperCollins, 2006), 28.

24. Ibid., 137.

25. Ibid., 8.

26. There are obviously exceptions. An example in education is educator, author, and developmental psychologist Mel Levine, *A Mind at a Time* (New York: Simon & Schuster, 2003). He is gaining a bit of momentum in certain educational circles by trying to shift the educational mind-set from the classroom and star students to an individual commitment to each child (see "Misunderstood Minds," a PBS documentary that first aired on March 27, 2002, and that has a companion website at www.pbs .org/misunderstoodminds), but the tide is strongly against his viewpoint.

27. David L. DuBois and Michael J. Karcher, "Youth Mentoring: Theory, Research, and Practice," in *Handbook of Youth Mentoring*, ed. D. L. DuBois and M. J. Karcher (Thousand Oaks, CA: Sage, 2005), 10.

28. Jean B. Grossman and Jean E. Rhodes, "The Test of Time: Predictors and Effects of Duration in Youth Mentoring Relationships," *American Journal of Community Psychology* 30 (2002): 213.

29. Renée Spencer, "'It's Not What I Expected': A Qualitative Study of Youth Mentoring Relationship Failures," *Journal of Adolescent Research* 22 (2007): 348.

30. Walt Mueller, *Youth Culture 101* (Grand Rapids: Zondervan/Youth Specialties, 2007), 38.

31. This will be discussed in more detail in chapter 3. Keep in mind that this was a macro-analysis study, and there will be notable exceptions to most of what I affirm. But few students even hinted that my conclusions were off target.

32. Paul Willis, *Common Culture: Symbolic Work at Play in the Everyday Cultures of the Young* (Boulder, CO: Westview, 1990), 1.

33. Denise Clark Pope, *Doing School: How We Are Creating a Generation of Stressed Out, Materialistic, and Miseducated Students* (New Haven: Yale University Press, 2001).

34. Chapman R. Clark, "Fathers' Participation in Their Adolescent Sons' Athletic Events: A Qualitative Study" (unpublished paper, Fuller Theological Seminary, Youth, Family, and Culture Department, Pasadena, CA, 1994).

35. Elkind, *Ties That Stress*.

36. Examples of this devastating effect abound in the research literature. See, for instance, the explicit connection between lack of positive adult involvement and violence in schools reported in Darlene R. Wright and Kevin M. Fitzpatrick, "Social Capital and Adolescent Violent Behavior: Correlates of Fighting and Weapon Use among Secondary School Students," *Social Forces* 84, no. 3 (March 2006): 1448. Similarly, Katherine Newman has reported that the number one necessary condition that is present in teens who resort to the kind of mass violence that has been seen in school shootings is "the shooter's perception of himself as *extremely marginal* in the social worlds that matter to him" (my emphasis). See Katherine Newman, *Rampage: The Social Roots of School Shootings* (New York: Basic Books, 2004), 230. For reporting on the link between other high-risk behaviors and the lack of social capital, see Lisa Smylie, Sheri Medaglia, and Eleanor Maticka-Tyndale, "The Effect of Social Capital and Socio-demographics on Adolescent Risk and Sexual Health Behaviours," *Canadian Journal of Human Sexuality* 15, no. 2 (Summer 2006): 95–112.

37. One reviewer made the observation that the lack of disagreement regarding my conclusions among the adolescents I talked to could be an example of them saying what I wanted to hear, or another form of layered living. Granted, that possibility exists. I do believe, however, that the different ways I triangulated the data provide at least some level of validity to the responses of the adolescents themselves.

38. Mary Pipher, *Reviving Ophelia: Saving the Selves of Adolescent Girls* (New York: Ballantine Books, 1994), 22.

39. As quoted in Powers, "Apocalypse of Adolescence."

40. Elkind, *Sympathetic Understanding of the Child*.

41. As an example, see the research of Ellen Galinsky of the Work and Family Institute of New York. One thousand children and adolescents from grades three to twelve were interviewed, as reported in Robert D. Strom, Troy E. Beckert, and Paris S. Strom, "Evaluating the Success of Caucasian Fathers in Guiding Adolescents," *Adolescence* 37 (Spring 2002): 131–49.

42. Stacey Richardson and Marita P. McCabe, "Parental Divorce during Adolescence and Adjustment in Early Adulthood," *Adolescence* 36 (Fall 2001): 467–89.

43. Ibid.

44. James E. Côté and Anton L. Allahar, *Generation on Hold: Coming of Age in the Late Twentieth Century* (Toronto: Stoddart, 1994), 71.

45. Carla Barnhill, "How Good Parents Give Up on Their Teens," *Books & Culture* (May–June 2002): 29, www.christianitytoday.com/bc/2002/003/14.27.html (accessed February 16, 2004).

46. Hersch, *Tribe Apart*, 20.

47. Ibid., 247. See also my discussion in chapter 1.

48. Allen and Allen, *Escaping the Endless Adolescence*, x.

49. Ibid., 13.

50. Mahedy and Bernardi, *Generation Alone*, 32.

51. See Enrico Gnaulati and Barb J. Heine, "Separation-Individuation in Late Adolescence: An Investigation of Gender and Ethnic Differences," *Journal of Psychology* 135, no. 1 (January 2001): 59–70; Mark T. Greenberg, Judith M. Siegel, and Cynthia J. Leitch, "The Nature and Importance of Attachment Relationships to Parents and Peers during Adolescence," *Journal of Youth and Adolescence* 12, no. 5 (1983): 373–86; and J. Eccles et al., "Self-Evaluations of Competence, Task Values, and Self-Esteem," in *Beyond Appearance: A New Look at Adolescent Girls*, ed. N. G. Johnson, M. C. Roberts, and J. Worell (Washington, DC: American Psychological Association, 1999), 53–83.

52. Cassandra Halleh Delaney, "Rites of Passage in Adolescence," *Adolescence* 30 (Winter 1995): 891–97.

53. Hersch, *Tribe Apart*, 21.

54. Don Martin and Maggie Martin, "Understanding Dysfunctional and Functional Family Behaviors for the At-Risk Adolescent," *Adolescence* 35 (Winter 2000): 785–92.

55. Alexander Wolff, "Special Report: The High School Athlete, Part 1," *Sports Illustrated*, November 18, 2002, sportsillustrated.cnn.com/si_online/news/2002/11/12/high_school (accessed February 13, 2004).

56. As reported in the *Los Angeles Times*, November 13, 2002, D2.

Chapter 3 The World Beneath

1. Jeffrey Lashbrook, "Fitting In: Exploring the Emotional Dimension of Adolescent Peer Pressure," *Adolescence* 35 (Winter 2000): 754.

2. For an example of this concern, see Pope, *Doing School*, xi.

3. An example of this concern is raised in Michael T. Ungar, "The Myth of Peer Pressure," *Adolescence* 35 (Spring 2000): 167–80.

4. Hersch, *Tribe Apart*, viii.

5. Solarz, *American Psychological Association*, 3.

6. A decade before the first edition of *Hurt* was published, Côté and Allahar, in *Generation on Hold*, 21, had already noted that adolescents had developed a secret side to their world in reaction to rejection from adults: "Because they are not allowed to participate fully in adult culture, youths develop their own culture in an attempt to find a more meaningful identity." Christian Smith has recently affirmed the basic vision of Côté and Allahar: "Teenagers are forever waiting, continually preparing, perpetually coming of age, and are meanwhile for the most part socially superfluous. Thus, they experience a disconnect from the adult world not only in the structures of their routine and activities and schedules, but also through the many years of limbo through which they must hang in suspension before passing into full-fledged adulthood" (Christian Smith, *Soul Searching: The Religious and Spiritual Lives of American Teenagers* [New York: Oxford University Press, 2005], 185).

7. This further illustrates the difference between the innocuous withdrawal adolescents have typically created—as in *Saved by the Bell* or Danny Zuko and the T Birds in *Grease*—and the place of separation and the uniqueness of the midadolescent subculture into which the withdrawal has developed today. Since the first edition of *Hurt*, most people who worked closely with adolescents easily recognized this reality, and yet there remain those who have a hard time grasping the difference between a more traditional understanding of the generation gap and the world beneath. During a doctoral seminar an African-American grad student helped connect the dots of this line of thinking, and since then, the sociological research on this phenomenon has greatly influenced my thinking on the world beneath.

8. The detailed chronology of this progression depends on a myriad of factors, such as the part of the country in which one lived, but this study revealed that it has caught up to all of us today. The world beneath appears to be true of nearly every sector of American society, if not the entire urbanized world (meaning wherever there is ready access to radio, CDs, television, and films).

9. I realize that the language I am slipping into is universal and therefore may cause the reader to look for exceptions that will disprove my observations. I have chosen to generalize in strong terms instead of continuing to use a qualifying statement such as "nearly all" or "the vast majority."

10. Putnam, *Bowling Alone*. To access the data used in *Bowling Alone*, see www.bowlingalone .com/socialcapital.php3 (accessed July 30, 2006). This URL is no longer accessible, but the concepts are expressed currently throughout the website and in the book.

11. Putnam, *Bowling Alone*, 312.

12. See Delaney, "Rites of Passage in Adolescence"; and Lashbrook, "Fitting In."

13. Quoted in John R. Chapin, "Adolescent Sex and Mass Media: A Developmental Approach," *Adolescence* 35 (Winter 2000): 799–811.

14. Mahedy and Bernardi, *Generation Alone*, 31.

15. Lashbrook, "Fitting In."

16. Delaney, "Rites of Passage in Adolescence."

17. Ibid.

18. Anita Hunter has noted that "resilience in adolescence may not be an adaptable, flexible, competent process of overcoming adversity but a process of defense using such tactics as insulation, isolation, disconnecting, denial, and aggression" ("Adolescent Resilience," *Journal of Nursing Scholarship* 31, no. 3 [1999]: 243–47, quotation from p. 246). When unsupported, adolescents tend not to reach a stage of recovery, but instead stall in survival and self-protection. Further, "the mediating variable appears to be the presence of a consistent, caring, loving adult who teaches the adolescent how to traverse the adversities in life and is there to help him or her pick themselves up, learn and grow from the experience, and move forward because they know they are loved, respected, and valued" (Anita Hunter, "A Cross-Cultural Comparison of Resilience in Adolescents," *Journal of Pediatric Nursing* 16, no. 3 [June 2001]: 172–79, quotation from p. 178).

19. Delaney, "Rites of Passage in Adolescence."

20. Chapin, "Adolescent Sex and Mass Media," 802.

21. S. Harter et al., "The Complexity of the Self in Adolescence," in Arnett, *Readings on Adolescence*, 112.

22. "The proliferation of 'selves' and concern over 'who is the real me?' ratchets up in middle adolescence," writes Madeline Levine. My perspective is that teens are sometimes somewhat aware of contradictions in their sense of self, but because they know they have to present and "be someone" the emphasis for them is not dealing with the incongruities but rather surviving in the moment. When

confronted with the reality of their "multiple selves," they generally fall into a confused malaise, wondering, as Levine notes, "how they will ever integrate the curious kid at school, the rowdy kid with friends, the quiet kid in new situations, and the crabby kid at home into a single comfortable person. Their internal landscape is cluttered with multiple selves, some in contradiction with each other. . . . While there have been many advances in their thinking, it is still just beyond their reach to integrate opposing characteristics" (Price of Privilege, 120). See also Catherine E. Amiot et al., "Integration of Social Identities in the Self: Toward a Cognitive-Developmental Model," Personality and Social Psychology Review 11, no. 4 (2007): 364–88.

23. Hersch, Tribe Apart, 306.

24. J. S. Phinney and M. Devich-Navarro, "Variations in Bicultural Identification among African American and Mexican American Adolescents," in Arnett, Readings on Adolescence, 120–31.

25. Solarz, American Psychological Association, 3. A 2009 study from the Centers for Disease Control and Prevention revealed that by the time the North American teenager reaches twelfth grade, nearly half of his/her classmates have used marijuana; over three in five have engaged in vaginal intercourse; and four in five have consumed at least one full drink of alcohol. For full results, see the Centers for Disease Control and Prevention, "2009 National Youth Risk Behavior Survey," http://www.cdc.gov/healthyyouth/yrbs/index.htm (accessed July 3, 2010). Also, a December 2009 study by the Pew Research Center found that 15 percent of high school students—and 30 percent of seniors—had received nude or semi-nude pictures on their mobile phone. See "Teens and Sexting," Pew Research Center, http://pewinternet.org/Reports/2009/Teens-and-Sexting.aspx (accessed November 30, 2010).

26. Levine, Price of Privilege, 35.

27. See Pete Ward, God at the Mall (Peabody, MA: Hendrickson, 1999), 87: "For Stuart Hall and those in the CCCS, the concept of subculture was used to explain the existence of 'resistant cultures' within society. Drawing on the work of the Italian theorist Gramsci, Hall argued that culture provided an arena within which different groups in society carried out a struggle. Those groups which are economically and socially dominant seek to extend their authority by using culture to support their power. Culture then becomes a means for dominant groups in society to seek the assent of subordinate groups. . . . Hall's understanding of youth culture was that it was an attempt to resist 'hegemony' by creating subcultures. These subcultures are created by the use of particular kinds of dress, ways of behaving, and ways of speaking which are laden with symbols and signs. . . . The symbols when correctly understood reveal a style of life which is an attempt to create identity apart from that offered by the dominant culture; it is therefore 'resistant.'" The source he cites here is Stuart Hall and Tony Jefferson, Resistance through Rituals (London: Hutchinson, 1975): 5–8.

28. Pipher, Reviving Ophelia, 28.

29. Hersch, Tribe Apart, 30.

30. One example of this is the work of William Strauss and Neil Howe (The Fourth Turning: An American Prophecy [New York: Broadway Books, 1997]), who claim that because generations generally cycle the same characteristics every four generations, the present emerging generation will therefore be more spiritual, more collaborative, and more able to "reconstruct a positive reputation for American adolescents" (327). Based on this study, I could not disagree more strongly. Yes, this emerging generation appears to be all of these things and more, but in reality, our society is facing an abandoned, on-their-own generation, which has unprecedented consequences for the future.

31. Mahedy and Bernardi, Generation Alone, 32.

32. Pipher, Reviving Ophelia, 285.

33. For over three decades, resilience researchers have emphasized that social capital given by adults to adolescents who have experienced trauma is a key mitigating factor toward recovery. For a brief review, see Michael Rutter, "Protective Factors in Children's Responses to Stress and Disadvantage," in Primary Prevention of Psychopathology, vol. 3, Social Competence in Children, ed. M. W. Kent and Jon E. Rolf (Hanover, NH: University Press of New England, 1979); Anne C. Peterson et al., "Resilience in Adolescence," in The Adolescent in Turmoil: A Monograph for the International Society for Adolescent Psychiatry, ed. Allan Z. Schwartzberg (Westport, CT: Praeger, 1998); Suniya Luthar, Dante Cicchetti, and Bronwyn Becker, "The Construct of Resilience: A Critical Evaluation and Guidelines for Future Work," Child Development 71, no. 3 (May/June 2000): 543–62; Hunter, "Cross-Cultural Comparison of Resilience in Adolescents," n. 19; Robin D. Everall, Jessica Altrows, and Barbara L. Paulson, "Creating a Future: A Study of Resilience in Suicidal Female Adolescents," Journal of Counseling and Development 84 (Fall 2006): 461–70.

Chapter 4 Peers

1. Susan Harter et al., "The Development of Multiple Role-Related Selves during Adolescence," *Development and Psychopathology* 9 (1997): 844.

2. Peter Blos, "Second Individuation Process."

3. I chose in this study not to investigate in depth such demographic distinctions as ethnicity and socioeconomic stratification as I looked at the high school social environment. Some may argue that this makes many of my observations illegitimate and lacking in texture. I am attempting, however, to describe life as it is from a macro perspective. The vast majority of those in various subgroups, while displaying distinctness, were also functioning members of the social setting and as such displayed behaviors that were consistent with my observations of the adolescent community as a whole. See the appendix for a more detailed description of this decision.

4. Donald C. Posterski, *Friendship: A Window on Ministry to Youth* (Scarborough, ON: Project Teen Canada, 1985), 8.

5. See Eugene R. Oetting and F. Beauvais, "Peer Cluster Theory: Drugs and the Adolescent," *Journal of Counseling and Development* 65 (1986): 17–22; and Eugene R. Oetting and F. Beauvais, "Peer Cluster Theory, Socialization Characteristics and Adolescent Drug Use: A Path Analysis," *Journal of Counseling Psychology* 34 (1987): 205–13.

6. Examples abound and are cited throughout this book.

7. While some peer studies focus on early adolescence and a few on adolescence in general, to date there has not been adequate comprehensive research identifying distinguishing characteristics of the three stages of adolescence (see chap. 1). In numerous studies, however, the differences are clearly implied.

8. For examples of clustering as an idea while not using the actual term, see Curran, Stice, and Chassin, "Relation between Adolescent Alcohol Use and Peer Alcohol Use," 131; K. A. Urberg, S. M. Degirmencioglu, and C. Pilgrim, "Close Friend and Group Influence on Adolescent Cigarette Smoking and Alcohol Use," *Developmental Psychology* 33 (1997): 834–44; R. R. Kafka and P. London, "Communication in Relationships and Adolescent Substance Abuse: The Influence of Parents and Friends," *Adolescence* 26 (1991): 587–98; M. S. Tisak, J. Tisak, and M. Rogers, "Adolescents' Reasoning about Authority and Friendship Relations in the Context of Drug Use," *Journal of Adolescence* 17 (1994): 265–82; Kimberly L. Henry, Eugene R. Oetting, and Michael D. Slater, "The Role of Attachment to Family, School, and Peers in Adolescents' Use of Alcohol: A Longitudinal Study of Within-Person and Between-Persons Effects," *Journal of Counseling Psychology* 56, no. 4 (2009): 564–72; and Ricardo Stanton-Salazar and Stephanie Urso Spina, "Adolescent Peer Networks as a Context for Social and Emotional Support," *Youth & Society* 36, no. 4 (2005): 379–417.

9. B. B. Brown, M. S. Mory, and D. Kinney, "Casting Crowds in a Relational Perspective: Caricature, Channel, and Context," in Arnett, *Readings on Adolescence*, 161–72.

10. For examples, see Maja Dekovic and Wim Meeus, "Peer Relations in Adolescence: Effects of Parenting and Adolescents' Self-Concept," *Journal of Adolescence* 20 (1997): 163–76; and D. C. Rowe, E. J. Woulbroun, and B. L. Gulley, "Peer and Friends as Nonshared Environmental Influence," in *Separate Social World of Siblings*, ed. E. M. Hethington, D. Reiss, and R. Plomin (Hillsdale, NJ: Lawrence Erlbaum, 1994), 159–74.

11. For example, P. A. Cusick, *Inside High School* (New York: Holt, Rinehart & Winston, 1973); and R. W. Larkin, *Suburban Youth in Cultural Crisis* (New York: Oxford University Press, 1979) were both used to triangulate data compiled by ethnographic researchers in the mid-1990s (Brown, Mory, and Kinney, "Casting Crowds," 166).

12. See Barney G. Glaser, *Basics of Grounded Theory Analysis: Emergence vs. Forcing* (Mill Valley, CA: Sociology Press, 1992); and Linda Jo Calloway and Constance A. Knapp, "Using Grounded Theory to Interpret Interviews," csis.pace.edu/~knapp/AIS95.htm (accessed November 30, 2010).

13. Jean Piaget, *The Psychology of Intelligence* (New York: International Universities Press, 1950); and E. Erikson, *Identity*.

14. Crystal R. Tani, Ernest L. Chavez, and Jerry L. Deffenbacher, "Peer Isolation and Drug Use among White Non-Hispanic and Mexican American Adolescents," *Adolescence* 36 (Spring 2001): 127–39.

15. Joseph A. Micucci, *The Adolescent in Family Therapy: Breaking the Cycle of Conflict and Control* (New York: Guilford, 1998).

16. J. A. Bishop and Heidi Inderbitzen, "Peer Acceptance and Friendship: An Investigation of Their Relationship to Self-Esteem," *Journal of Early Adolescence* 15 (1995): 476–89.

17. Daniel K. Lapsley and Jason Edgerton, "Separation-Individuation, Adult Attachment Style, and College Adjustment," *Journal of Counseling and Development* 80 (2002): 484.

18. Lashbrook, "Fitting In."

19. Urie Bronfenbrenner, *The Ecology of Human Development: Experiments by Nature and Design* (Cambridge, MA: Harvard University Press, 1979).

20. Elkind, *Hurried Child*, 3rd ed.

21. Elkind, *Ties That Stress*.

22. See note 32 of chapter 1.

23. Dekovic and Meeus, "Peer Relations in Adolescence," 173. See also L. B. Whitbeck, R. D. Conger, and M. Kao, "The Influence of Parental Support, Depressed Affect, and Peers on the Sexual Behavior of Adolescent Girls," *Journal of Family Issues* 14 (1993): 261-78.

24. Levine, *Price of Privilege*, 8.

25. See chapter 2.

26. Denis W. Jarvinen and John G. Nicholls, "Adolescents' Social Goals, Beliefs about the Causes of Social Success, and Satisfaction in Peer Relations," *Developmental Psychology* 32, no. 3 (1996): 440.

27. In their study of Mexican-origin students in San Diego, Stanton-Salazar and Spina observed that "enriching and supportive peer relationships and networks appear to buffer the adolescent from environmental stressors," such as difficult family life, neighborhood violence, or inadequately resourced schools. See Stanton-Salazar and Spina, "Adolescent Peer Networks," 411.

28. Ibid., 386.

29. One of the reviewers responded to this by noting, "Is this really true? In my experience, even kids in clusters seem driven by the same flights of emotion as they always have. A kid is cool and thus clustered, as long as he doesn't screw up. If he does, he is ostracized from the whole group." In my observation, one of the primary differences between clusters and previous adolescent social structures is that the cluster becomes for a season the most powerful community for the midadolescent, with the possible exception of the family. The bonds formed, then, are not as easily severed as high school friendships in the past.

30. Christopher Daddis, "Influence of Close Friends on the Boundaries of Adolescent Personal Authority," *Journal of Research on Adolescence* 18 (2008): 91.

31. See, for example, Lara Mayeux and Antonius H. N. Cillessen, "It's Not Just Being Popular, It's Knowing It, Too: The Role of Self-Perceptions of Status in the Associations between Peer Status and Aggression," *Social Development*, no. 17 (2008): 871-88; and Irene J. Kim, Nolan W. S. Zane, and Sehee Hong, "Protective Factors against Substantive Use among Asian American Youth: A Test of the Peer Cluster Theory," *Journal of Community Psychology* 30, no. 5 (2002): 565-84.

32. For examples of this, see Curran, Stice, and Chassin, "Relation between Adolescent Alcohol Use and Peer Alcohol Use"; R. H. Aseltine, "A Reconsideration of Parental and Peer Influence on Adolescent Deviance," *Journal of Health and Social Behavior* 36 (1995): 103-21; W. H. Buysse, "Behavior Problems and Relationships with Family and Peers during Adolescence," *Journal of Adolescence* 20 (1997): 645-59; and Kathryn E. Hoff, George J. Dupaul, and Michael L. Handwerk, "Rejected Youth in Residential Treatment: Social Affiliation and Peer Group Configuration," *Journal of Emotional and Behavioral Disorders* 11, no. 2 (2003): 112-21, esp. 113.

33. Urberg, Degirmencioglu, and Pilgrim, "Close Friend and Group Influence," 843.

34. There is no clear-cut academic resource for this view, but several scholars are leaning toward this as an interesting typology for dealing with the nature versus nurture debate while maintaining the integrity of the uniqueness of each person.

35. Dekovic and Meeus, "Peer Relations in Adolescence."

36. For a comprehensive summary of Mary Ainsworth and John Bowlby's attachment theory, see Inge Bretherton, "The Origins of Attachment Theory: John Bowlby and Mary Ainsworth," *Developmental Psychology* 28, no. 5 (1992): 759-75.

37. Dekovic and Meeus, "Peer Relations in Adolescence"; see also Gareth R. Schott and Wynford Bellin, "The Relational Self-Concept Scale: A Context-Specific Self-Report Measure for Adolescents," *Adolescence* 36 (Spring 2001): 85-103. They argue that "to be truly effective for education [and presumably any other desired use], measurement of the self needs to be linked directly to the social processes of the school environment" (99), thus affirming an additional need for my study.

38. B. B. Brown, N. Mounts, S. D. Lamborn, and L. Steinberg, "Parenting Practices and Peer Group Affiliation in Adolescence," *Child Development* 64 (1993): 469.

39. Ibid.

40. Dekovic and Meeus, "Peer Relations in Adolescence," 164.

41. Historically, however, this shift was assumed to be from early to late adolescence (a two-stage view) rather than from early to middle (in a three-stage view).

42. For a complete description of this metaphor used for the adolescent journey, see Clark, "Changing Face of Adolescence."

43. I believed this because that is what it was like when I was in high school. What I observed was a very different process.

44. See D. Bender and F. Losel, "Protective and Risk Effects of Peer Relations and Social Support on Antisocial Behavior in Adolescents from Multi-Problem Milieus," *Journal of Adolescence* 20 (1997): 661–78.

45. The notion of "cousin clusters" was first developed through a comprehensive literature review on clustering by PhD student Andy Root as a requirement for an independent study course with me in June 2000. In summarizing the literature regarding peer relationships, Root concluded that there are indeed groups of students who band together beyond their clusters and get along quite well. These are what he calls "cousin clusters."

46. In my view, a tragic and painful example of what happens when authorities are not aware of (or ignore the signs of) this social hierarchy and fragmentation is what occurred leading up the Columbine massacre in 1999. While this has not been, to my knowledge, explored as a significant contributing factor, the sociological landscape of Columbine High School in the two years preceding the events of April 20 played at least some role in how the shooters came to violently lash out at their classmates.

Chapter 5 School

1. *The Class*, dir. Laurent Cantet, original title *Entre les Murs* (France) (Culver City, CA: Sony Pictures, 2008), video recording.

2. This has been somewhat difficult for me as a researcher, as my own sister, brother-in-law, sister-in-law, and mother-in-law are all lifelong members of the public educational system and guild. I have great respect for them, as well as all those teachers and educators I have met over the years. I do not desire to offend or hurt any public school official by what I report in this study. If in the course of attempting to present what I found in this study I unfairly offend anyone, I sincerely apologize.

3. Greg J. Duncan, Johanne Boisjoly, and Kathleen Mullan Harris, "Sibling, Peer, Neighbor, and Schoolmate Correlations as Indicators of the Importance of Context for Adolescent Development," *Demography* 38, no. 3 (August 2001): 437–47.

4. Administrators also obviously play an important role in the healthy development of children and adolescents, but to the majority of students, administrators do not play as key a role as do teachers.

5. For an example of this perspective, see Dudley J. Wiest, Eugene H. Wong, and Joseph M. Cervantes, "Intrinsic Motivation among Regular, Special, and Alternative Education High School Students," *Adolescence* 36 (Spring 2001): 111–26.

6. Parker Palmer, *The Courage to Teach: Exploring the Inner Landscape of a Teacher's Life* (Hoboken, NJ: Jossey-Bass, 1997).

7. Solarz, *American Psychological Association*, 27.

8. Michael Nakkula and Michael Sadowski, eds., *Adolescents at School: Perspectives on Youth, Identity, and Education* (Cambridge, MA: Harvard Education Press, 2008), 19.

9. Elliot Currie, *The Road to Whatever: Middle Class Culture and the Crisis of Adolescence* (New York: Metropolitan Books, 2004), 193–94.

10. I attended this banquet three years in a row, one as a parent and two during the course of this research project.

11. This is also true in the area of volunteerism. Although a standard line from educational and academic circles is that volunteerism "fosters a sense of purpose and meaning and enhances moral development" (Solarz, *American Psychological Association*, 32), what I observed is that most of the students who do volunteer service, especially as a part of their school curriculum, are almost always motivated by forces other than altruistic concern and genuine service to others. The most common reasons for volunteering are to fulfill a class or school requirement, please teachers, or contribute to a college résumé. Because I consistently observed this widespread tendency, I chose not to spend time discussing volunteerism as a major aspect of midadolescence or detailing the exemplary students who are noted for being volunteers.

12. In the school where I studied, the administration was generally exempt from this view. Most teachers felt as though the coprincipals were "teacher-administrators," meaning that they were educators and colleagues first and bureaucrats second, which went a long way toward maintaining a minimum level of morale in the face of much professional discouragement.

13. As reported by the Associated Press, "Unruly Students Top Public's List of School Worries," *New York Times*, April 23, 2003, D3. Other recent studies also reveal teachers' feelings of powerlessness over policies that directly affect what happens in their classrooms. See, for example, Jeffrey S.

Brooks, Roxanne M. Hughes, and Melanie C. Brooks, "Fear and Trembling in the American High School: Educational Reform and Teacher Alienation," *Educational Policy* 22 (January 2008): 45–62.

14. See Carl E. Larson and Frank M. J. LaFasto, *Teamwork: What Must Go Right, What Can Go Wrong* (Newbury Park, CA: Sage, 1989).

15. Duncan, Boisjoly, and Harris, "Sibling, Peer, Neighbor, and Schoolmate Correlations."

16. In a study on adolescent delinquency, Monique Matherne and Adrian Thomas placed a major emphasis on the schools', and especially the teachers', responsibility to avert potential delinquency in at-risk students. The supporting literature cited carried an equally strong message endorsing the teacher's role as an important link. See Monique M. Matherne and Adrian Thomas, "Family Environment as a Predictor of Adolescent Delinquency," *Adolescence* 36 (Winter 2001): 655–64.

17. Many studies cite teachers' affirmation regarding the educational necessity of parental support, and yet parents have increasingly backed away from direct involvement in the high school system. See, for example, Strom, Beckert, and Strom, "Evaluating the Success of Caucasian Fathers," 131–49.

18. Robert Crosnoe and Glen H. Elder Jr., "Family Dynamics, Supportive Relationships, and Educational Resilience during Adolescence," *Journal of Family Issues* 25 (July 2004): 573.

19. I realize that this description of the teacher-parent relationship is a gross overstatement and generalization. The essence of this dynamic is drawn here, however, to ensure that the reader will understand that there is a real problem. We do not have a system in which a healthy partnership can easily take place.

20. In "a report released by Public Agenda, a nonprofit research and policy organization, . . . teachers said a lack of parental involvement is a serious problem, with 78% of teachers saying too many parents don't know what is going on with their child's education. Only 19% said parental involvement is strong in their high school" (Associated Press, "Unruly Students Top Public's List").

21. It is true that parents are notorious in educational circles for not returning phone calls, not responding to letters, and the like. Yet in light of the difficulties and dynamics of raising midadolescents, it is easy to see how their busyness and fear of more pressure and possible ridicule generally foster a retreatism mentality. The parent-teacher relationship is a classic case of both needing each other, but both remaining skeptical of and intimidated by the other. Teachers, however, are in a much less precarious position than parents, and therefore I agree with educational leaders who advocate the teacher's role as the initiator. See Strom, Beckert, and Strom, "Evaluating the Success of Caucasian Fathers."

22. Associated Press, "Unruly Students Top Public's List."

23. *The Class*, dir. Laurent Cantet.

24. Ruben Garza, "Latino and White High School Students' Perceptions of Caring Behaviors: Are We Culturally Responsive to Our Students?" *Urban Education* 44 (May 2009): 298.

25. Alison Cook-Sather, "What Would Happen If We Treated Students as Those with Opinions That Matter? The Benefits to Principals and Teachers of Supporting Youth Engagement in School," *NASSP Bulletin* 91 (December 2007): 348. See also the conclusions of Louie F. Rodriguez, "'Teachers Know You Can Do More': Understanding How School Cultures of Success Affect Urban High School Students," *Educational Policy* 22 (September 2008): 758–80.

26. David Brooks, "Making It: Love and Success at America's Finest Universities," *Weekly Standard* 8, no. 15, www.weeklystandard.com/Content/Public/Articles/000/000/002/017ickdp.asp (accessed December 23, 2002).

27. See Wiest, Wong, and Cervantes, "Intrinsic Motivation."

28. P. Jackson, *Life in Classrooms*, rev. ed. (New York: Teachers College Press, 1990), 27.

29. Donald Lee McCabe, "Academic Dishonesty among High School Students," *Adolescence* 34 (Winter 1999): 681–87.

30. Jackson, *Life in Classrooms*, 26–28.

31. McCabe, "Academic Dishonesty." See also Jackson, *Life in Classrooms*; and Pope, *Doing School*.

32. For a more detailed argument for this statement, see chapter 10.

33. Andrea Solarz notes that "adolescent perception of teacher fairness has also been found to be associated with positive adolescent development" (*American Psychological Association*, 27). See also J. D. Klein, "The National Longitudinal Study on Adolescent Health: Preliminary Results—Great Expectations," *Journal of the American Medical Association* 278 (1997): 864–65. According to my observations, this is one of the more frequent arguments for rationalizing the widespread practice of cheating: "Teachers aren't fair, so we should be able to cheat."

34. L. Jensen, J. Arnett, S. Feldman, and E. Cauffman, "It's Wrong, but Everybody Does It: Academic Dishonesty among High School and College Students," *Contemporary Educational Psychology* 27, no. 2 (2002): 209–28.

35. Ibid.

36. Pope, *Doing School*, 156.

37. This is the designation given to those who were born in their country of origin but have been raised in their immigrant nation.

38. In the community where this study took place, many Asian students felt the pressure and the expectation to attend classes all day Saturday and to maintain the highest levels of academic achievement.

39. Some schools even require a certain minimum of volunteer hours, regardless of the personal or familial circumstances of the student.

40. Pope, *Doing School*, 150.

41. As recorded in Pope, ibid.

42. There have been a few attempts to train students to work in teams, although, primarily due to the self-focused perspective of midadolescents, how to use this as an effective teaching technique has yet to be discovered. See Solarz, *American Psychological Association*. As David Elkind quipped in a speech at the National Youth Workers' Convention in October 1988, "We should close all junior high schools and take all those kids and have them go somewhere and build a boat for two years!"

43. Solarz, *American Psychological Association*, 15.

44. On July 31, 2003, the *New York Times* ran a front-page story on "pushouts," those students who, for whatever reason, may bring down a school's overall test scores and are therefore being forced to drop out of school prematurely.

45. Solarz, *American Psychological Association*, 10. See also H. Gardner, *Multiple Intelligences: The Theory in Practice* (New York: Basic Books, 1993).

46. I do not subscribe to the notion that every child has unlimited potential, for that maintains the myth that all are equally capable of achieving anything. This is an overly optimistic cultural myth that is destructive to individuals who may not be designed for a given dream. What is more appropriate is to alter our system and train each child to believe that he or she is the only one capable of being himself or herself, the person he or she is designed to become.

47. Levine, *A Mind at a Time*.

Chapter 6 Family

1. Richardson and McCabe, "Parental Divorce during Adolescence," 467–89; Strom, Beckert, and Strom, "Evaluating the Success of Caucasian Fathers"; Matherne and Thomas, "Family Environment"; and Robert H. Bradley and Robert F. Corwyn, "Home Environment and Behavioral Development during Early Adolescence: The Mediating and Moderating Roles of Self-Efficacy Beliefs," *Merrill-Palmer Quarterly* 47, no. 2 (2001): 165–87.

2. Clifford L. Broman, Xin Li, and Mark Reckase, "Family Structure and Mediators of Adolescent Drug Use," *Journal of Family Issues* 28 (August 2008): 1626–49; Sara E. Goldstein, Pamela E. Davis-Kean, and Jacquelynne S. Eccles, "Parents, Peers, and Problem Behavior: A Longitudinal Investigation of the Impact of Relationship Perceptions and Characteristics on the Development of Adolescent Problem Behavior," *Developmental Psychology* 41, no. 2 (March 2005): 401–13; Jennifer Manlove et al., "Pathways from Family Religiosity to Adolescent Sexual Activity and Contraceptive Use," *Perspectives on Sexual and Reproductive Health* 40, no. 2 (2008): 105–17.

3. Solarz, *American Psychological Association*, 25.

4. In attempting to strengthen this book, I elicited editorial and conceptual input from students, colleagues, and friends. The one I relied on the most heavily, corporate executive Jim Collins, took me to task in this section. I decided his point did not fit the stream of thought in this section, but his words are noteworthy: "This is not true really—especially outside the Judeo-Christian culture. Many Pacific island cultures swap kids pretty freely—they all have different terms for it—with little stigma or impact. The problem in our culture is the coincident facts of the accepted norm and cultural change. That is to say, the family is changing in a fashion that is convenient for selfish adults. But there remain distinct social mores that weigh upon the children of 'abnormal' families. It is this penalty that I believe has the deepest effect. I personally disagree with the notion, for example, that lesbian parents are bad for kids in and of themselves. What is bad for kids is the social stigma that is an undeniable outgrowth of their familial situation. While society may want to allow people to be free to pursue their own wants and desires, the simple fact is that the children subjected to these environments at home bear their weight alone when they are not at home. The selfish parent exacerbates this situation by making discussion of their pain difficult or by belittling the opinions and feelings of their children." I would like to add to this the reason I struggle with lesbian parents: the implied notion that fathers are inherently unnecessary is a concept that objective empirical research does not allow for.

5. This is how the U.S. Census Bureau defines a family. This definition was selected by only 22 percent of a random sample of twelve hundred adults in a 1990 survey conducted by the Massachusetts Mutual Insurance Company. See Kearl's *Guide to the Sociology of the Family*, www.trinity.edu/mkearl /family.html (accessed August 1, 2003).

6. Although the European concept of the extended family with the parents as the primary nurturers of their own children can be traced back several thousand years to the early Israelites, many assert that the notion of the traditional dual-parent family harkens back only as far as black-and-white television. An example of this kind of revisionist rejection of the dual-parent family is found in Stephanie Coontz, *The Way We Never Were*: "It is worth noting that the word family originally meant a band of slaves. Even after the word came to apply to people affiliated by blood and marriage, for many centuries the notion of family referred to authority relations rather than loved ones. The sentimentalization of family life and female nurturing was historically and functionally linked to the emergence of competitive individualism and formal egalitarianism for men" (*The Way We Never Were: American Families and the Nostalgia Trap* [New York: Basic Books, 1992], 43–44). There is ample evidence of a long, consistent history of family life in European societies, which is the basis for American family life. This began to erode in the early to mid-1830s when observers began to notice a shift (some would say a decline or decay) in American family life. According to Yale University professor John Demos, this period sowed seeds that flourished over one hundred years later—divorce and desertion increased, child rearing became decidedly casual, authority in the household was questioned and challenged, and the family experienced generally less time together (John Demos, *Past, Present, and Personal: The Family and the Life Course in America* [New York: Oxford University Press, 1986]).

7. Susan L. Brown, "How Cohabitation Is Reshaping American Families," *Contexts* 4, no. 3 (Summer 2005), www.proquest.com (accessed December 11, 2009).

8. Ibid.

9. Amy G. Langekamp and Michelle L. Frisco, "Family Transitions and Adolescent Severe Emotional Distress: The Salience of Family Context," *Social Problems* 55, no. 2 (May 2008), www.proquest.com (accessed December 11, 2009).

10. This is confirmed by many studies on parent behaviors. For one example, see Strom, Beckert, and Strom, "Evaluating the Success of Caucasian Fathers."

11. Currie, *Road to Whatever*, 45.

12. Matherne and Thomas, "Family Environment," 663. See also Elizabeth Bertera, "The Role of Positive and Negative Social Exchanges between Adolescents, Their Peers and Family as Predictors of Suicide Ideation," *Child and Adolescent Social Work Journal* 24, no. 6 (December 2007), www .proquest.com (accessed December 11, 2009).

13. Solarz, *American Psychological Association*, 26.

14. Ibid.

15. Jeffrey J. Arnett, "Adolescent Storm and Stress, Reconsidered," in *Readings on Adolescence*, 10.

16. Ibid.

17. Solarz, *American Psychological Association*, 27.

18. Mary Eastham, "Healing the Wounded Adolescent," *Compass* 43, no. 2 (Winter 2009), www .proquest.com (accessed December 11, 2009).

19. Strom, Beckert, and Strom, "Evaluating the Success of Caucasian Fathers."

20. While some studies have demonstrated that strong support from siblings may to some extent compensate for low levels of support from parents, this should never be seen as an excuse for parents to abdicate their primary responsibility. See Avidan Milevsky, "Compensatory Patterns of Sibling Support in Emerging Adulthood: Variations in Loneliness, Self-Esteem, Depression and Life Satisfaction," *Journal of Social and Personal Relationships* 22 (2005): 751.

21. Solarz, *American Psychological Association*, 4.

22. Mark D. Regnerus, "Friends' Influence on Adolescent Theft and Minor Delinquency: A Developmental Test of Peer-Reported Effects," *Social Science Research* 13, no. 4 (December 2002): 681–706.

23. Mary Eastham, "Healing the Wounded Adolescent." See also the conclusions of William S. Aquilino and Andrew J. Supple: "Successful individuation coupled with continued support from parents leads to positive psychosocial competence beyond adolescence" ("Long-Term Effects of Parenting Practices during Adolescence on Well-Being Outcomes in Young Adulthood," *Journal of Family Issues* 22 [April 2001]: 291); and the conclusions of Simon Eltringham and Jan Aldridge, "Parenting on Shifting Sands: The Transfer of Responsibility for Safely Managing Danger," *Clinical Child Psychology and Psychiatry* 7 (2002): 143.

Chapter 7 Sports

1. Not surprisingly, this sort of social labeling satisfies a significant developmental need for these students, as "peer group membership and activity involvement are linked to identity exploration and to a sense of belonging to a particular type of peer group and having a particular activity-based persona" (Bonnie L. Barber, Jacquelynne S. Eccles, and Margaret R. Stone, "Whatever Happened to the Jock, the Brain, and the Princess? Young Adult Pathways Linked to Adolescent Activity Involvement and Social Identity," *Journal of Adolescent Research* 16, no. 5 [September 2001]: 429–55, quotation on 431).

2. Solarz, *American Psychological Association*, 18.

3. See Barber, Eccles, and Stone, "Whatever Happened?"; Patricia A. Harrison and Narayan Gopal-akrishnan, "Differences in Behavior, Psychological Factors, and Environmental Factors Associated with Participation in School Sports and Other Activities in Adolescence," *Journal of School Health* 9, no. 3 (March 2003): 113; Karen Trew et al., "Sport, Leisure and Perceived Self-Competence among Male and Female Adolescents," *European Physical Education Review* 5, no. 1 (1999): 53–74.

4. See Lina A. Ricciardelli, Marita P. McCabe, and Damien Ridge, "The Construction of the Ado-lescent Male Body through Sport," *Journal of Health Psychology* 11, no. 4 (2006): 577–87.

5. For a subtle yet honest look at the way high school sports have become a powerful, consuming, and demanding institution in our country, see Wolff, "Special Report"; and Mark Hyman, *Until It Hurts: America's Obsession with Youth Sports and How It Harms Our Kids* (Boston: Beacon, 2009).

6. Merrill J. Melnick, Kathleen E. Miller, and Donald F. Sabo, "Tobacco Use among High School Athletes and Nonathletes: Results of the 1997 Youth Risk Behavior Survey," *Adolescence* 36 (Winter 2001): 730. See also Barber, Eccles, and Stone, "Whatever Happened?"; Lynn A. Barnett, "Flying High or Crashing Down: Girls' Accounts of Trying Out for Cheerleading and Dance," *Journal of Adolescent Research* 21, no. 5 (September 2006): 514–41; Margo Gardner, Jodie Roth, and Jeanne Brooks-Gunn, "Sports Participation and Juvenile Delinquency: The Role of the Peer Context among Adolescent Boys and Girls with Varied Histories of Problem Behavior," *Developmental Psychology* 45, no. 2 (2009): 341–53.

7. Elkind, *Hurried Child*, 30.

8. John Underwood, "A Game Plan for America," *Sports Illustrated*, February 23, 1981, quoted in ibid.

9. Hyman, *Until It Hurts*, 1–14.

10. Eric Sondheimer, "Soccer Players Face Split Decision: Some Elite Southland Athletes Must Choose between Their High School and Club Teams," *Los Angeles Times*, January 16, 2008, http://articles.latimes.com/2008/jan/16/sports/sp-academy16 (accessed March 8, 2010). While Sondheimer's article focused primarily on soccer clubs in southern California, the statement holds true in regards to other sports clubs across the United States, including the amount of annual club dues.

11. See U.S. Soccer Development Academy, http://ussda.demosphere.com/Profiles/index_E.html (accessed March 12, 2010).

12. Sondheimer, "Soccer Players." He goes on: "With more than 7 million students participating in high school sports, [Assistant Director of the National Federation of State High School Associations, Mark] Koski said his organization's main objective is to produce 'lifelong positive citizens' and not necessarily Olympic champions. But the proliferation of club programs nationwide shows there's a growing pursuit of athletic excellence."

13. Hyman, *Until It Hurts*, 66.

14. Ibid., 38. Hyman also includes an interesting look at the famed "Tommy John surgery," pioneered by Dr. Frank Jobe in 1974, which repairs a torn ulnar collateral ligament—a devastating injury for a baseball pitcher—by replacing it from a tendon harvested from another part of the body. John's career, thought to be over, was extended by over ten years. Once thought to be exotic and highly risky, the surgery has become increasingly commonplace for athletes of all ages: "From 1988 to 1994, renowned Alabama-based surgeon James Andrews performed Tommy John surgery on just seven high school players. From 2000 to 2004, that figure climbed to 124. Today more than half of the Tommy John operations that Andrews does are on high school and college athletes" (ibid., 84). As for Tommy John himself? He explains to Hyman that "what [parents] don't understand, and will never understand, unfortunately, is it makes no difference whether you start pitching at eight or eighteen. I can take a kid who has never pitched in his life until he's seventeen. By the time he's nineteen he'll throw as well or better than the kid who's been pitching since he was eight—and have less wear and tear on his arm" (ibid., 21).

15. Writes Hyman: "For adults, youth sports can become something of a social register. When a child is named to an elite or travel team there can be an unmistakable boost to an entire family's social standing" (ibid., 22).

16. I chose not to interview nonathlete preadolescents because I did not want to add to their insecurity or feelings of inadequacy by discussing these potentially delicate issues. For the purposes of this experiment, it was not necessary to include this particular voice.

17. A serious reconsideration of the idea that students like Grant receive long-term benefits from a "tough-love, truth-telling" coaching style is long overdue. Feedback that focuses primarily on social comparisons—to say nothing of negative feedback—undermines motivation and leads to greater self-consciousness and contingent self-worth on the part of students. On the other hand, autonomy-supportive coaching—which includes providing choice for athletes, avoiding controlling behaviors like criticisms, acknowledging athletes' feelings and perspectives, providing a rationale for tasks and limits, and giving opportunity for athletes to show initiative and independence—has been shown to influence motivation, physical activity, and psychological well-being. See J. Douglas Coatsworth and David E. Conroy, "The Effects of Autonomy-Supportive Coaching, Need Satisfaction, and Self-Perceptions on Initiative and Identity in Youth Swimmers," *Developmental Psychology* 45, no. 2 (2009): 320–28.

18. A recent study of college football players in the Midwest revealed that those who reported higher on the need to win at all costs, to subjugate personal needs, and to dominate one's opponent also reported higher hegemonic, rigid stereotype male gender norms, which put them at risk for depression, anxiety, and decreased interpersonal intimacy. See Jesse A. Steinfeldt et al., "Gender Role Conflict and Stigma toward Help-Seeking among College Football Players," *Psychology of Men and Masculinity* 10, no. 4 (2009): 261–72.

Chapter 8 Sex

1. Human subject research, especially with children and adolescents, is difficult at best and dangerous at worst. In the area of adolescent sexuality, by far the most common form of data collection is self-report, in which a young person responds in a survey or reveals in an interview the sexual experiences he or she has had or how he or she feels or thinks about sex. Research methodologies that are used to investigate attitudes and even expressed behaviors, even the most rigorous and thorough, nonetheless require a multidimensional matrix of data inputs to even begin to accurately assemble meaningful conclusions. Yet in the popular media, and generally with the blessing of researchers, the results of these types of studies can be presented as hard, cold, undeniable fact when in reality there may be much, much more to the picture than the method was able to discern or uncover.

2. Here is a blogger's description of the 2005 ad: "Dr. Pepper is running a new ad. The ad features the song 'Stacy's mom' (. . . has got it going on), which is sung by a teen who flirts back and forth with his girlfriend's mom. The Dr. Pepper ad shows a group of boys about 10–12 years old playing in a park when a mini-van drives up. Very close shots of the driver as she gets out of the van, a sneaker, keys jingling, a 'tease' as the wind blows her blouse a few inches above her belt. Subtle, sexy stuff. The kids stop and look as she pulls the side door open and pops the top on a cooler of Dr. Pepper. The kids smile and race to the cooler. The last few quick shots have the words from the song 'I'm in love with Stacy's mom . . .' [as] one child gazes reverently up at the woman, who gives back a knowing smirk" (http://right-mind.us/blogs/blog_0/archive/2005/02/07/1534.aspx [accessed June 17, 2010]).

3. I declined to discuss this with young women individually to maintain a margin of distance.

4. A handful of students in one focus group who attend a Christian youth ministry started the discussion with relatively expected answers. Then one of them broke the ice with the statement, "C'mon, be honest, you guys! You know what it's like!" At that point, the group fell into line with replies that matched those of students who were not religiously connected.

5. See Snopes.com for a description of the fad (http://www.snopes.com/risque/school/bracelet.asp, accessed November 30, 2010). As Young Life Rancho Del Sol area director, Rob Clark, in an email to me about this fad, mentions that they are widely being displayed by middle school girls in his community. "Although this fad is usually taken as a tongue and cheek gimmick at best," Rob wrote, "when middle school students are flirting with their use, it at least becomes something to watch."

6. Peggy Orenstein, "Playing at Sexy: Do Gyrating Little Girls Become Sexting Young Women?" *New York Times Magazine,* June 13, 2010, 11.

7. Chapin, "Adolescent Sex and Mass Media."

8. See especially Mark Regnerus, *Forbidden Fruit: Sex and Religion in the Lives of American Teenagers* (New York: Oxford University Press, 2007).

9. Solarz, *American Psychological Association,* 24.

10. I was careful about not directly discussing sexuality, especially sexual behavior, with a student one-on-one, and I remained cautious in group settings. What I report in this chapter is a summary of random comments from a variety of students in different settings.

11. Orenstein, quoting Deborah Tolman, "Playing at Sexy," 7.

12. Ibid.

13. It is difficult to discern the actual reality of sexual intercourse among adolescents. Studies do vary, and yet the trend seems to be down for intercourse across the best of the current data. There is a rich database of those attempting to pull together the numbers in a meaningful way. For example, the landmark study of teenage sex and religion is Regnerus, *Forbidden Fruit*. For Canadian youth, see Smylie, Medaglia, and Maticka-Tyndale, "The Effect of Social Capital and Socio-demographics on Adolescent Risk and Sexual Health Behaviours."

14. Rita Rubin, "Survey Finds U.S. Abortion Rate Hits Lowest Level since 1974," *USA Today*, January 15, 2003, 8D.

15. Data obtained from Child Trends, www.childtrends.org/PDF/FAAG2002.pdf (accessed April 24, 2003).

16. Cathy Gulli et al., "Suddenly Teen Pregnancy Is Cool?" *Maclean's* 121, no. 3 (January 28, 2008): 40–44. Available online at http://www.macleans.ca/culture/lifestyle/article.jsp?content=20080117_99497_99497 (accessed on November 30, 2010).

17. Joseph M. Strayhorn and Jillian C. Strayhorn, "Religiosity and Teen Birth Rate in the United States," *Reproductive Health*, September 2009, www.reproductive-health-journal.com/content/6/1/14 (accessed November 13, 2009).

18. Ibid.

19. "One in Four Female Adolescents Is Infected with At Least One Sexually Transmitted Infection, New CDC Study Finds," Oral Abstract D4a—Prevalence of Sexually Transmitted Infections and Bacterial Vaginosis among Female Adolescents in the United States: Data from the National Health and Nutritional Examination Survey (NHANES) 2003–2004, http://www.cdc.gov/stdconference/2008/press/summaries-11march2008.htm (accessed June 15, 2010).

20. Advertisement, *USA Today*, March 25, 2008, 8A.

21. There is ample evidence of this. For more, see Sharlene Azam, *Oral Sex Is the New Goodnight Kiss*, a book that also includes a documentary film (DVD) and other online tools and resources, available at http://www.thenewgoodnightkiss.com/ (accessed August 5, 2010).

22. "Slightly more than one-half of adolescents have engaged in heterosexual oral sex (55% overall); in fact, higher proportions of teens have engaged in this activity than have engaged in vaginal sex (50%) (*p-value <.000*, not shown). Substantially fewer (11%) had ever had anal sex. . . . 54% of adolescent females and 55% of adolescent males have ever had oral sex, and one in 10 has ever had anal sex. Both oral sex and anal sex were much more common among adolescents who had initiated vaginal sex as compared to virgins." Laura Duberstein Lindberg et al., "Non-coital Sexual Activities among Adolescents," *Journal of Adolescent Health* 42, no. 7 (May 2008), http://www.guttmacher.org/pubs/JAH_Lindberg.pdf (accessed December 10, 2009).

23. Paige D. Martin, Don Martin, and Maggie Martin, "Adolescent Premarital Sexual Activity, Cohabitation, and Attitudes toward Marriage," *Adolescence* 36 (Fall 2001): 601–9.

24. Mara Brendgen, Frank Vitaro, and Anna Beth Doyle, "Same-Sex Peer Relations and Romantic Relationships during Early Adolescence: Interactive Links to Emotional, Behavioral, and Academic Adjustment," *Merrill-Palmer Quarterly* 48, no. 1 (January 2002): 77–103. See also Chapin, "Adolescent Sex and Mass Media."

25. In discussions with two pediatricians at a conference, I was told that there are several medical and psychological researchers who are looking into making a connection between the earlier onset of menses worldwide and the ever-increasing sexual images of the world culture. Others have made this same connection. I have, however, had difficulty finding a print source for this.

26. L. Remez, "Oral Sex among Adolescents: Is It Sex or Is It Abstinence?" *Family Planning Perspectives* 32, no. 6 (2000): 298–304.

27. Solarz, *American Psychological Association*, 23.

28. Quoted in Michael D. Lemonick, *Time* magazine interview, *Time*, October 30, 2000, www.time.com/time/magazine/0,9263,1101001030,00.html (accessed February 13, 2004).

29. Martin, Martin, and Martin, "Adolescent Premarital Sexual Activity"; see also Terri D. Fisher, "Teen Romance under the Microscope," review of *The Development of Romantic Relationships in Adolescence*, ed. Wyndol Furman, B. Bradford Brown, and Candice Feiring, *Journal of Sex Research* 37, no. 4 (November 2000): 383.

30. Brooks, "Making It."

31. I am reminded of the rise in "reality" television shows in which (usually) twentysomethings perform outrageous acts just for the thrill (and money). These are the people who have been experimenting

with sexuality for years if not decades and now need another high to make sense out of life. This also may have something to do with extreme sports and even "Jackass" stunts of MTV fame.

32. Stuart Pfeifer, "3 Teenagers Will Be Tried as Adults in Videotape Rape Case," *Los Angeles Times*, January 30, 2003, B5.

33. Smylie, Medaglia, and Maticka-Tyndale, "The Effect of Social Capital and Socio-demographics," 97.

Chapter 9 Busyness and Stress

1. For a comprehensive discussion of this, see Mary A. Carskadon, ed., *Adolescent Sleep Patterns: Biological, Social, and Psychological Influences* (Cambridge: Cambridge University Press, 2002).

2. According to a poll conducted by the Associated Press, one in five undergraduate students is constantly stressed to the point that even spring break adds to the list of anxieties that they feel. Associated Press, "1 in 5 Undergrads Is Constantly Stressed," msnbc.com, http://www.msnbc.msn.com/id/23693229 (accessed July 10, 2010).

3. Brooks, "Making It."

4. Ibid.

5. Suniya S. Luthar and Shawn J. Latendresse, "Adolescent Risk: The Costs of Affluence," *New Directions for Youth Development* 95 (Fall 2002): 103.

6. Ibid., 108.

7. Levine, *Price of Privilege*, 18.

8. Solarz, *American Psychological Association*, 29.

9. Elkind, *Hurried Child*, 3rd ed., 166.

10. Ibid., 184.

11. Shannon M. Suldo et al., "Sources of Stress for Students in High School College Preparatory and General Education Programs: Group Differences and Associations with Adjustment," *Adolescence* 44 (Winter 2009): 925–48. By way of contrast, the study also revealed that students in advanced "college prep" programs indicated academic stress as the greatest strain. See also Vivien S. Huan et al., "The Impact of Adolescent Concerns on Their Academic Stress," *Educational Review* 60, no. 2 (May 2008): 169–78.

12. On the impact of family stress, see the recent study by Floor V. A. van Oort et al., "Prospective Community Study of Family Stress and Anxiety in (Pre)adolescents," *European Child and Adolescent Psychiatry* 19, no. 6 (June 2010): 483–91. See also the interesting study on the physiological impact of parental support in the midst of stress by Agnes M. Willemen et al., "Physiological Reactivity to Stress and Parental Support: Comparison of Clinical and Non-clinical Adolescents," *Clinical Psychology and Psychotherapy* 15, no. 5 (September–October 2008): 340–51.

13. Lawrence Steinberg, "We Know Some Things: Parent-Adolescent Relations in Retrospect and Prospect," *Journal of Research in Adolescence* 11, no. 1 (2001): 1–19.

14. Solarz, *American Psychological Association*, 34.

15. Pipher, *Reviving Ophelia*, 283.

16. Hersch, *Tribe Apart*, 364.

17. See Bradley and Corwyn, "Home Environment and Behavioral Development during Early Adolescence," 165–87.

18. Albert Bandura, *Social Foundations of Thought and Action: A Social Cognitive Theory* (Englewood Cliffs, NJ: Prentice-Hall, 1986), 178.

19. Bradley and Corwyn, "Home Environment," 167.

20. Luthar and Latendresse, "Adolescent Risk"; Selena T. Nguyen-Rodriguez, Jennifer B. Unger, and Donna Spruijt-Metz, "Psychological Determinants of Emotional Eating in Adolescence," *Eating Disorders* 17 (2009): 211–24; Dena Phillips Swanson et al., "Identity Processes and the Positive Youth Development of African Americans: An Explanatory Framework," *New Directions for Youth Development* 95 (Fall 2002): 73–99. See also the discussion in Archibald D. Hart and Catherine Hart Weber, *Stressed or Depressed: A Practical and Inspirational Guide for Parents of Hurting Teens* (Brentwood, TN: Integrity, 2005).

21. E. David Klonsky and Jennifer Meuhlenkamp, "Self-Injury: A Research Review for the Practitioner," *Journal of Clinical Psychology* 63, no. 11 (2007): 1045–56.

22. Cornell University, "Self-Injury Is Prevalent Among College Students, Survey Shows," *Science Daily*, June 5, 2006, http://www.sciencedaily.com/releases/2006/06/060605155351.htm (accessed July 9, 2008).

23. Ibid. For more on self-injury, see John D. Guerry and Mitchell J. Prinstein, "Longitudinal Prediction of Adolescent Nonsuicidal Self-Injury: Examination of a Cognitive Vulnerability-Stress Model," *Journal of Clinical Child and Adolescent Psychology* 39, no. 1 (January/February 2010): 77–89;

Catherine R. Glenn and E. David Klonsky, "The Role of Seeing Blood in Non-Suicidal Self-Injury," *Journal of Clinical Psychology* 66, no. 4 (April 2010): 466–73; and L. Webb, "Deliberate Self-Harm in Adolescence: A Systematic Review of Psychological and Psychosocial Factors," *Journal of Advanced Nursing* 38, no. 3 (May 2002): 235–44.

24. Nguyen-Rodriguez, Unger, and Spruijt-Metz, "Psychological Determinants of Emotional Eating"; Swanson, "Identity Processes and Positive Youth Development." See also Samantha Miller et al., "Habitual Response to Stress in Recovering Adolescent Anorexic Patients," *Child Psychiatry and Human Development* 40, no. 1 (2009): 43–54.

25. Associated Press, "1 in 5 Undergrads Is Constantly Stressed."

Chapter 10 Ethics and Morality

1. Males, "New Demons."

2. Thucydides, *The History of the Peloponnesian War*, trans. Richard Crawley, The Internet Classics Archive, http://classics.mit.edu/Thucydides/pelopwar.2.second.html (accessed February 16, 2004).

3. Karen S. Peterson, "Youthful Pessimism Gives Rise to Generation Vexed," *USA Today*, October 19, 2000, 12D.

4. One of the reviewers inserted here, "They have also been deluged by media that teaches kids at an early age that adults are colossally imperfect buffoons whose moral and ethical foundation can be shaken by the merest temptation."

5. Erin Curry, "American Youth More Conservative but Less Moral, Studies Report," www.bpnews.net/bpnews.asp?ID=14511 (accessed October 24, 2002).

6. Jean Piaget, *The Moral Judgment of the Child* (New York: Harcourt, Brace, Jovanovich, 1932).

7. Lawrence Kohlberg, *Essays on Moral Development: The Philosophy of Moral Development*, vols. 1 and 2 (San Francisco: Harper & Row, 1981, 1984).

8. Solarz, *American Psychological Association*, 11.

9. Cathy Stonehouse, "Moral Development: The Process and the Pattern," *Counseling and Values* 24 (1979): 6.

10. A different approach to the stage theories of moral development is Abraham Maslow's "hierarchy of needs" (*Motivation and Personality* [New York: Harper, 1954]), which brings into the moral developmental process an explanation as to why stage theories seem lacking, as in the case of midadolescents when they are operating out of the needs of the world beneath. According to Maslow, general types of needs (physiological, safety, love, and esteem) must be satisfied before a person can move from being self-focused to other-focused.

11. See Robert N. Barger, *A Summary of Lawrence Kohlberg's Stages of Moral Development* (Notre Dame, IN: University of Notre Dame, 2000), http://www.qcc.cuny.edu/socialsciences/ppecorino/INTRO_TEXT/Chapter%208%20Ethics/Reading-Barger-on-Kohlberg.htm: "The first level of moral thinking (pre-conventional) is that generally found at the elementary school level. In the first stage of this level, people behave according to socially acceptable norms because they are told to do so by some authority figure (e.g., parent or teacher). This obedience is compelled by the threat or application of punishment. The second stage of this level is characterized by a view that right behavior means acting in one's own best interests."

12. David Knox, Marty E. Zusman, and Kristen McGinty, "Deception of Parents during Adolescence," *Adolescence* 36 (Fall 2001): 611–14.

13. Ibid.

14. Lene Arnett Jensen, Jeffrey Jensen Arnett, S. Shirley Feldman, and Elizabeth Cauffman, "The Right to Do Wrong: Lying to Parents among Adolescents and Emerging Adults," *Journal of Youth and Adolescence* 33, no. 2 (April 2004): 101–12. See also Mark Warr, "The Tangled Web: Delinquency, Deception, and Parental Attachment," *Journal of Youth and Adolescence* 36, no. 5 (2007): 607–22.

15. Ibid.

16. For an example of a study that reports a similar conclusion, see Kang Lee and Hollie J. Ross, "The Concept of Lying in Adolescents and Young Adults: Testing Sweetser's Folkloristic Model," *Merrill-Palmer Quarterly* 43, no. 2 (1997): 255–70.

17. Lashbrook, "Fitting In," 747–57.

18. Gerald Zelizer, "Break Cheating Pattern Early," *USA Today*, November 20, 2002. See also ibid.

19. Over the course of this study, I became increasingly jaded in my trust in much of the research methodology employed in the study of adolescent behaviors. I believe that even in so-called qualitative studies that rely on interviews to supplement quantitative empirical research, midadolescents may respond to questions out of one of the surface layers. Just because an adolescent tells a researcher

something in an interview in her home, for example, does not necessarily mean that how she describes her life is an accurate or even trustworthy portrayal.

20. McCabe, "Academic Dishonesty."

21. Eric M. Anderman, Tripp Griesinger, and Gloria Westerfield, "Motivation and Cheating during Early Adolescence," *Journal of Educational Psychology* 90 (1998): 84–93.

22. McCabe, "Academic Dishonesty."

23. Ibid.

24. "Disciplinary action alone will not solve the problem. Effectively dealing with cheating in the classroom must begin with changing the culture of the classroom" (Daniel E. Lee, "Cheating in the Classroom: Beyond Policing," *The Clearing House* 82, no. 4 [March/April 2009], http://proquest.umi .com/pqdweb?did=1651769121&Fmt=3&clientId=29876&RQT=309&VName=PQD [accessed December 11, 2009]).

25. Tamera B. Murdock, Anne S. Beauchamp, and Amber M. Hinton, "Predictors of Cheating and Cheating Attributions: Does Classroom Context Influence Cheating and Blame for Cheating?" *European Journal of Psychology of Education* 23, no. 4 (2008): 477–92.

26. Eric M. Anderman, "The Effects of Personal, Classroom and School Goal Structures on Academic Cheating," in *Psychological Perspectives on Academic Cheating*, ed. Eric M. Anderman and Tamera B. Murdock (San Diego: Elsevier, 2007), 87–106.

27. McCabe, "Academic Dishonesty," 684.

28. Christine A. Tanner, "Moral Decline or Pragmatic Decision Making? Cheating and Plagiarism in Perspective," *Journal of Nursing Education* 43, no. 7 (July 2004): 291–92.

29. Zelizer, "Break Cheating Pattern Early."

30. Josephson Institute of Ethics, "Survey Documents Decade of Moral Deterioration: Kids Are More Likely to Cheat, Steal, and Lie than Kids 10 Years Ago," www.josephsoninstitute.org/Survey2002 /survey2002–pressrelease.htm (accessed October 24, 2002). In 2008, the Josephson Institute of Ethics reported that 64% of respondents admitted to cheating on an exam in the past year, and 38% did so two or more times. This represents a decline from the 2002 figures represented here but an increase from 2006 data, which reported 60% as having cheated on an exam in the past year and 35% having done so two or more times ("The Ethics of American Youth: 2008," http://charactercounts.org/programs /reportcard/2008/index.html [accessed June 18, 2010]).

31. Chris Dogra (sophomore, Fairfax High School, Los Angeles), *Los Angeles Times*, November 2, 2002, B23.

32. Zelizer, "Break Cheating Pattern Early."

33. Ibid.

34. See Solarz, *American Psychological Association*, 16: "For most teens, telling them to 'just say no' is not helpful advice for dealing with sexually stressful interpersonal situations in which they are anxious to be liked."

35. Ibid., 33.

36. William Damon, director of Adolescent Research Center (lecture given at Fuller Theological Seminary, Pasadena, CA, February 15, 2000). See also William Damon, *The Moral Child* (New York: Free Press, 1988).

37. See Barger, *Summary of Lawrence Kohlberg's Stages of Moral Development*, http://www .qcc.cuny.edu/socialsciences/ppecorino/INTRO_TEXT/Chapter%208%20Ethics/Reading-Barger-on -Kohlberg.htm (accessed November 30, 2010).

Chapter 11 Partying, Gaming, and Social Networking

1. For data reported by teenagers to the Centers for Disease Control and Prevention, please see chapter 3. Also: "In the 2004 Canadian Addiction Survey, 77% of 15- to 17-year-olds and 97% of 18- to 19-year-olds reported that they had used alcohol at some time in their lives, with 62% and 91% respectively reporting use in the past year. It is notable that among those who had used alcohol in the past year, 29% and 42% respectively reported regular binge drinking (5 or more drinks on a single occasion) (Demers & Poulin, 2005)" (Smylie, Medaglia, and Maticka-Tyndale, "The Effect of Social Capital," 96).

2. Tao Ruspoli, "Drugs and Technicity: A Heideggerian Inquiry into the Evolution of Drug Use," www.ruspoli.com/drugs.html (accessed February 16, 2004).

3. A 2010 longitudinal study of 12,067 persons found that "changes in the alcohol consumption behavior of a person's social network had a statistically significant effect on that person's subsequent alcohol consumption behavior" (J. Niels Rosenquist et al., "The Spread of Alcohol Consumption Behavior in a Large Social Network," *Annals of Internal Medicine* 152, no. 7 [April 6, 2010]: 426).

4. Some studies attempt to understand how this process works. Karl E. Bauman and Susan T. Ennett, for example, after reviewing research that looks at how peers influence drug and alcohol use, stated that "peers are believed to contribute to adolescent drug use both directly and indirectly through several complex mechanisms: by modeling drug use; by shaping norms, attitudes, and values; and by providing opportunities and support for drug use" (Bauman and Ennett, "On the Importance of Peer Influence for Adolescent Drug Use: Commonly Neglected Considerations," *Addiction* 91, no. 2 [1996]: 184). See also Jeffrey J. Arnett, "Reckless Behavior in Adolescence: A Developmental Perspective," *Developmental Review* 12 (1992): 339–73; and Jeffrey J. Arnett and L. Balle-Jensen, "Cultural Bases of Risk Behavior," *Child Development* 64 (1993): 1842–55.

5. Arnett, *Adolescence and Emerging Adulthood.*

6. Franca Beccaria and Allan Sande, "Drinking Games and Rite of Life Projects: A Social Comparison of the Meaning and Functions of Young People's Use of Alcohol during the Rite of Passage to Adulthood in Italy and Norway," *Young* 11 (2003): 101.

7. Jodi Dworkin, "Risk Taking as Developmentally Appropriate Experimentation for College Students," *Journal of Adolescent Research* 20 (March 2005): 232.

8. Katie Hafner, "Texting May Be Taking a Toll," *New York Times*, May 25, 2009, www.nytimes.com/2009/05/26/health/26teen.html (accessed April 11, 2010).

9. Amanda Lenhart, "Teens and Mobile Phones over the Past Five Years: Pew Internet Looks Back," Pew Internet & American Life Project, August 19, 2009, http://www.pewinternet.org/Reports/2009/14--Teens-and-Mobile-Phones-Data-Memo.aspx (accessed April 11, 2010).

10. To parents, one of the more bizarre expressions of the technological world our kids grow up in is the almost universal way teenagers place their charged phone next to their ear on their pillow before they go to sleep. Parents simply do not understand why the phone has to be so close to their teenager's ear, especially when there is good reason to believe that the practice may be harmful. Teens typically reply, "In case someone needs me," which is their way of saying, "This is my lifeline, and my friends' lifeline. You just don't understand us at all."

11. Livingstone, "Taking Risky Opportunities."

12. Maria Frostling-Henningsson, "First-Person Shooter Games as a Way of Connecting to People: 'Brothers in Blood,'" *CyberPsychology and Behavior* 12, no. 5 (2009): 561.

13. Huon Longman, Erin O'Connor, and Patricia Obst, "The Effect of Social Support Derived from World of Warcraft on Negative Psychological Symptoms," *CyberPsychology and Behavior* 12, no. 5 (2009): 563. The study also found that those who played the most—from forty-four to eighty-two hours per week—had much less offline social support and greater incidence of negative psychological symptoms.

14. Helene Cole and Mark D. Griffiths, "Social Interactions in Massively Multiplayer Online Role-Playing Games," *CyberPsychology and Behavior* 10, no. 4 (2007): 583.

Chapter 12 Kids at the Margins

1. See Epstein, *Teen 2.0.*

2. D. Wayne Osgood, E. Michael Foster, and Mark E. Courtney, "Vulnerable Populations and the Transition to Adulthood," *Future of Children* 20, no. 1 (Spring 2010): 210.

3. Osgood, Foster, and Courtney, "Vulnerable Populations."

4. Ibid.

5. K. A. S. Wickrama, Samuel Noh, and Chalandra M. Bryant, "Racial Differences in Adolescent Distress: Differential Effects of the Family and Community for Blacks and Whites," *Journal of Community Psychology* 33, no. 3 (2005): 276.

6. Amanda Barczyk and Sanna Thompson, "Alcohol/Drug Dependency in Homeless Youth," *Alcoholism: Clinical and Experimental Research* 32, supp. 1 (June 2008): 367A.

7. Many terms have been used over the years to describe those teenagers who are not included by their peers in the mainstream of life, like "nerd" and "dork." When the first edition of *Hurt* was released, in many schools and communities those in the band and drama were sometimes considered part of this group. Interestingly, there has been a recent resurgence of interest in the "nerd," as exhibited by the overwhelming popularity of the television show *Glee*. This category, however, remains an important one, because in almost every setting, there are those who do not "fit" with the majority of other young people and are therefore shunned by their peers.

8. These descriptors do not even need to be objectively determined, because they may apply primarily in the eyes of the family and other systems that view themselves and therefore their offspring as elite.

9. Levine, *Price of Privilege*, 64.

10. David Moshman, *Adolescent Psychological Development: Rationality, Morality, and Identity,* (New York: Guilford, 2004).

11. Lalitha Vasudevan and Gerald Campano, "The Social Production of Adolescent Risk and the Promise of Adolescent Literacies," *Review of Research Education* 33 (2009): 323.

12. Catherine A. Taylor et al., "Cumulative Experiences of Violence among High-Risk Urban Youth," *Journal of Interpersonal Violence* 23, no. 11 (2008): 1618–35.

13. Michael Ungar, "The Importance of Parents and Other Caregivers to the Resilience of High-Risk Adolescents," *Family Process* 43, no. 1 (2004): 33–34.

14. Joanne O'Sullivan Oliveira and Pamela J. Burke, "Lost in the Shuffle: Culture of Homeless Adolescents," *Pediatric Nursing* 35, no. 3 (May–June 2009): 154–61.

15. Vasudevan and Campano, "The Social Production of Adolescent Risk," 323.

16. I am certain that even the potential critique of the well-entrenched practice of separating out the "gifted and talented" from other children will cause concern among its supporters. But, on the other hand, is it possible that attempting to draw attention to the development of an educational system that adapts to the needs of one slice of our young can also simultaneously deny the rest the chance to develop their unique potential? It seems to me that to defend the extremely narrow criteria of the American educational system that labels only some as either gifted *or* talented is problematic at best. To add fuel to this discussion, I encourage the reader to peruse the National Association for Gifted Children website (www.nagc.org). Some will certainly celebrate the history and perspective, while others, myself included, will find the most narrow, pejorative, and dangerous argumentation for a cause in our culture. Regardless, this chapter looks primarily at the effect that labels have on developing adolescents, regardless of their pedigree, lineage, or test scores.

17. Levine, *Price of Privilege,* 9.

18. Ibid., 14.

19. Ibid.

20. Ibid., 48.

21. Curtis Miller, "The Way of Privilege: What You Need to Know about the Issues Facing Afflu- ent Youth," *Fuller Youth Institute eJournal,* July 13, 2008, http://fulleryouthinstitute.org/2008/07 /the-way-of-privilege/ (accessed June 28, 2010).

22. Scot D. Evans, "Youth Sense of Community: Voice and Power in Community Contexts," *Journal of Community Psychology* 35, no. 6 (2007): 704.

23. Ibid., 705.

24. As an example of this, "Parents who praised their children's efforts and ability and encouraged independent problem solving had children who preferred more challenging tasks" (Joel M. Hektner, "Family, School, and Community Predictors of Adolescent Growth-Conducive Experiences: Global and Specific Approaches," *Applied Developmental Science* 5, no. 3 [2001]: 180–81).

25. The reader may not be satisfied or agree with my editorial decision on this point, but perhaps it helps to know that I am not either.

26. Ruta Valaitis, "'They Don't Trust Us; We're Just Kids.' Views about Community from Pre- dominantly Female Inner City Youth," *Health Care for Women International* 23, no. 3 (2002): 256–57.

27. Vulnerable kids with severe physical disabilities are a possible exception, as many peers dem- onstrate a rare compassion and deference toward these who are most needy. I have noticed an interesting twist on the issue of how many mainstream peers view and treat those with severe disabilities, and also sometimes those who are so different they receive a kind of respect for walking outside the box, like those who present as gay or lesbian but do not attempt to flaunt or hide behind their lifestyle. When compared with how mainstream youth view and treat their other marginalized peers—like those with social or emotional disabilities or those whose lifestyle is perceived as being offensive or disruptive to the mainstream social structure—there is a much greater sensitivity and even protectionistic feel toward those with physical disabilities (the assumption being, perhaps, that they "can't help it") and often an outright disdain and ridicule for those with other forms of less obvious disabilities or struggles. I am convinced that this is what goes on, yet it will take further careful and deliberate research to arrive at any type of definitive understanding or conclusion of my observation.

28. There is a growing body of evidence that demonstrates that young people who have a strong "internal sense of purpose" as well as a significant adult support system will develop greater resiliency, especially when facing obstacles. See, for example, Ann S. Masten, "Ordinary Magic: Resilience Pro- cesses in Development," *American Psychologist* 56, no. 3 (March 2001): 227–38.

29. Maria Drews, "Bouncing Back: Increasing Resilience for Hurting Kids," *Fuller Youth Institute eJournal,* August 3, 2009, http://fulleryouthinstitute.org/2009/08/bouncing-back/#footnote_10_8354 (accessed July 6, 2010). See also Ann S. Masten and J. Douglas Coatsworth, "The Development of

Competence in Favorable and Unfavorable Environments: Lessons from Research on Successful Children," *American Psychologist* 53, no. 2 (February 1998): 213, 215; and Masten, "Ordinary Magic," 232, 235.

30. According to the University of Pennsylvania Positive Psychology Center, positive psychology is defined as "the scientific study of the strengths and virtues that enable individuals and communities to thrive" (http://www.ppc.sas.upenn.edu/ [accessed July 6, 2010]).

31. U.S. Department of Health and Human Services, "Positive Youth Development," http://www.acf.hhs.gov/programs/fysb/content/positiveyouth/index.htm (accessed May 13, 2009).

32. Reed Larson, "Positive Youth Development, Willful Adolescents, and Mentoring," *Journal of Community Psychology* 34, no. 6 (2006): 678–79.

33. For examples of her work, see N. A. Ansary and S. S. Luthar, "Distress and Academic Achievement among Adolescents of Affluence: A Study of Externalizing and Internalizing Problem Behaviors and School Performance," *Development and Psychopathology* 21 (2009): 319–41, and T. M. Yates, A. J. Tracy, and S. S. Luthar, "Nonsuicidal Self-Injury among 'Privileged' Youth: Longitudinal and Cross-sectional Approaches to Developmental Processes," *Journal of Consulting and Clinical Psychology* 76 (2008): 52–62.

34. Suniya S. Luthar and Shawn J. Latendresse, "Children of the Affluent: Challenges to Well-Being," *Current Directions in Psychological Science* 14, no. 1 (February 2005): 49–53.

35. Levine, *Price of Privilege*, 38–48.

36. In one Canadian longitudinal study of teenagers reflecting on the most difficult life experience they had yet faced as a teenager at seventeen years of age and then again at twenty-six, researchers discovered that those who had reported "positive parenting" experiences were more likely to develop a narrative that resulted in a "positive resolution" to the situation, and conversely, those who reported relatively negative parenting experiences expressed a narrative that indicated a far more difficult resolution of the situation. The researchers note that, "As predicted, a significant relationship was found between perceptions of positive parenting in late adolescence and the subsequent tendency to narrate low points with a clear and positive resolution in emerging adulthood" (Alessio Vieno et al., "Parenting and Antisocial Behavior: A Model of the Relationship between Adolescent Self-Disclosure, Parental Closeness, Parental Control, and Adolescent Antisocial Behavior," *Developmental Psychology* 45, no. 6 [2009]: 1516).

37. Ungar, "The Importance of Parents and Other Caregivers," 36.

38. There is a difference between the helicopter parent who rescues and overly controls his or her child's life and responsibilities, and those parents who are available and active in relationship with their child, adolescent, and emerging adult. College freshman parent briefings, for example, tend to lump both kinds of parenting practices into the same camp, and strongly advise against them, sometimes telling parents that "your kids are now adults, let them grow up without you." In my view, college freshmen need to maintain a strong relationship to their parents, but those parents need to avoid stepping into what the adolescent must handle, for their own sake.

39. For more information, see studies cited throughout this chapter.

40. Abraham H. Maslow, *Toward a Psychology of Being*, 3rd ed. (New York: Wiley, 1998), 27.

41. Few would argue that on the whole American private schools have this as a central goal, but there are significant exceptions, such as in certain charter and private schools, or where there is an administration or faculty that advances racial equality as a core agenda.

42. *Time*, http://www.time.com/time/magazine/article/0,9171,1948619-3,00.html (accessed November 30, 2010).

43. G. Orfield, "Reviving the Goal of an Integrated Society: A 21st Century Challenge," The Civil Rights Project/Proyecto Derechos Civiles at UCLA, January 1, 2009, http://civilrightsproject.ucla.edu/research/k-12-education/integration-and-diversity/reviving-the-goal-of-an-integrated-society-a-21st-century-challenge (accessed August 12, 2010).

44. Levine, *Price of Privilege*, 48–53.

Part 3 Where Do We Go from Here?

1. For a lengthy discussion of this concept, especially in a father-child relationship during adolescence, see Chap and Dee Clark, *Daughters and Dads* (Colorado Springs: NavPress, 1998).

Chapter 13 What Do Midadolescents Need?

1. Stanford University's William Damon has been successful at translating theoretical perspectives and conclusions into practical action. See, for example, William Damon, ed., *Bringing in a New*

Era in Character Education (Stanford, CA: Hoover Institute Press, 2002); Damon, *Moral Child*; and Damon, *Youth Charter*.

2. As mentioned in chapter 8, the embrace I refer to here is the antithesis of the embrace of romance or sexuality. For many young people, men and women alike, being sexually active rarely relieves the pain of abandonment and generally only adds to a deeper sense of disillusionment and despair. The embrace that Sara and every other adolescent is subconsciously clamoring for is the warmth of a safe place and a secure relationship.

Chapter 14 Five Strategies to Turn the Tide of Systemic Abandonment

1. Robert S. Griffin, *Sports in the Lives of Children and Adolescents: Success on the Field and in Life* (Westport, CT: Praeger, 1998).

2. I am aware that Big Brothers and Big Sisters take great pains to avoid having this happen too quickly, and they report that many Big Brothers and Big Sisters stay in touch with their kids long after they grow up. But in general, most of them play a rather temporary role in the life of a child.

3. Damon, *Youth Charter*.

Appendix

1. Paula Saukko, "Methodologies for Cultural Studies: An Integrative Approach," in *The Sage Handbook of Qualitative Research*, ed. Norman K. Denzin and Yvonna S. Lincoln, 3rd ed. (Thousand Oaks, CA: Sage, 2005), 346.

2. The website *www.parenTeen.com* is where our team will make available new research, conclusions, insights, articles, and the like for those wishing to stay abreast of what is happening in the world of today's teenagers.

3. An example of this is Michelle Fine and Lois Weis's report on injustice toward American high school youth. Through their own ethnographic, close-up investigation they were able to see that "Unlike most students in U.S. schools, youth in desegregated schools must theorize their own identities relationally all the time and every day, because they are making selves in spaces where 'difference' matters. That is, they are learning, claiming, and negotiating their places in a microcosmic racial/ classed hierarchy on a daily basis" (Fine and Weis, "Compositional Studies in Two Parts: Critical Theorizing and Analyzing on Social (In)Justice," in Denzin and Lincoln, *Sage Handbook*, 75). This level of observation could not have come solely from the more typical forms of studying teenagers, like a survey. There is too much insight and too intimate a familiarity with the circumstances of those they were studying to have been discovered without some form and level of participant-observation.

4. Patricia A. Adler and Peter Adler, "Teen Scenes: Ethnographies of Adolescent Cultures," *Journal of Contemporary Ethnography* 31 (October 2002): 653.

5. Kathy Charmaz, "Grounded Theory in the 21st Century: Applications for Advancing Social Justice Studies," in Denzin and Lincoln, *Sage Handbook*, 517.

6. "Traditional researchers' concern with process and method, therefore, has been supplemented with (but by no means supplanted by) an interest in the ways in which ethnographic observers interact with, or enter into a dialogic relationship with, members of the group being studied" (Michael V. Angrosino, "Recontextualizing Observation: Ethnography, Pedagogy, and the Prospects for a Progressive Political Agenda," in Denzin and Lincoln, *Sage Handbook*, 734).

7. "Ethnography's 'self-correcting investigative process' has typically included adequate and appropriate sampling procedures, systematic techniques for gathering and analyzing data, validation of data, avoidance of observer bias, and documentation of findings" (Angrosino, "Recontextualizing Observation," 733).

8. George Kamberelis and Greg Dimitriadis, "Focus Groups: Strategic Articulations of Pedagogy, Politics, and Inquiry," in Denzin and Lincoln, *Sage Handbook*, 887–907.

9. As Kamberelis and Dimitriadis note, "And perhaps most important, the dialogic possibilities afforded by focus groups help researchers to work against premature consolidation of their understandings and explanations, thereby signaling the limits of reflexivity and the importance of intellectual/ empirical modesty as forms of ethics and praxis. Such modesty allows us to engage in 'doubled practices' where we listen to the attempts of others as they make sense of their lives. It also allows us to resist the seductive qualities of 'too easy' constructs such as 'voice' as we trouble experience itself, which is always already constituted within one 'grand narrative' or another" (Kamberelis and Dimitriadis, "Focus Groups," in Denzin and Lincoln, *Sage Handbook*, 903).

10. Ibid.

11. By "population pools" I refer to groupings of students, like a high school, ethnic group, neighborhood, etc.

12. "Groupthink occurs when a homogenous highly cohesive group is so concerned with maintaining unanimity that they fail to evaluate all their alternatives and options" (http://oregonstate.edu /instruct/theory/grpthink.html [accessed May 15, 2010]). See also I. Janis, *Groupthink: Psychological Studies of Policy Decisions and Fiascoes* (Boston: Houghton Mifflin, 1982).

13. Since I began this study, I have worked with dozens of students, grads, and others who have deeply invested in this research, and therefore the term I use to include them all is "teams."

14. According to the State of Washington Department of Personnel, for example, competencies are defined as "the measurable or observable knowledge, skills, abilities, and behaviors (KSABs) critical to successful job performance" (http://www.dop.wa.gov/strategichr/workforceplanning/competencies /pages/default.aspx [accessed May 19, 2010]).

bibliography

Books

Adler, Patricia A., and Peter Adler. "Observational Techniques." In Denzin and Lincoln, *Handbook of Qualitative Research*, 377–92.

Alan Guttmacher Institute. *Teen Sex and Pregnancy*. New York: Alan Guttmacher Institute, 1995.

Allen, Joseph, and Claudia Worrell Allen. *Escaping the Endless Adolescence: How We Can Help Our Teenagers Grow Up before They Grow Old*. New York: Ballantine Books, 2009.

Anderman, Eric M. "The Effects of Personal, Classroom and School Goal Structures on Academic Cheating." In *Psychological Perspectives on Academic Cheating*, edited by Eric M. Anderman and Tamera B. Murdock, 87–106. San Diego: Elsevier, 2007.

Angrosino, Michael V. "Recontextualizing Observation: Ethnography, Pedagogy, and the Prospects for a Progressive Political Agenda." In Denzin and Lincoln, *Sage Handbook of Qualitative Research*, 729–46.

Arnett, Jeffrey J. *Adolescence and Emerging Adulthood: A Cultural Approach*. Upper Saddle River, NJ: Pearson Education, 2000.

———. "Adolescent Storm and Stress, Reconsidered." In Arnett, *Readings on Adolescence*, 6–14.

———, ed. *Readings on Adolescence and Emerging Adulthood*. Upper Saddle River, NJ: Prentice-Hall, 2002.

Atkinson, Paul, and Martyn Hammersley. "Ethnography and Participant Observation." In Denzin and Lincoln, *Handbook of Qualitative Research*, 248–61.

Augustine. *Confessions*. Translated by Rex Warner. New York: Signet Classics, 2001.

Azam, Sharlene. *Oral Sex Is the New Goodnight Kiss*. http://www.thenewgoodnightkiss.com/ (accessed August 5, 2010).

Bandura, Albert. *Social Foundations of Thought and Action: A Social Cognitive Theory.* Englewood Cliffs, NJ: Prentice-Hall, 1986.

Barger, Robert N. *A Summary of Lawrence Kohlberg's Stages of Moral Development.* Notre Dame, IN: University of Notre Dame, 2000, http://www.qcc.cuny.edu/socialsciences/ppecorino/INTRO_TEXT/Chapter%208%20Ethics/Reading-Barger-on-Kohlberg.htm, (accessed November 30, 2010).

Barnes, G. M., M. P. Farrell, and S. Banerjee. "Family Influences on Alcohol Abuse and Other Problem Behaviors among Black and White Americans." In *Alcohol Problems among Adolescents,* edited by G. M. Boyd, J. Howard, and R. A. Zucker, 13–32. Hillsdale, NJ: Lawrence Erlbaum, 1995.

Besharov, D. J., ed. *America's Disconnected Youth: Toward a Preventative Strategy.* Washington, DC: CWLA Press, 1999.

Blos, Peter. *The Adolescent Passage.* New York: International Universities Press, 1979.

———. "The Second Individuation Process of Adolescence." In *The Adolescent Passage,* 141–70. New York: International Universities Press, 1979.

Bronfenbrenner, Urie. *The Ecology of Human Development: Experiments by Nature and Design.* Cambridge, MA: Harvard University Press, 1979.

Brown, B. B., M. S. Mory, and D. Kinney. "Casting Crowds in a Relational Perspective: Caricature, Channel, and Context." In Arnett, *Readings on Adolescence,* 161–72.

Buechner, Frederick. *Whistling in the Dark.* San Francisco: Harper, 1993.

Carroll, Colleen. *The New Faithful: Why Young Adults Are Embracing Christian Orthodoxy.* Chicago: Loyola, 2002.

Carskadon, Mary A., ed. *Adolescent Sleep Patterns: Biological, Social, and Psychological Influences.* Cambridge: Cambridge University Press, 2002.

Charmaz, Kathy. "Grounded Theory in the 21st Century: Applications for Advancing Social Justice Studies." In Denzin and Lincoln, *Sage Handbook of Qualitative Research,* 507–35.

Child Trends. *Facts at a Glance.* Washington, DC: Child Trends, 1999.

Chodorow, Nancy. *The Reproduction of Mothering: Psychoanalysis and the Sociology of Gender.* Berkeley: University of California Press, 1978.

Clark, Chap. "The Changing Face of Adolescence: A Theological View of Human Development." In *Starting Right: Thinking Theologically about Youth Ministry,* edited by Kenda C. Dean, Chap Clark, and Dave Rahn, 41–62. Grand Rapids: Zondervan/Youth Specialties, 2000.

Clark, Chap, and Dee Clark. *Daughters and Dads.* Colorado Springs: NavPress, 1998.

———. *Disconnected: Parenting Teens in a MySpace World.* Grand Rapids: Baker Books, 2007.

Clark, Chap, and Steve Rabey. *When Kids Hurt: Help for Adults Navigating the Adolescent Maze.* Grand Rapids: Baker Books, 2009.

————. *The Youth Worker's Handbook to Family Ministry.* Grand Rapids: Zondervan/Youth Specialties, 1997.

Coleman, J. C., and L. B. Hendry. *The Nature of Adolescence.* 3rd ed. New York: Routledge, 1999.

Conger, R. D., and W. Chao. "Adolescent Depressed Mood." In *Understanding Differences between Divorced and Intact Families: Stress, Interaction, and Child Outcome,* edited by R. L. Simons, 157–75. Thousand Oaks, CA: Sage, 1996.

Coontz, Stephanie. *The Way We Never Were: American Families and the Nostalgia Trap.* New York: Basic Books, 1992.

Côté, James E., and Anton L. Allahar. *Generation on Hold: Coming of Age in the Late Twentieth Century.* Toronto: Stoddart, 1994.

Currie, Elliot. *The Road to Whatever: Middle Class Culture and the Crisis of Adolescence.* New York: Metropolitan Books, 2004.

Cusick, P. A. *Inside High School.* New York: Holt, Rinehart & Winston, 1973.

Damon, William. *The Moral Child: Nurturing Children's Natural Moral Growth.* New York: Free Press, 1988.

————. *The Youth Charter.* New York: Free Press, 1997.

————, ed. *Bringing In a New Era in Character Education.* Stanford, CA: Hoover Institute Press, 2002.

Damon, William, Deanna Kuhn, and Robert S. Siegler, eds. *Handbook of Child Psychology.* Vol. 2, *Cognition, Perception, and Language.* 5th ed. New York: Wiley, 1998.

Debold, E., L. M. Brown, W. Weseen, and G. K. Brookins. "Cultivating Hardiness Zones for Adolescent Girls: A Reconceptualization of Resilience in Relationships with Caring Adults." In Johnson, Roberts, and Worell, *Beyond Appearance,* 181–204.

Demos, John. *Past, Present, and Personal: The Family and the Life Course in America.* New York: Oxford University Press, 1986.

Denmark, F. L. "Enhancing the Development of Adolescent Girls." In Johnson, Roberts, and Worell, *Beyond Appearance,* 377–404.

Denzin, Norman K. *The Research Act: A Theoretical Introduction to Sociological Methods.* 2nd ed. New York: McGraw-Hill, 1978.

Denzin, Norman K., and Yvonna S. Lincoln, eds. *Handbook of Qualitative Research.* Thousand Oaks, CA: Sage, 1994.

————, eds. *The Sage Handbook of Qualitative Research.* 3rd ed. Thousand Oaks, CA: Sage, 2005.

DeVries, Mark. *Family-Based Youth Ministry.* Downers Grove, IL: InterVarsity, 1994.

Dryfoos, J. G. *Safe Passage: Making It through Adolescence in a Risky Society.* New York: Oxford University Press, 1998.

DuBois, David L., and Michael J. Karcher. "Youth Mentoring: Theory, Research, and Practice." In *Handbook of Youth Mentoring,* edited by D. L. DuBois and M. J. Karcher, 2–12. Thousand Oaks, CA: Sage, 2005.

Eccles, J., B. Barber, D. Jozefowicz, O. Malenchuk, and M. Vida. "Self-Evaluations of Competence, Task Values, and Self-Esteem." In Johnson, Roberts, and Worell, *Beyond Appearance*, 53–83.

Elkind, David. *All Grown Up and No Place to Go*. Reading, MA: Addison-Wesley, 1984.

———. *The Hurried Child: Growing Up Too Fast Too Soon*. 2nd ed. Reading, MA: Addison-Wesley, 1988.

———. *The Hurried Child: Growing Up Too Fast Too Soon*. 3rd ed. Cambridge, MA: Perseus, 2001.

———. *Reinventing Childhood: Raising and Educating Children in a Changing World*. Rosemont, NJ: Modern Learning, 1998.

———. *A Sympathetic Understanding of the Child: Birth to Sixteen*. Needham Heights, MA: Allyn & Bacon, 1994.

———. *Ties That Stress: The New Family Imbalance*. Cambridge, MA: Harvard University Press, 1994.

Epstein, Robert. *The Case against Adolescence: Rediscovering the Adult in Every Teen*. Sanger, CA: Quill Driver Books, 2007.

———. *Teen 2.0: Saving Our Children and Families from the Torment of Adolescence*. Fresno, CA: Linden, 2010.

Erikson, Erik H. *Identity: Youth and Crisis*. New York: Norton, 1968.

Feldman, Shirley, and Glen R. Elliott. *At the Threshold: The Developing Adolescent*. New York: Knopf, 1996.

Fine, Michelle, and Lois Weis. "Compositional Studies in Two Parts: Critical Theorizing and Analyzing on Social (In)Justice." In Denzin and Lincoln, *Sage Handbook of Qualitative Research*, 65–84.

Garbarino, J. *Lost Boys: Why Our Sons Turn Violent and How We Can Save Them*. New York: Anchor Books, 1999.

Gardner, H. *Multiple Intelligences: The Theory in Practice*. New York: Basic Books, 1993.

Gesell, A., F. L. Ilg, and L. B. Ames. *Youth: The Years from Ten to Sixteen*. New York: Harper & Brothers, 1956.

Gilligan, Carol. *In a Different Voice*. Cambridge, MA: Harvard University Press, 1982.

Glaser, Barney G. *Basics of Grounded Theory Analysis: Emergence vs. Forcing*. Mill Valley, CA: Sociology Press, 1992.

Goleman, D. *Emotional Intelligence*. New York: Bantam, 1994.

Griffin, Robert S. *Sports in the Lives of Children and Adolescents: Success on the Field and in Life*. Westport, CT: Praeger, 1998.

Hall, G. Stanley. *Adolescence: Its Psychology and Its Relation to Physiology, Anthropology, Sociology, Sex, Crime, Religion, and Education*. 2 vols. Englewood Cliffs, NJ: Prentice-Hall, 1904.

Hall, Stuart, and Tony Jefferson. *Resistance through Rituals*. London: Hutchinson, 1975.

Hamilton, D. "Traditions, Preferences, and Postures in Applied Qualitative Research." In Denzin and Lincoln, *Handbook of Qualitative Research*, 60–69.

Handel, Gerald, and Gail G. Whitchurch, eds. *The Psychosocial Interior of the Family.* New York: Aldine De Gruyter, 1994.

Hart, Archibald D., and Catherine Hart Weber. *Stressed or Depressed: A Practical and Inspirational Guide for Parents of Hurting Teens.* Brentwood, TN: Integrity, 2005.

Harter, S., S. Bresnick, H. A. Boushey, and N. R. Whitesell. "The Complexity of the Self in Adolescence." In Arnett, *Readings on Adolescence*, 111–18.

Herman, Judith. *Trauma and Recovery: The Aftermath of Violence—From Domestic Abuse to Political Terror.* New York: Basic Books, 1992.

Hersch, Patricia. *A Tribe Apart: A Journey into the Heart of American Adolescence.* New York: Ballantine Books, 1998.

Hyman, Mark. *Until It Hurts: America's Obsession with Youth Sports and How It Harms Our Kids.* Boston: Beacon, 2009.

Jackson, P. *Life in Classrooms.* Rev. ed. New York: Teachers College Press, 1990.

Jaffe, M. L. *Adolescence.* New York: Wiley, 1998.

Janesick, Valerie J. "The Dance of Qualitative Research Design: Metaphor, Methodolatry, and Meaning." In Denzin and Lincoln, *Handbook of Qualitative Research*, 209–19.

Janis, I. *Groupthink: Psychological Studies of Policy Decisions and Fiascoes.* Boston: Houghton Mifflin, 1982.

Johnson, N. G., M. C. Roberts, and J. Worell, eds. *Beyond Appearance: A New Look at Adolescent Girls.* Washington, DC: American Psychological Association, 1999.

Kamberelis, George, and Greg Dimitriadis. "Focus Groups: Strategic Articulations of Pedagogy, Politics, and Inquiry." In Denzin and Lincoln, *Sage Handbook of Qualitative Research*, 887–907.

Kann, L., S. A. Kitchen, B. I. Williams, J. G. Ross, R. Lowry, J. A. Grunbaum, and L. J. Kolbe. *Youth Risk Behavior Surveillance—United States, 1999.* Atlanta: Centers for Disease Control and Prevention, 1999.

Kaufman, P., M. N. Alt, and C. D. Chapman. *Dropout Rates in the United States: 2000.* Washington, DC: U.S. Department of Education National Center for Educational Statistics, 2001.

Kegan, Robert. *The Evolving Self.* Cambridge, MA: Harvard University Press, 1983.

———. *In Over Our Heads: The Mental Demands of Modern Life.* Cambridge, MA: Harvard University Press, 1994.

Kerber, August. *Quotable Quotes on Education.* Detroit: Wayne State University Press, 1968.

Kipke, M., ed. *Adolescent Development and the Biology of Puberty: Summary of a Workshop on New Research.* Washington, DC: National Academy Press, 1999.

Kohlberg, Lawrence. *Essays on Moral Development: The Philosophy of Moral Development.* 2 vols. San Francisco: Harper & Row, 1981–84.

Larkin, R. W. *Suburban Youth in Cultural Crisis.* New York: Oxford University Press, 1979.

Larson, Carl E., and Frank M. J. LaFasto. *Teamwork: What Must Go Right, What Can Go Wrong.* Newbury Park, CA: Sage, 1989.

Levine, Madeline. *The Price of Privilege: How Parental Pressure and Material Advantage Are Creating a Generation of Disconnected and Unhappy Kids.* New York: HarperCollins, 2006.

Levine, Mel. *A Mind at a Time.* New York: Simon & Schuster, 2003.

Mahedy, William, and Janet Bernardi. *A Generation Alone: Xers Making a Place in the World.* Downers Grove, IL: InterVarsity, 1994.

Mahler, Margaret. "Symbiosis and Individuation: The Psychological Birth of the Human Infant." In S*eparation-Individuation: Selected Papers of Margaret S. Mahler,* 149–65. Northvale, NJ: Jason Aronson, 1974.

Maslow, Abraham. *Motivation and Personality.* New York: Harper, 1954.

———. *Toward a Psychology of Being.* 3rd ed. New York: Wiley, 1998.

Micucci, J. A. *The Adolescent in Family Therapy: Breaking the Cycle of Conflict and Control.* New York: Guilford, 1998.

Moshman, David. *Adolescent Psychological Development: Rationality, Morality, and Identity.* New York: Guilford Press, 2004.

Mueller, Walt. *Understanding Today's Youth Culture.* Wheaton: Tyndale, 1999.

———. *Youth Culture 101.* Grand Rapids: Zondervan/Youth Specialties, 2007.

Mussen, Paul H., John J. Conger, Jerome Kagan, and James Geiwitz. *Psychological Development: A Life-Span Approach.* New York: Harper & Row, 1979.

Nakkula, Michael, and Michael Sadowski, eds. *Adolescents at School: Perspectives on Youth, Identity, and Education.* Cambridge, MA: Harvard Education Press, 2008.

Newman, Katherine. *Rampage: The Social Roots of School Shootings.* New York: Basic Books, 2004.

Palmer, Parker. *The Courage to Teach: Exploring the Inner Landscape of a Teacher's Life.* Hoboken, NJ: Jossey-Bass, 1997.

Peterson, Anne C., Pamela Sarigiani, Nancy Leffert, and Phame Camarena. "Resilience in Adolescence." In *The Adolescent in Turmoil: A Monograph for the International Society for Adolescent Psychiatry,* edited by Allan Z. Schwartzberg, 52–70. Westport, CT: Praeger, 1998.

Phinney, J. S., and M. Devich-Navarro. "Variations in Bicultural Identification among African American and Mexican American Adolescents." In Arnett, *Readings on Adolescence,* 120–31.

Piaget, Jean. *The Moral Judgment of the Child.* New York: Harcourt, Brace, Jovanovich, 1932.

———. *The Psychology of Intelligence.* New York: International Universities Press, 1950.

Pipher, Mary. *Reviving Ophelia: Saving the Selves of Adolescent Girls.* New York: Ballantine Books, 1994.

Plato. *Platonis Opera.* Edited by John Burnet. New York: Oxford University Press, 1903.

Pollack, W., and T. Shuster. *Real Boys' Voices.* New York: Random House, 2000.

Ponton, L. E. *The Romance of Risk: Why Teenagers Do the Things They Do.* New York: Basic Books, 1997.

Pope, Denise Clark. *Doing School: How We Are Creating a Generation of Stressed Out, Materialistic, and Miseducated Students.* New Haven: Yale University Press, 2001.

Posterski, Donald C. *Friendship: A Window on Ministry to Youth.* Scarborough, ON: Project Teen Canada, 1985.

Powers, Ron. *Tom and Huck Don't Live Here Anymore: Searching for the Lost American Childhood.* New York: St. Martin's Press, 2001.

Putnam, Robert D. *Bowling Alone: The Collapse and Revival of American Community.* New York: Simon & Schuster, 2000.

Raphael, Ray. *The Men from the Boys.* Lincoln: University of Nebraska Press, 1988.

Regnerus, Mark. *Forbidden Fruit: Sex and Religion in the Lives of American Teenagers.* New York: Oxford University Press, 2007.

Rowe, D. C., E. J. Woulbroun, and B. L. Gulley. "Peer and Friends as Nonshared Environmental Influence." In *Separate Social Worlds of Siblings*, edited by E. M. Hetherington, D. Reiss, and R. Plomin, 159–74. Hillsdale, NJ: Lawrence Erlbaum, 1994.

Rutter, Michael. "Protective Factors in Children's Responses to Stress and Disadvantage." In *Primary Prevention of Psychopathology*, vol. 3, *Social Competence in Children*, edited by M. W. Kent and Jon E. Rolf, 220–47. Hanover, NH: University Press of New England, 1979.

Santrock, John W. *Adolescence.* 8th ed. New York: McGraw-Hill, 2001.

Saukko, Paula. "Methodologies for Cultural Studies: An Integrative Approach." In Denzin and Lincoln, *Sage Handbook of Qualitative Research*, 343–56.

Scales, P. C., P. L. Benson, and E. C. Roehlkepartain. *Grading Grown-ups: American Adults Report on Their Real Relationships with Kids.* Minneapolis: Lutheran Brotherhood and Search Institute, 2001.

Shandler, S. *Ophelia Speaks.* New York: Harper, 1999.

Simeonsson, Rune J., ed. *Risk, Resilience, and Prevention: Promoting the Well-Being of All Children.* Baltimore: Brookes, 1994.

Smith, Christian. *Soul Searching: The Religious and Spiritual Lives of American Teenagers.* New York: Oxford University Press, 2005.

Solarz, Andrea. *American Psychological Association Healthy Adolescents Project: Adolescent Development Project.* Washington, DC: American Psychological Association, 2002.

Stanfield, John H. "Ethnic Modeling in Qualitative Research." In Denzin and Lincoln, *Handbook of Qualitative Research*, 175–88.

Strauss, William, and Neil Howe. *The Fourth Turning: An American Prophecy.* New York: Broadway Books, 1997.

Strommen, Merton. *Five Cries of Youth.* Rev. ed. New York: Harper & Row, 1988.

Thompson, J. K., and L. Smolak, eds. *Body Image, Eating Disorders, and Obesity in Children and Adolescents.* Washington, DC: American Psychological Association, 2003.

Thucydides. *The History of the Peloponnesian War.* Translated by Richard Crawley. The Internet Classics Archive, http://classics.mit.edu/Thucydides /pelopwar.2.second.html (accessed February 16, 2004).

U.S. Council of Economic Advisors. *Teens and Their Parents in the Twenty-first Century: An Examination of Trends in Teen Behavior and the Role of Parental Involvement.* Washington, DC: White House, 2000.

U.S. Department of Health and Human Services. *Trends in the Well-Being of America's Children and Youth.* Washington, DC: U.S. Government Printing Office, 1999.

van Gennep, Arnold. *The Rites of Passage.* Translated by Monika B. Vizedom and Gabrielle L. Caffe. Chicago: University of Chicago Press, 1960.

Wallbridge, H. R., and T. A. G. Osachuk. "Therapy with Adolescents." In *Basics of Clinical Practice*, edited by D. G. Martin and A. D. Moore, 208–22. Pacific Grove, CA: Brooks Cole, 208.

Wallerstein, Judith, Julia M. Lewis, and Sandra Blakeslee. *The Unexpected Legacy of Divorce: A Twenty-Five-Year Landmark Study.* New York: Hyperion, 2000.

Ward, Pete. *God at the Mall.* Peabody, MA: Hendrickson, 1999.

White House Council on Youth Violence. *Helping Your Children Navigate Their Teenage Years: A Guide for Parents.* Washington, DC: U.S. Department of Health and Human Services, 2000.

Willis, Paul. *Common Culture: Symbolic Work at Play in the Everyday Cultures of the Young.* Boulder, CO: Westview, 1990.

Articles

ACAeNews. "Solution Focused Counseling in Middle and High Schools, Part 2: What the Research Says about What Works." *School Counseling and Psychology*, American Counseling Association 1, no. 2, January 29, 1998, www .counseling.org/enews/volume_1/0102b.htm (accessed February 26, 1998).

Adler, Patricia A., and Peter Adler. "Teen Scenes: Ethnographies of Adolescent Cultures." *Journal of Contemporary Ethnography* 31 (October 2002): 652–60.

Ainsworth, Mary D. S. "Infant-Mother Attachment." *American Psychologist* 34 (1979): 932–37.

Ainsworth, Mary D. S., and John Bowlby. "An Ethological Approach to Personality Development." *American Psychologist* 46, no. 4 (1991): 333–41.

Allen, J. P., S. Philliber, S. Herrling, and G. P. Kuperminc. "Preventing Teen Pregnancy and Academic Failure: Experimental Evaluation of a Developmentally Based Approach." *Child Development* 64, no. 4 (1997): 729–42.

Allen, Joseph P., Penny Marsh, Christy McFarland, Kathleen Boykin McElhaney, Deborah J. Land, Kathleen M. Jodl, and Sheryl Peck. "Attachment and Autonomy as Predictors of the Development of Social Skills and Delinquency during Midadolescence." *Journal of Consulting and Clinical Psychology* 70, no. 1 (2002): 56–66.

Amiot, Catherine E., Roxane de la Sablonnière, Deborah J. Terry, and Joanne R. Smith. "Integration of Social Identities in the Self: Toward a Cognitive-Developmental Model." *Personality and Social Psychology Review* 11, no. 4 (2007): 364–88.

Anderman, Eric M., Tripp Griesinger, and Gloria Westerfield. "Motivation and Cheating during Early Adolescence." *Journal of Educational Psychology* 90 (1998): 84–93.

Ansary, N. A., and S. S. Luthar. "Distress and Academic Achievement among Adolescents of Affluence: A Study of Externalizing and Internalizing Problem Behaviors and School Performance." *Development and Psychopathology* 21 (2009): 319–41.

Aquilino, William S., and Andrew J. Supple. "Long-Term Effects of Parenting Practices during Adolescence on Well-Being Outcomes in Young Adulthood." *Journal of Family Issues* 22 (April 2001): 289–308.

Archibald, A. B., J. A. Graber, and J. Brooks-Gunn. "Associations among Parent-Adolescent Relationships, Pubertal Growth, Dieting, and Body Image in Young Adolescent Girls: A Short-Term Longitudinal Study." *Journal of Research on Adolescence* 9 (1999): 395–415.

Arnett, Jeffrey J. "Reckless Behavior in Adolescence: A Developmental Perspective." *Developmental Review* 12 (1992): 339–73.

Arnett, Jeffrey J., and L. Balle-Jensen. "Cultural Bases of Risk Behavior." *Child Development* 64 (1993): 1842–55.

Aseltine, R. H. "A Reconsideration of Parental and Peer Influence on Adolescent Deviance." *Journal of Health and Social Behavior* 36 (1995): 103–21.

Associated Press. "1 in 5 Undergrads Is Constantly Stressed." MSNBC, http://www.msnbc.msn.com/id/23693229 (accessed July 10, 2010).

———. "Unruly Students Top Public's List of School Worries." *New York Times*, April 23, 2003, D3.

Bakan, David. "Adolescence in America: From Idea to Social Fact." *Daedalus* 100 (1971): 979–95.

Barber, Bonnie L., Jacquelynne S. Eccles, and Margaret R. Stone. "Whatever Happened to the Jock, the Brain, and the Princess? Young Adult Pathways Linked to Adolescent Activity Involvement and Social Identity." *Journal of Adolescent Research* 16, no. 5 (September 2001): 429–55.

Barber, J. G., and P. Delfabbro. "Predictors of Adolescent Adjustment: Parent-Peer Relationships and Parent-Child Conflict." *Child and Adolescent Social Work Journal* 17, no. 4 (2000): 275–88.

Barczyk, Amanda, and Sanna Thompson. "Alcohol/Drug Dependency in Homeless Youth." *Alcoholism: Clinical and Experimental Research* 32, supp. 1 (June 2008): 367A.

Barnett, Lynn A. "Flying High or Crashing Down: Girls' Accounts of Trying Out for Cheerleading and Dance." *Journal of Adolescent Research* 21, no. 5 (September 2006): 514–41.

Barnhill, Carla. "How Good Parents Give Up on Their Teens." *Books & Culture* (May–June 2002): 29, www.christianitytoday.com/bc/2002/003/14.27.html (accessed February 16, 2004).

Bauman, Karl E., and Susan T. Ennett. "On the Importance of Peer Influence for Adolescent Drug Use: Commonly Neglected Considerations." *Addiction* 91, no. 2 1996: 185–98.

Beccaria, Franca, and Allan Sande. "Drinking Games and Rite of Life Projects: A Social Comparison of the Meaning and Functions of Young People's Use of Alcohol during the Rite of Passage to Adulthood in Italy and Norway." *Young* 11 (2003): 99–119.

Bender, D., and F. Losel. "Protective and Risk Effects of Peer Relations and Social Support on Antisocial Behavior in Adolescents from Multi-Problem Milieus." *Journal of Adolescence* 20 (1997): 661–78.

Bertera, Elizabeth. "The Role of Positive and Negative Social Exchanges between Adolescents, Their Peers and Family as Predictors of Suicide Ideation." *Child and Adolescent Social Work Journal* 24, no. 6 (December 2007), www.proquest.com (accessed December 11, 2009).

Bishop, J. A., and H. M. Inderbitzen. "Peer Acceptance and Friendship: An Investigation of Their Relationship to Self-Esteem." *Journal of Early Adolescence* 15 (1995): 476–89.

Boles, S. A. "A Model of Parental Representations, Second Individuation, and Psychological Adjustment in Late Adolescents." *Journal of Clinical Psychology* 55, no. 4 (1999): 497–513.

Boyd, M. P., and Z. Yin. "Cognitive-Affective Sources of Sport Enjoyment in Adolescent Sports Participants." *Adolescence* 31 (1996): 383–95.

Bradley, Robert H., and Robert F. Corwyn. "Home Environment and Behavioral Development during Early Adolescence: The Mediating and Moderating Roles of Self-Efficacy Beliefs." *Merrill-Palmer Quarterly* 47, no. 2 (2001): 165–87.

Brendgen, Mara, Frank Vitaro, and Anna Beth Doyle. "Same-Sex Peer Relations and Romantic Relationships during Early Adolescence: Interactive Links to Emotional, Behavioral, and Academic Adjustment." *Merrill-Palmer Quarterly* 48, no. 1 (2002): 77–103.

Bretherton, Inge. "The Origins of Attachment Theory: John Bowlby and Mary Ainsworth." *Developmental Psychology* 28, no. 5 (1992): 759–75.

Broman, Clifford L., Xin Li, and Mark Reckase. "Family Structure and Mediators of Adolescent Drug Use." *Journal of Family Issues* 28 (August 2008): 1626–49.

Brooks, David. "Making It: Love and Success at America's Finest Universities." *Weekly Standard* 8, no. 15, www.weeklystandard.com/Content/Public/Articles/000/000/002/017ickdp.asp (accessed December 23, 2002).

Brooks, Jeffrey S., Roxanne M. Hughes, and Melanie C. Brooks. "Fear and Trembling in the American High School: Educational Reform and Teacher Alienation." *Educational Policy* 22 (January 2008): 45–62.

Brown, B. B., N. Mounts, S. D. Lamborn, and L. Steinberg. "Parenting Practices and Peer Group Affiliation in Adolescence." *Child Development* 64 (1993): 467–82.

Brown, J. D., and J. Cantor. "An Agenda for Research on Youth and the Media." *Journal of Adolescent Health* 27, no. 2, supp. (2000): 2–7.

Brown, Susan L. "How Cohabitation Is Reshaping American Families." *Contexts* 4, no. 3 (Summer 2005), www.proquest.com (accessed December 11, 2009).

Buysse, W. H. "Behavior Problems and Relationships with Family and Peers during Adolescence." *Journal of Adolescence* 20 (1997): 645–59.

Calloway, Linda Jo, and Constance A. Knapp. "Using Grounded Theory to Interpret Interviews." csis.pace.edu/~knapp/AIS95.htm (accessed November 30, 2010).

Centers for Disease Control. "2009 National Youth Risk Behavior Survey." http://www.cdc.gov/healthyyouth/yrbs/index.htm (accessed July 3, 2010).

Chapin, John R. "Adolescent Sex and Mass Media: A Developmental Approach." *Adolescence* 35 (Winter 2000): 799–811.

Chubb, N. H., C. I. Fertman, and J. L. Ross. "Adolescent Self-Esteem and Locus of Control: A Longitudinal Study of Gender and Age Differences." *Adolescence* 32 (1997): 113–30.

Clark, Chap. "Entering Their World: A Qualitative Look at the Changing Face of Contemporary Adolescence." *Journal of Youth Ministry* 1, no. 1 (2002): 9–22.

———. "Fathers' Participation in Their Adolescent Sons' Athletic Events: A Qualitative Study." Unpublished paper, Fuller Theological Seminary, Youth, Family, and Culture Department, Pasadena, CA, 1994.

———. "From Fragmentation to Integration: A Theology for Contemporary Youth Ministry." *American Baptist Quarterly* 19, no. 1 (2000): 45–55.

Coatsworth, J. Douglas, and David E. Conroy. "The Effects of Autonomy-Supportive Coaching, Need Satisfaction, and Self-Perceptions on Initiative and Identity in Youth Swimmers." *Developmental Psychology* 45, no. 2 (2009): 320–28.

Cohen, Patricia. "Long Road to Adulthood Is Growing Even Longer." *New York Times*, June 11, 2010, http://www.nytimes.com/2010/06/13/us/13generations.html?_r=1 (accessed November 30, 2010).

Cole, Helene, and Mark D. Griffiths. "Social Interactions in Massively Multiplayer Online Role-Playing Games." *CyberPsychology and Behavior* 10, no. 4 (2007): 575–83.

Cook-Sather, Alison. "What Would Happen If We Treated Students as Those with Opinions That Matter? The Benefits to Principals and Teachers of Supporting Youth Engagement in School." *NASSP Bulletin* 91 (December 2007): 343–62.

Cornell University. "Self-Injury Is Prevalent among College Students, Survey Shows." *Science Daily*, June 5, 2006, http://www.sciencedaily.com/releases /2006/06/060605155351.htm (accessed July 9, 2008).

Crosnoe, Robert, and Glen H. Elder Jr. "Family Dynamics, Supportive Relationships, and Educational Resilience during Adolescence." *Journal of Family Issues* 25 (July 2004): 571–602.

Curran, P. J., E. Stice, and L. Chassin. "The Relation between Adolescent Alcohol Use and Peer Alcohol Use: A Longitudinal Random Coefficient Model." *Journal of Consulting and Clinical Psychology* 65 (1997): 130–40.

Curry, Erin. "American Youth More Conservative but Less Moral, Studies Report." www.bpnews.net/bpnews.asp?ID=14511 (accessed October 24, 2002).

Daddis, Christopher. "Influence of Close Friends on the Boundaries of Adolescent Personal Authority." *Journal of Research on Adolescence* 18 (2008): 75–98.

Dekovic, Maja, and Wim Meeus. "Peer Relations in Adolescence: Effects of Parenting and Adolescents' Self-Concept." *Journal of Adolescence* 20 (1997): 163–76.

Delaney, Cassandra H. "Rites of Passage in Adolescence." *Adolescence* 30 (Winter 1995): 891–97.

Drews, Maria. "Bouncing Back: Increasing Resilience for Hurting Kids." *Fuller Youth Institute eJournal*, August 3, 2009, http://fulleryouthinstitute.org /2009/08/bouncing-back/#footnote_10_8354 (accessed July 6, 2010).

Duncan, Greg J., Johanne Boisjoly, and Kathleen Mullan Harris. "Sibling, Peer, Neighbor, and Schoolmate Correlations as Indicators of the Importance of Context for Adolescent Development." *Demography* 38, no. 3 (August 2001): 437–47.

Dworkin, Jodi. "Risk Taking as Developmentally Appropriate Experimentation for College Students." *Journal of Adolescent Research* 20 (March 2005): 232.

Eastham, Mary. "Healing the Wounded Adolescent." *Compass* 43, no. 2 (Winter 2009), www.proquest.com (accessed December 11, 2009).

Eltringham, Simon, and Jan Aldridge. "Parenting on Shifting Sands: The Transfer of Responsibility for Safely Managing Danger." *Clinical Child Psychology and Psychiatry* 7 (2002): 137–45.

Evans, Scot D. "Youth Sense of Community: Voice and Power in Community Contexts." *Journal of Community Psychology* 35, no. 6 (2007): 693–709.

Everall, Robin D., Jessica Altrows, and Barbara L. Paulson. "Creating a Future: A Study of Resilience in Suicidal Female Adolescents." *Journal of Counseling and Development* 84 (Fall 2006): 461–70.

Federal Interagency Forum on Child and Family Statistics. "Family Structure and Children's Living Arrangements." *America's Children: Key National Indicators of Well-Being, 2009*, http://www.childstats.gov/americaschildren /famsoc1.asp (accessed November 22, 2009).

Fergusson, D., and M. Lynskey. "Adolescent Resiliency to Family Adversity." *Journal of Child Psychology and Psychiatry* 37 (1996): 281–92.

Fisher, Terri D. "Teen Romance under the Microscope." Review of *The Development of Romantic Relationships in Adolescence*, edited by Wyndol Furman, B. Bradford Brown, and Candice Feiring. *Journal of Sex Research* 37, no. 4 (November 2000): 383–85.

Flor, D. L., and N. F. Knapp. "Transmission and Transaction: Predicting Adolescents' Internalization of Parental Religious Values." *Journal of Family Psychology* 15, no. 4 (2001): 627–45.

Frostling-Henningsson, Maria. "First-Person Shooter Games as a Way of Connecting to People: 'Brothers in Blood.'" *CyberPsychology and Behavior* 12, no. 5 (2009): 557–62.

Garbarino, J., J. P. Gaa, P. Swank, R. McPherson, and L. V. Gratch. "The Relation of Individuation and Psychosocial Development." *Journal of Family Psychology* 9 (1995): 311–18.

Gardner, Margo, Jodie Roth, and Jeanne Brooks-Gunn. "Sports Participation and Juvenile Delinquency: The Role of the Peer Context among Adolescent Boys and Girls with Varied Histories of Problem Behavior." *Developmental Psychology* 45, no. 2 (2009): 341–53.

Garza, Ruben. "Latino and White High School Students' Perceptions of Caring Behaviors: Are We Culturally Responsive to Our Students?" *Urban Education* 44 (May 2009): 297–321.

Glenn, Catherine R., and David E. Klonsky. "The Role of Seeing Blood in Non-Suicidal Self-Injury." *Journal of Clinical Psychology* 66, no. 4 (April 2010): 466–73.

Gnaulati, Enrico, and Barb J. Heine. "Separation-Individuation in Late Adolescence: An Investigation of Gender and Ethnic Differences." *Journal of Psychology* 135, no. 1 (January 2001): 59–70.

Goldstein, Sara E., Pamela E. Davis-Kean, and Jacquelynne S. Eccles. "Parents, Peers, and Problem Behavior: A Longitudinal Investigation of the Impact of Relationship Perceptions and Characteristics on the Development of Adolescent Problem Behavior." *Developmental Psychology* 41, no. 2 (March 2005): 401–13.

Good Schools Pennsylvania. "Education History: A Timeline of Public Education in America." www.goodschoolspa.org/students/index.cfm?fuseaction=history (accessed August 13, 2003).

Gottsegen, Emile, and William W. Philliber. "Impact of a Sexual Responsibility Program on Young Males." *Adolescence* 36 (Fall 2001): 427–33.

Greenberg, Mark T., Judith M. Siegel, and Cynthia J. Leitch. "The Nature and Importance of Attachment Relationships to Parents and Peers during Adolescence." *Journal of Youth and Adolescence* 12, no. 5 (1983): 373–86.

Grossman, Jean B., and Jean E. Rhodes. "The Test of Time: Predictors and Effects of Duration in Youth Mentoring Relationships." *American Journal of Community Psychology* 30 (2002): 199–219.

Guerry, John D., and Mitchell J. Prinstein. "Longitudinal Prediction of Adolescent Nonsuicidal Self-Injury: Examination of a Cognitive Vulnerability-Stress Model." *Journal of Clinical Child and Adolescent Psychology* 39, no. 1 (January/February 2010): 77–89.

Gulli, Cathy. "Suddenly Teen Pregnancy Is Cool?" *Maclean's* 121, no. 3 (January 28, 2008): 40–44.

Hafner, Katie. "Texting May Be Taking a Toll." *New York Times*, May 25, 2009, http://www.nytimes.com/2009/05/26/health/26teen.html (accessed April 11, 2010).

Harrison, Patricia A., and Narayan Gopalakrishnan. "Differences in Behavior, Psychological Factors, and Environmental Factors Associated with Participation in School Sports and Other Activities in Adolescence." *Journal of School Health* 9, no. 3 (March 2003): 113–20.

Harter, Susan, Shelly Bresnick, Heather A. Bouchey, and Nancy R. Whitesell. "The Development of Multiple Role-Related Selves During Adolescence." *Development and Psychopathology* 9 (1997): 835–53.

Hektner, Joel M. "Family, School, and Community Predictors of Adolescent Growth-Conducive Experiences: Global and Specific Approaches." *Applied Developmental Science* 5, no. 3 (2001): 180–81.

Henrich, C. C., G. P. Kuperminc, A. Sack, S. J. Blatt, and B. J. Leadbeater. "Characteristics and Homogeneity of Early Adolescent Friendship Groups: A Comparison of Male and Female Clique and Nonclique Members." *Applied Developmental Science* 4, no. 1 (2000): 15–26.

Henry, Kimberly L., Eugene R. Oetting, and Michael D. Slater. "The Role of Attachment to Family, School, and Peers in Adolescents' Use of Alcohol: A Longitudinal Study of Within-Person and Between-Persons Effects." *Journal of Counseling Psychology* 56, no. 4 (2009): 564–72.

Hoff, Kathryn E., George J. Dupaul, and Michael L. Handwerk. "Rejected Youth in Residential Treatment: Social Affiliation and Peer Group Configuration." *Journal of Emotional and Behavioral Disorders* 11, no. 2 (2003): 112–21.

Hogan, M. "Media Matters for Youth Health." *Journal of Adolescent Health* 27, no. 2, supp. (2000): 73–76.

Huan, Vivien S., Yeo Lay See, Rebecca P. Ang, and Chong Wan Har. "The Impact of Adolescent Concerns on Their Academic Stress." *Educational Review* 60, no. 2 (May 2008): 169–78.

Hunter, Anita. "Adolescent Resilience." *Journal of Nursing Scholarship* 31, no. 3 (1999): 243–47.

———. "A Cross-Cultural Comparison of Resilience in Adolescents." *Journal of Pediatric Nursing* 16, no. 3 (June 2001): 172–79.

Hussong, A. M. "Differentiating Peer Contexts and Risk for Adolescent Substance Use." *Journal of Youth and Adolescence* 31, no. 3 (2002): 207–20.

———. "Perceived Peer Context and Adolescent Adjustment." *Journal of Research on Adolescents* 10, no. 4 (2000): 391–415.

Jarvinen, Denis W., and John G. Nicholls. "Adolescents' Social Goals, Beliefs about the Causes of Social Success, and Satisfaction in Peer Relations." *Developmental Psychology* 32, no. 3 (1996): 440.

Jensen, L., J. Arnett, S. Feldman, and E. Cauffman. "It's Wrong, but Everybody Does It: Academic Dishonesty among High School and College Students." *Contemporary Educational Psychology* 27, no. 2 (2002): 209–28.

———. "The Right to Do Wrong: Lying to Parents among Adolescents and Emerging Adults." *Journal of Youth and Adolescence* 33, no. 2 (April 2004): 101–12.

Josephson Institute of Ethics. "The Ethics of American Youth: 2002." http://charactercounts.org/programs/reportcard/2002/index.html (accessed October 24, 2002).

———. "The Ethics of American Youth: 2008." http://charactercounts.org/programs/reportcard/2008/index.html (accessed June 18, 2010).

———. "Survey Documents Decade of Moral Deterioration: Kids Are More Likely to Cheat, Steal, and Lie than Kids 10 Years Ago." www.josephsoninstitute.org/Survey2002/survey2002–pressrelease.htm (accessed October 24, 2002).

Kafka, R. R., and P. London. "Communication in Relationships and Adolescent Substance Abuse: The Influence of Parents and Friends." *Adolescence* 26 (1991): 587–98.

Kandel, D. B. "The Parental and Peer Contexts of Adolescent Deviance: An Algebra of Interpersonal Influences." *Journal of Drug Issues* 26, no. 2 (1996): 289–315.

Kim, Irene J., Nolan W. S. Zane, and Sehee Hong. "Protective Factors against Substantive Use among Asian American Youth: A Test of the Peer Cluster Theory." *Journal of Community Psychology* 30, no. 5 (2002): 565–84.

Klein, J. D. "The National Longitudinal Study on Adolescent Health: Preliminary Results—Great Expectations." *Journal of the American Medical Association* 278 (1997): 864–65.

Klonsky, E. David, and Jennifer Meuhlenkamp. "Self-Injury: A Research Review for the Practitioner." *Journal of Clinical Psychology* 63, no. 11 (2007): 1045–56.

Knox, David, Marty E. Zusman, and Kristen McGinty. "Deception of Parents during Adolescence." *Adolescence* 36 (Fall 2001): 611–14.

Knox, Richard. "The Teen Brain: It's Just Not Grown Up Yet." National Public Radio, March 1, 2010, www.npr.org/templates/story/story.php?storyId=124119468 (accessed July 1, 2010).

Langekamp, Amy G., and Michelle L. Frisco. "Family Transitions and Adolescent Severe Emotional Distress: The Salience of Family Context." *Social Problems* 55, no. 2 (May 2008), www.proquest.com (accessed December 11, 2009).

Lapsley, Daniel K., and Jason Edgerton. "Separation-Individuation, Adult Attachment Style, and College Adjustment." *Journal of Counseling and Development* 80 (2002): 484–92.

Larson, Reed. "Positive Youth Development, Willful Adolescents, and Mentoring." *Journal of Community Psychology* 34, no. 6 (2006): 678–79.

Lashbrook, Jeffrey. "Fitting In: Exploring the Emotional Dimension of Adolescent Peer Pressure." *Adolescence* 35 (Winter 2000): 747–57.

Lee, Daniel E. "Cheating in the Classroom: Beyond Policing." *The Clearing House* 82, no. 4 (March/April 2009), www.proquest.umi.com/pdqweb?did= 1651769121&Fmt=3&clientId=29876&RQT=309&VName=PQD (accessed December 11, 2009).

Lee, Kang, and Hollie J. Ross. "The Concept of Lying in Adolescents and Young Adults: Testing Sweetser's Folkloristic Model." *Merrill-Palmer Quarterly* 43, no. 2 (1997): 255–70.

Leibenluft, E., D. L. Gardner, and R. W. Cowdry. "The Inner Experience of the Borderline Self-Mutilator." *Journal of Personality Disorders* 1 (1987): 317–24.

Lenhart, Amanda. "Teens and Mobile Phones over the Past Five Years: Pew Internet Looks Back." Pew Internet & American Life Project, August 19, 2009, http://www.pewinternet.org/Reports/2009/14--Teens-and-Mobile-Phones -Data-Memo.aspx (accessed April 11, 2010).

Leventhal, T., and J. Brooks-Gunn. "The Neighborhoods They Live In: The Effects of Neighborhood Residence on Child and Adolescent Outcomes." *Psychological Bulletin* 126, no. 2 (March 2000): 309–27.

Lindberg, Laura Duberstein, Rachel Jones, and John S. Santelli. "Non-coital Sexual Activities among Adolescents." *Journal of Adolescent Health* 42, no. 7 (May 2008), http://www.guttmacher.org/pubs/JAH_Lindberg.pdf (accessed December 10, 2009).

Livingstone, Sonia. "Taking Risky Opportunities in Youthful Content Creation: Teenagers' Use of Social Networking Sites for Intimacy, Privacy and Self-Expression." *New Media Society* 10 (2008): 393–411.

Lock, J. "Acting Out and the Narrative Function: Reconsidering Peter Blos's Concept of the Second Individuation Process." *American Journal of Psychotherapy* 39 (1995): 548–57.

Longman, Huon, Erin O'Connor, and Patricia Obst. "The Effect of Social Support Derived from World of Warcraft on Negative Psychological Symptoms." *CyberPsychology and Behavior* 12, no. 5 (2009): 563–66.

Luthar, Suniya S., and Shawn J. Latendresse. "Adolescent Risk: The Costs of Affluence." *New Directions for Youth Development* 95 (Fall 2002): 101–21.

———. "Children of the Affluent: Challenges to Well-Being." *Current Directions in Psychological Science* 14, no. 1 (February 2005): 49–53.

Luthar, Suniya, Dante Cicchetti, and Bronwyn Becker. "The Construct of Resilience: A Critical Evaluation and Guidelines for Future Work." *Child Development* 71, no. 3 (May/June 2000): 543–62.

Males, Mike. "The New Demons: Ordinary Teens." *Los Angeles Times*, April 21, 2002, home.earthlink.net/~mmales/epheb.htm (accessed March 13, 2003).

Manlove, Jennifer, Cassandra Logan, Kristen A. Moore, and Erum Ikramullah. "Pathways from Family Religiosity to Adolescent Sexual Activity and Contraceptive Use." *Perspectives on Sexual and Reproductive Health* 40, no. 2 (2008): 105–17.

Manolis, C., A. Levin, and R. Dahlstrom. "A Generation X Scale: Creation and Validation." *Educational and Psychological Measurement* 57, no. 4 (1997): 666–84.

Martin, Don, and Maggie Martin. "Understanding Dysfunctional and Functional Family Behaviors for the At-Risk Adolescent." *Adolescence* 35 (Winter 2000): 785–92.

Martin, Paige D., Don Martin, and Maggie Martin. "Adolescent Premarital Sexual Activity, Cohabitation, and Attitudes toward Marriage." *Adolescence* 36 (Fall 2001): 601–9.

Masten, Ann S. "Ordinary Magic: Resilience Processes in Development." *American Psychologist* 56, no. 3 (March 2001): 227–38.

Masten, Ann S., and J. Douglas Coatsworth. "The Development of Competence in Favorable and Unfavorable Environments: Lessons from Research on Successful Children." *American Psychologist* 53, no. 2 (February 1998): 205–20.

Matherne, Monique M., and Adrian Thomas. "Family Environment as a Predictor of Adolescent Delinquency." *Adolescence* 36 (Winter 2001): 655–64.

Matkovic, V., Jasminka Z. Ilich, Mario Skugor, Nancy E. Badenhop, Prem Goel, Albert Clairmont, Dino Klisovic, Ramzi W. Nahhas, and John D. Landoll. "Leptin Is Inversely Related to Age at Menarche in Human Females." *Journal of Clinical Endocrinology and Metabolism* 82, no. 10 (October 1997): 3239–45.

Mayeux, Lara, and Antonius H. N. Cillessen. "It's Not Just Being Popular, It's Knowing It, Too: The Role of Self-Perceptions of Status in the Associations between Peer Status and Aggression." *Social Development* 17, no. 4 (2008): 871–88.

McCabe, Donald Lee. "Academic Dishonesty among High School Students." *Adolescence* 34 (Winter 1999): 681–87.

Melnick, Merrill J., Kathleen E. Miller, and Donald F. Sabo. "Tobacco Use among High School Athletes and Nonathletes: Results of the 1997 Youth Risk Behavior Survey." *Adolescence* 36 (Winter 2001): 730.

Milevsky, Avidan. "Compensatory Patterns of Sibling Support in Emerging Adulthood: Variations in Loneliness, Self-Esteem, Depression and Life Satisfaction." *Journal of Social and Personal Relationships* 22 (2005): 744–55.

Miller, Curtis. "The Way of Privilege: What You Need to Know about the Issues Facing Affluent Youth." *Fuller Youth Institute eJournal*, July 13, 2008, http://fulleryouthinstitute.org/2008/07/the-way-of-privilege/ (accessed June 28, 2010).

Miller, Samantha, Sarah J. Ericksen, Christina Barnom, and Hans Steiner. "Habitual Response to Stress in Recovering Adolescent Anorexic Patients." *Child Psychiatry and Human Development* 40, no. 1 (2009): 43–54.

Murdock, Tamera B., Anne S. Beauchamp, and Amber M. Hinton. "Predictors of Cheating and Cheating Attributions: Does Classroom Context Influence Cheating and Blame for Cheating?" *European Journal of Psychology of Education* 23, no. 4 (2008): 477–92.

National Health and Nutritional Examination Survey (NHANES). "One in Four Female Adolescents Is Infected with At Least One Sexually Transmitted

Infection, New CDC Study Finds." http://www.cdc.gov/stdconference/2008
/press/summaries-11march2008.htm (accessed June 15, 2010).

Nguyen-Rodriguez, Selena T., Jennifer B. Unger, and Donna Spruijt-Metz. "Psychological Determinants of Emotional Eating in Adolescence." *Eating Disorders* 17 (2009): 211–24.

Oetting, Eugene R., and F. Beauvais. "Peer Cluster Theory: Drugs and the Adolescent." *Journal of Counseling and Development* 65 (1986): 17–22.

———. "Peer Cluster Theory, Socialization Characteristics, and Adolescent Drug
Use: A Path Analysis." *Journal of Counseling Psychology* 34 (1987): 205–13.

Oliveira, Joanne O'Sullivan, and Pamela J. Burke. "Lost in the Shuffle: Culture of
Homeless Adolescents." *Pediatric Nursing* 35, no. 3 (May–June 2009): 154–61.

Orenstein, Peggy. "Playing at Sexy: Do Gyrating Little Girls Become Sexting
Young Women?" *New York Times Magazine*, June 13, 2010, 11.

Orfield, G. "Reviving the Goal of an Integrated Society: A 21st Century Challenge." The Civil Rights Project/Proyecto Derechos Civiles at UCLA, January
1, 2009, http://civilrightsproject.ucla.edu/research/k-12-education/integration
-and-diversity/reviving-the-goal-of-an-integrated-society-a-21st-century
-challenge (accessed August 12, 2010).

Osgood, D. Wayne, E. Michael Foster, and Mark E. Courtney. "Vulnerable Populations and the Transition to Adulthood." *Future of Children* 20, no. 1 (Spring
2010): 209–29.

Peterson, Karen S. "Youthful Pessimism Gives Rise to Generation Vexed." *USA
Today*, October 19, 2000, 12D.

Pew Research Center. "Teens and Sexting." http://pewinternet.org/Reports/2009
/Teens-and-Sexting.aspx (accessed November 30, 2010).

Pfeifer, Stuart. "3 Teenagers Will Be Tried as Adults in Videotape Rape Case."
Los Angeles Times, January 30, 2003, B5.

Powers, Ron. "The Apocalypse of Adolescence," *Atlantic*, March 2002, www
.theatlantic.com/issues/2002/03/powers.htm (accessed May 3, 2003).

Regnerus, Mark D. "Friends' Influence on Adolescent Theft and Minor Delinquency: A Developmental Test of Peer-Reported Effects." *Social Science
Research* 13, no. 4 (December 2002): 681–706.

Remez, L. "Oral Sex among Adolescents: Is It Sex or Is It Abstinence?" *Family
Planning Perspectives* 32, no. 6 (2000): 298–304.

Resnick, M. D., P. S. Bearman, R. W. Blum, K. E. Bauman, K. M. Harris, J. Jones,
J. Tabor, T. Beuhring, R. E. Sieving, M. Shew, M. Ireland, L. H. Bearinger, and
J. R. Udry. "Protecting Adolescents from Harm: Findings from the National
Longitudinal Study on Adolescent Health." *Journal of the American Medical
Association* 278 (1997): 823–32.

Ricciardelli, Lina A., Marita P. McCabe, and Damien Ridge. "The Construction
of the Adolescent Male Body through Sport." *Journal of Health Psychology*
11, no. 4 (2006): 577–87.

Richardson, Stacey, and Marita P. McCabe. "Parental Divorce during Adolescence
and Adjustment in Early Adulthood." *Adolescence* 36 (Fall 2001): 467–89.

Roberts, Donald F. "Media and Youth: Access, Exposure, and Privatization." *Journal of Adolescent Health* 27, no. 2, supp. (2000): 8–14.

Rodriguez, Louie F. "'Teachers Know You Can Do More': Understanding How School Cultures of Success Affect Urban High School Students." *Educational Policy* 22 (September 2008): 758–80.

Rosenquist, J. Niels, Joanne Murabito, James H. Fowler, and Nicholas A. Christakis. "The Spread of Alcohol Consumption Behavior in a Large Social Network." *Annals of Internal Medicine* 152, no. 7 (April 6, 2010): 426–33.

Roth, J., and J. Brooks-Gunn. "What Do Adolescents Need for Healthy Development? Implications for Youth Policy." *Social Policy Report* 14 (2000): 3–19.

Rubin, Rita. "Survey Finds U.S. Abortion Rate Hits Lowest Level since 1974." *USA Today*, January 15, 2003, 8D.

Ruspoli, Tao. "Drugs and Technicity: A Heideggerian Inquiry into the Evolution of Drug Use." www.ruspoli.com/drugs.html (accessed February 16, 2004).

Schott, Gareth R., and Wynford Bellin. "The Relational Self-Concept Scale: A Context-Specific Self-Report Measure for Adolescents." *Adolescence* 36 (Spring 2001): 85–103.

Schvaneveldt, Paul L., Brent C. Miller, and Helen E. Berry. "Academic Goals, Achievement, and Age at First Sexual Intercourse: Longitudinal, Bidirectional Influences." *Adolescence* 36 (Winter 2001): 767–87.

Smylie, Lisa, Sheri Medaglia, and Eleanor Maticka-Tyndale. "The Effect of Social Capital and Socio-demographics on Adolescent Risk and Sexual Health Behaviours." *Canadian Journal of Human Sexuality* 15, no. 2 (Summer 2006): 95–112.

Sondheimer, Eric. "Soccer Players Face Split Decision: Some Elite Southland Athletes Must Choose between Their High School and Club Teams." *Los Angeles Times*, January 16, 2008, http://articles.latimes.com/2008/jan/16/sports/sp-academy16 (accessed March 8, 2010).

Spencer, Renée. "'It's Not What I Expected': A Qualitative Study of Youth Mentoring Relationship Failures." *Journal of Adolescent Research* 22 (2007): 331–54.

Stanton-Salazar, Ricardo, and Stephanie Urso Spina. "Adolescent Peer Networks as a Context for Social and Emotional Support." *Youth & Society* 36, no. 4 (2005): 379–417.

Steinberg, L. "We Know Some Things: Parent-Adolescent Relations in Retrospect and Prospect." *Journal of Research in Adolescence* 11, no. 1 (2001): 1–19.

Steinfeldt, Jesse A., M. Clint Steinfeldt, Bre England, and Quentin L. Speight. "Gender Role Conflict and Stigma toward Help-Seeking among College Football Players." *Psychology of Men and Masculinity* 10, no. 4 (2009): 261–72.

Stice, E., C. Hayward, R. Cameron, J. Killen, and B. Taylor. "Body Image and Eating Disturbances Predict Onset of Depression among Female Adolescents: A Longitudinal Study." *Journal of Abnormal Psychology* 109, no. 3 (2000): 438–44.

Stonehouse, Cathy. "Moral Development: The Process and the Pattern." *Counseling and Values* 24 (1979): 6.

Strayhorn, Joseph M., and Jillian C. Strayhorn. "Religiosity and Teen Birth Rate in the United States." *Reproductive Health*, September 2009, www.reproductive -health-journal.com/content/6/1/14 (accessed November 13, 2009).

Strom, Robert D., Troy E. Beckert, and Paris S. Strom. "Evaluating the Success of Caucasian Fathers in Guiding Adolescents." *Adolescence* 37 (Spring 2002): 131–49.

Suldo, Shannon M., Elizabeth Shaunessy, Amanda Thalji, Jessica Michalowski, and Emily Shaffer. "Sources of Stress for Students in High School College Preparatory and General Education Programs: Group Differences and Associations with Adjustment." *Adolescence* 44 (Winter 2009): 925–48.

Svetaz, M. V., M. Ireland, and M. Blum. "Adolescents with Learning Disabilities: Risk and Protective Factors Associated with Emotional Well-Being: Findings from the National Longitudinal Study of Adolescent Health." *Journal of Adolescent Health* 27 (2000): 340–48.

Swanson, Dena Phillips, Margaret B. Spencer, Tabitha Dell'Angelo, Vinay Harpalani, and Tirzah R. Spencer. "Identity Processes and the Positive Youth Development of African Americans: An Explanatory Framework." *New Directions for Youth Development* 95 (Fall 2002): 73–99.

Taffle, Ron. *Childhood Unbound: Saving Our Kids' Best Selves—Confident Parenting in a World of Change.* New York: Free Press, 2009.

Tani, Crystal R., Ernest L. Chavez, and Jerry L. Deffenbacher. "Peer Isolation and Drug Use among White Non-Hispanic and Mexican American Adolescents." *Adolescence* 36 (Spring 2001): 127–39.

Tanner, Christine A. "Moral Decline or Pragmatic Decision Making? Cheating and Plagiarism in Perspective." *Journal of Nursing Education* 43, no. 7 (July 2004): 291–92.

Taylor, Catherine A., Neil W. Boris, Sherryl Scott Heller, Gretchen A. Clum, Janet C. Rice, and Charles H. Zeanah. "Cumulative Experiences of Violence among High-Risk Urban Youth." *Journal of Interpersonal Violence* 23, no. 11 (2008): 1618–35.

Tisak, M. S., J. Tisak, and M. Rogers. "Adolescents' Reasoning about Authority and Friendship Relations in the Context of Drug Use." *Journal of Adolescence* 17 (1994): 265–82.

Trew, Karen, Deidre Scully, John Kremer, and Shaun Ogle. "Sport, Leisure and Perceived Self-Competence among Male and Female Adolescents." *European Physical Education Review* 5, no. 1 (1999): 53–74.

U.S. Department of Health and Human Services. "Positive Youth Development." http://www.acf.hhs.gov/programs/fysb/content/positiveyouth/index.htm (accessed May 13, 2009).

Ungar, Michael T. "The Importance of Parents and Other Caregivers to the Resilience of High-Risk Adolescents." *Family Process* 43, no. 1 (2004): 23–41.

———. "The Myth of Peer Pressure." *Adolescence* 35 (Spring 2000): 167–80.

Urberg, K. A., S. M. Degirmencioglu, and C. Pilgrim. "Close Friend and Group Influence on Adolescent Cigarette Smoking and Alcohol Use." *Developmental Psychology* 33 (1997): 834–44.

Valaitis, Ruta. "'They Don't Trust Us; We're Just Kids': Views about Community from Predominantly Female Inner City Youth." *Health Care for Women International* 23, no. 3 (2002): 256–57.

van der Kolk, B. A., J. C. Perry, and J. L. Herman. "Childhood Origins of Self-Destructive Behavior." *American Journal of Psychiatry* 148 (1991): 1665–71.

van Oort, Floor V. A., Frank C. Verhulst, Johan Ormel, and Anja C. Huizink. "Prospective Community Study of Family Stress and Anxiety in (Pre)adolescents." *European Child and Adolescent Psychiatry* 19, no. 6 (June 2010): 483–91.

Vasudevan, Lalitha, and Gerald Campano. "The Social Production of Adolescent Risk and the Promise of Adolescent Literacies." *Review of Research Education* 33 (2009): 310–53.

Vieno, Alessio, Nation Maury, Pastore Massimiliano, and Santinello Massimo. "Parenting and Antisocial Behavior: A Model of the Relationship between Adolescent Self-Disclosure, Parental Closeness, Parental Control, and Adolescent Antisocial Behavior." *Developmental Psychology* 45, no. 6 (2009): 1509–19.

Warr, Mark. "The Tangled Web: Delinquency, Deception, and Parental Attachment." *Journal of Youth and Adolescence* 36, no. 5 (2007): 607–22.

Webb, L. "Deliberate Self-Harm in Adolescence: A Systematic Review of Psychological and Psychosocial Factors." *Journal of Advanced Nursing* 38, no. 3 (May 2002): 235–44.

Weir, E. "Raves: A Review of the Culture, the Drugs, and the Prevention of Harm." *Canadian Medical Association Journal* 162, no. 13 (2000): 1843–48.

Whitbeck, L. B., R. D. Conger, and M. Kao. "The Influence of Parental Support, Depressed Affect, and Peers on the Sexual Behavior of Adolescent Girls." *Journal of Family Issues* 14 (1993): 261–78.

Wickrama, K. A. S., Samuel Noh, and Chalandra M. Bryant. "Racial Differences in Adolescent Distress: Differential Effects of the Family and Community for Blacks and Whites." *Journal of Community Psychology* 33, no. 3 (2005): 261–82.

Wiest, Dudley J., Eugene H. Wong, and Joseph M. Cervantes. "Intrinsic Motivation among Regular, Special, and Alternative Education High School Students." *Adolescence* 36 (Spring 2001): 111–26.

Willemen, Agnes M., Carlo Schuengel, and Hans M. Koot. "Physiological Reactivity to Stress and Parental Support: Comparison of Clinical and Non-clinical Adolescents." *Clinical Psychology and Psychotherapy* 15, no. 5 (September–October 2008): 340–51.

Wineburgh, A. L. "Treatment of Children with Absent Fathers." *Child and Adolescent Social Work Journal* 17, no. 4 (2000): 255–73.

Wolff, Alexander. "Special Report: The High School Athlete, Part 1." *Sports Illustrated*, November 18, 2002, sportsillustrated.cnn.com/si_online/news /2002/11/12/high_school (accessed February 13, 2004).

Wright, Darlene R., and Kevin M. Fitzpatrick. "Social Capital and Adolescent Violent Behavior: Correlates of Fighting and Weapon Use among Secondary School Students." *Social Forces* 84, no. 3 (March 2006): 1435–52.

Yates, T. M., A. J. Tracy, and S. S. Luthar. "Nonsuicidal Self-Injury among 'Privileged' Youth: Longitudinal and Cross-sectional Approaches to Developmental Processes." *Journal of Consulting and Clinical Psychology* 76 (2008): 52–62.

Zelizer, Gerald. "Break Cheating Pattern Early." *USA Today*, November 20, 2002.

Ziller, Curtis M. "The Way of Privilege: What You Need to Know about the Issues Facing Affluent Youth." *Fuller Youth Institute eJournal*, July 13, 2008, http://fulleryouthinstitute.org/2008/07/the-way-of-privilege (accessed June 28, 2010).

index